A DUBIOUS
EXPEDIENCY

A DUBIOUS EXPEDIENCY

HOW RACE PREFERENCES DAMAGE HIGHER EDUCATION

EDITED BY

Gail Heriot and
Maimon Schwarzschild

BOOKS

New York • London

First American edition published in 2021 by Encounter Books,
an activity of Encounter for Culture and Education, Inc.,
a nonprofit, tax-exempt corporation.
Encounter Books website address: www.encounterbooks.com

Manufactured in the United States and printed on
acid-free paper. The paper used in this publication meets
the minimum requirements of ANSI/NISO Z39.48–1992
(R 1997) (Permanence of Paper).

FIRST AMERICAN EDITION

LIBRARY OF CONGRESS CATALOGING-IN-PUBLICATION DATA

Names: Heriot, Gail, 1957– editor. | Schwarzschild, Maimon, 1951– editor.
Title: A dubious expediency: how race preferences damage higher education
/ edited by Gail Heriot and Maimon Schwarzschild.
Description: First American edition. | New York, NY: Encounter Books, 2021.
Includes bibliographical references and index.
Identifiers: LCCN 2020044107 (print) | LCCN 2020044108 (ebook)
ISBN 9781641771320 (cloth) | ISBN 9781641771337 (epub)
Subjects: LCSH: Discrimination in higher education—United States.
Racism in higher education—United States. | Universities and colleges
United States—Admission. | Education, Higher—Social aspects—United States.
Classification: LCC LC212.42.D83 2021 (print) | LCC LC212.42 (ebook)
DDC 379.2/6—dc23
LC record available at https://lccn.loc.gov/2020044107
LC ebook record available at https://lccn.loc.gov/2020044108

Interior page design and typesetting by Bruce Leckie

CONTENTS

INTRODUCTION

Race preferences, under the rubric of affirmative action, have been a matter of policy in American higher education for more than half a century. More students have attended college during these years than during the long Jim Crow era.

In its early academic incarnation, and recurrently ever since in the public statements of some of its supporters, affirmative action was to seek out, and perhaps mildly to boost, minority applicants to colleges and universities, primarily on behalf of African Americans. In 1965, for example, Harvard Law School created a "Special Summer Program" for juniors and seniors from what later came to be called historically black colleges in the South. Harvard's idea, modestly enough, was to encourage and try to qualify these students to enroll in its law school. Yet, in the same year, New York University's law faculty approved the admission of "ten to fifteen" students with test scores and college grades below the usual cutoff.

Preferential policies became more widespread, and far more aggressive, almost at once. By 1969, the American Association of Medical Colleges recommended that 12 percent of first-year medical students should be black. Affirmative-action programs, several of them financed by the Rockefeller Foundation, sought to recruit African American students from the inner city for admission to college and university, almost without concern for the students' academic preparation. That same year, New York's City University—known in earlier decades as the "Harvard of the proletariat" for its academic excellence—first created a "dual admissions" system whereby 50 percent of the class would still be admitted under academically selective standards but 50 percent would no longer be required to meet the standards; two months later, the City University dropped admissions standards altogether and introduced "open admissions" for all high school graduates.

At first, there was some tendency to acknowledge that preferences by race—and for other selected groups—were at odds with generally accepted, and usually desirable, principles of equal justice. Hence, preferences were often shrouded in euphemisms. As the "tough liberal" teachers' union leader Albert Shanker reported disapprovingly, after a conversation in 1972 with Democratic presidential candidate George McGovern, the candidate "is willing to abandon the word 'quota' but still endorse the practice."

In the ensuing years and decades, what had been introduced and justified as a temporary expedient, with perhaps mild preferences for blacks just emerging from the era of Jim Crow, became a permanent feature—and, increasingly, a predominating principle—of higher education, with sometimes dramatically relaxed standards for applicants and students from an array of newly favored groups.

From the outset in the 1960s and 1970s, there were voices warning that race preferences (and preferences by ethnicity and sex as well), once established, would not be temporary, would not be modest in scope, and would not conduce toward social integration or reconciliation, but rather quite the contrary. As early as 1967, Ralph J. Winter, a Yale law professor who was later appointed to the United States Court of Appeals, wrote of preferential programs: "Instead of helping to eliminate race from politics, they inject it. Instead of teaching tolerance and helping those forces seeking accommodation, they divide on a racial basis." In the mid-1970s, prominent public intellectual Nathan Glazer expressed his doubts in *Affirmative Discrimination: Ethnic*

Inequality and Public Policy. At the time, Glazer criticized both the factual claims underlying preferential affirmative action—such as the idea of "institutional racism"—and the implementation of preferences. These represented, said Glazer, a "withdrawal from the acceptance of common standards, a weakening of our sense of rightness or justice" in making academic judgments.

Fifty years and more have now elapsed, and race preferences—as well as preferences for other selected groups—have been thoroughly institutionalized in American higher education. Under the slogan of "diversity," they have become a way of life, even an article of faith. Proliferating campus bureaucracies oversee and promote preferential policies. Preferences are an important factor not only in undergraduate and graduate admissions, but in hiring and promoting faculty and administrators as well. Preferences, and the preoccupation with race and group identity that they engender, increasingly affect the academic curriculum: in some fields, they virtually transform it. And preferences create ongoing pressure for lower academic standards, as institutions try to disguise the educational gap between students admitted preferentially and those admitted with standard qualifications.

Is it now too late to assess the edifice of racial and group preferences honestly and to suggest that American higher education has taken a wrong turn? We hope—and think—not.

It is a matter of urgent current concern, as well as concern for the future, whether preferential affirmative action really fulfills its putative positive or desirable goals. These policies were first advanced—and are sometimes still defended—as promoting racial integration. Yet college and university campuses, far from being more racially integrated, are increasingly segregated: on many campuses there are now racially separate dormitories, racially separate orientation and graduation ceremonies, and racially separate social lives. Even entire academic departments are effectively set aside racially.

Preferential affirmative action is also supposed to put black students, in particular, on the road to high-status careers. Yet the evidence shows that students with entering academic credentials that are well below average at a given campus are likely to earn grades that are likewise well below average. Such students, through no fault of their own, have been "mismatched." In too many cases, they give up on tough but rewarding majors in science and engineering—in which they would have been competitive on campuses that might have admitted them on their academic merits—and opt for soft majors that are less likely to lead to prestigious and productive careers. Far from increasing the numbers of African Americans in such careers, preferential policies reduce the numbers relative to what they might be if colleges and universities followed race-neutral policies. As a result, there are fewer African American scientists, physicians, and engineers and likely fewer lawyers and college professors as well.

It might have been hoped that preferential policies would gradually reduce racial divisions and racial consciousness in America. Yet racial division, expressions of racial grievance, and identity politics have surged in recent years. Race looms ever larger in public and private life: at times, as in the spring and summer of 2020, with outbreaks of violence across the country.

Today, the question of race preferences remains contestable, and actively contested, both politically and legally. In mid-2020, the heavily Democratic California legislature voted to put a proposition on the November ballot to repeal California's constitutional provision—adopted by statewide referendum as Proposition 209 in 1996—that prohibits the state from discriminating, or granting preferential treatment, on the basis of race, sex, or ethnicity. The repeal effort was soundly defeated. A similar effort by a Democratic legislature failed in the state of Washington in 2019. Similar political contests are liable to arise elsewhere in the country, both over existing laws like those in California and Washington and over fresh proposals for or against preferential affirmative action.

In the courts, too, the legality and constitutionality of preferences can be expected to face further challenges. Supporters, as well as critics, of preferences are well aware of this prospect. When the Supreme Court decided *Bostock v. Clayton County* (2020), Justice Gorsuch's majority opinion held that Title VII of the Civil Rights Act of 1964 forbids employment discrimination on the basis of sexual orientation, because the plain text of the law prohibits discrimination based on "race,...sex, or national origin." If a male employee is penalized for engaging in sexual activity with another male that would be perfectly acceptable in the eyes of the employer if he were female, Gorsuch held, Title VII comes into play. Professor Cass Sunstein, a prominent liberal legal scholar and a supporter of race preferences, promptly published a column titled "Gay Rights Opinion Targets Affirmative Action," concluding that "If the text of Title VII condemns discrimination on the basis of sexual orientation, it might well be taken to condemn affirmative action as well." If a knowledgeable and sophisticated supporter of preferences reacts so anxiously to a decision on a different issue—a decision whose outcome he might otherwise applaud—it suggests the fragility of the courts' acquiescence in race preferences, not least in higher education, where racial and identity-group preferences seem so entrenched.

This volume offers frank assessments of American higher education's devotion to preferential treatment and identity politics. The authors do not necessarily agree on all points. Indeed, we two coeditors do not always agree. The authors do offer compelling reasons to reconsider educational policies that discriminate in favor of some and inevitably against others, that visibly corrupt educational life, and that set Americans against each other with bitter and angry consequences.

GH and MS
San Diego, California
December 2020

Starting Down the Slippery Slope

John M. Ellis

We have now had some fifty years of affirmative action on college campuses, long enough for the full extent of its destructive impact on higher education to become fully apparent: affirmative action has sharply increased the professoriate's normal leftward tilt and changed the character of the campus left, now as a result dominated not by liberalism but by an increasingly irrational radicalism; it has spawned mischievous new pseudo-disciplines that are in reality little more than collections of political activists who undermine the academic integrity of their institutions; it has damaged the campus climate for free expression, both through speech codes designed to protect the sensibilities of minorities and through the creation of a campus political monoculture; it has led to rampant grade inflation that is in large part a response to the problem of students mismatched with academic environments for which they are not prepared and in which they cannot compete; it has damaged the prospects and the morale of countless numbers of those mismatched students; it has been the largest factor among the pressures to dumb down college curricula by deemphasizing indispensable knowledge of the history and thought of Western civilization in general, and our own country in particular, and that in turn has produced a generation ignorant of much that previous generations knew with only a high school education; it has helped establish the campus hegemony of an intellectually vacuous and ignorant postmodern relativism; and, paradoxically, it has severely damaged the chance for its intended beneficiaries to enjoy the excellent education through which previous groups of "have-nots" (e.g., Italian Americans, Jews, Irish Americans) have been able to climb the social ladder to achieve full equality of opportunity.

And yet when it began, affirmative action seemed so modest and circumscribed, so limited in scope and so well-intended, that it was impossible to imagine the damage it would do. In retrospect, however, once the smallest first steps were taken, the future course of events was inevitable. As newly appointed dean of the Graduate Division at the University of California–Santa Cruz in 1977, I oversaw those first steps on my campus. This is a story of how a monster grew from seemingly innocuous beginnings and of how easy it was for federal agencies to use even quite minor pressures to induce university administrators to take those first steps down a slope whose disastrous slipperiness they never imagined. If there is one moral to this story, it is that there is no such thing as a little sin and no such thing as a small departure from principle.

As I began my term of office as dean, I faced the same pressures that all new professor-administrators face as they take what is in effect a time-out from their real work of teaching and research. Two aspects of those pressures are relevant to my story. First, to justify taking this detour from their actual work, academics instinctively feel that the rationale for their new job can only be that they are working to create the conditions in which colleagues who are still doing the primary work of teaching and research will be able to do the best that they are capable of. And that usually means finding more money—money that will translate into better students, better faculty, better facilities, and thus better teaching and research.

The second factor relevant to this story is the great variety of competing demands on their time that academic administrators face. This is not something they are used to. Professors are rather single-minded individuals: whether in teaching or research, they are concerned with a distinct set of ideas that dominate a single field of inquiry. Theirs is a life devoted to the pursuit of truth, a rather uncompromising notion and a sharply focused kind of pursuit. But when they are appointed as academic administrators, those same people suddenly face demands from people in all kinds of disciplines about all kinds of quite different issues, and they suddenly need to understand the value of small compromises that will allow them to get things done. When you have one goal in mind, you may need the help of someone who has something quite different on his mind, and so he may want something from you with respect to a completely unrelated matter. And so these seekers after truth in their fields have to get used to giving something here (even when they are not completely persuaded of the case for doing so) if it will get something bigger there. But since this is not the way they habitually think, they are not likely to be very good at it. Judging the different values of apples and oranges in a given situation is a valuable skill; it is not one that most academics have.

At the beginning of my term as graduate dean at UCSC, we had no affirmative-action program for graduate-student admissions. And so when my office chief of staff got wind of a soon-to-be-announced federal program of grants to campuses to provide fellowships for minority and female graduate students, we both had the same thought: of course we'd like more money to support our graduate students—but mostly we want more money, whatever it may be earmarked for.[1]

It does not take an administrator long to find out that getting money for a restricted use is first and foremost getting money, period: all money is green. If you get money that is restricted to a certain purpose, you were probably using some of your existing money on that purpose anyway, and already planning to use more, which means that the new money will free up a good deal of old money for other uses. Moreover, the simple act of spending more in one area (e.g., fellowships to support students) will often mean that there will be less pressure on other areas of the budget (e.g., funds to appoint graduate students as teaching or research assistants). But in the case of this particular federal program, the general notion that more money for one thing automatically means more for everything was even more true than usual, because with each block of money to be paid directly to the graduate students for their support came an equal sum for the administration's own use as a so-called "institutional allowance." The federal government certainly knew how to get the attention of administrators; this block of completely unrestricted money would—if we succeeded in getting our hands on it—mean that some of our most cherished plans could be implemented right away.

And so a large part of our response to the news was simply the standard administrator's response to any similar situation: there is money to be had, and we should get it. Of course the specific purpose seemed a worthy one, but so would many others; the main point was that to get anything worthwhile done we needed above all to increase the total office budget.

Hindsight tells us where all of this was leading, but at the time what was being asked of us was so modest that it was not at all difficult to believe in the usefulness of the program. Nor did this seem to be a question of a small compromise here to get a greater good there; there was barely any question of a compromise at all. All we needed to do to satisfy the federal bureaucrats (and so earn the money that was being offered) was establish a good outreach program. By now it is hard to imagine that there was once a time when it was still almost universally accepted that this would not involve preferences being given to minorities or women in admissions to graduate programs, but such was indeed the case at this time. Our job was to look diligently for potential minority and female graduate students in places and in ways we might not have before, and to motivate them to apply, but that was the end of the matter. They would sink or swim on their own merits in the application process. None of this was inconsistent with what would later become California's Proposition 209, and to this day campaigns to outlaw racial and gender preferences in admissions still insist they have nothing against "good" affirmative action (i.e., looking for and motivating minorities and women to apply).

To be sure, the new fellowships made available by the federal government were earmarked for minority and female students, which would not be allowed by Proposition 209; but, to any knowledgeable observer at the time, this would have seemed an unimportant point, because departments did not admit more graduate students than they could support in one way or another. From a practical point of view, what was important about the new program was not that the student support funds were earmarked, but rather the institution of an outreach program—one of finding and motivating more of certain kinds of applicants.

We exploited our advance warning of the new federal program by quickly putting together a proposal that outlined a vigorous outreach plan, and we sent it off to the program director almost before the program was officially announced. We were not the only ones anxious to get started: the program director, too, wanted to get things moving, and in a very short time we had received a large block of fellowships with all the attendant institutional grant money.

The outcome was exactly what might make academic administrators feel good about having temporarily abandoned their real work of teaching and research: we had kept a watchful eye for new sources of money, we had nimbly pounced on one just as soon as it came into view, to the great benefit—or so we thought—of our campus and its programs. The result looked to be something of a triumph: UCSC's graduate program was by far the smallest of all the nine UC campuses, yet we got more money than the other eight combined in this first year of the federal program, and that state of affairs even continued for a year or two. We had easily beaten to the punch all the larger, older, and more prestigious campuses of the UC system.

There is no greater truism than the old saying that nothing succeeds like success. With this outcome behind us, it was easy to persuade the campus administration to fund the staff we needed to do the job that we had outlined in our proposal, and we soon had an excellent man out on the road drumming up good minority graduate-program applications for us. Everything seemed to be going well—so well that the other UC campuses scrambled to catch up with us and get some of the federal money for themselves. But we had not seen deeply enough into the situation. What we did not grasp was that we now had staff within the graduate dean's office who had a real stake in a certain kind of outcome: their professional success and reputation was geared to a rise in minority and female graduate-student numbers. There's another word for this: a lobby. This was nothing to do with any personal characteristics of the individuals involved—it was simply a structural fact.

Regardless of this, in the short term, success continued to make for more success. The university's system-wide administration must have noticed what was happening, because it now joined in by making yet another large sum available for fellowships to support minority and female graduate students. And once again, the real effect of this was to make more support money available for all students. Further, since this followed hard on the heels of the increase brought by the federal program, departments began to notice that the amount of money that flowed from my office to support their students kept growing appreciably. We were gaining credibility and goodwill, and that in turn had the effect of making it easier to get other things done. I'll give a few illustrative examples of how this effect worked.

One day the phone rang, and when I picked it up there was an angry voice shouting at me. It belonged to a well-known member of the California state senate, and he was phoning to give me a good scolding over the fact that my campus was proposing to begin a new PhD program in a field in which (as he saw it) the state was already well served. Because of their budgetary implications, all new graduate programs were reviewed by the state government before approval. The senator had seen our program proposal and wanted to tell the guilty party—me—that this was a shameful waste of state resources when there were already so many PhD programs in that field in the state. He went on at some length about my lack of restraint. Finally, I managed to interrupt his harangue with a question: I asked him whether he knew that the federal government had liked our proposed graduate-student affirmative-action program so much that it had given us more money than the other eight UC campuses combined. He calmed down and wanted to know more. (The senator was Hispanic.) We talked—very pleasantly now—for some time about the matter. He ended the call by telling me to keep up the good work. We got our PhD program approved.

On another occasion, a rabble-rousing junior faculty member started to agitate publicly for formal ethnic representation in the appointment process for a senior position in my office. I knew that that way lay a dysfunctional appointment process, but the problem soon went away when I appealed to some senior ethnic faculty friends for help. I imagine they told him to pick on somebody else in the administration to harass—not someone who was already on the right side of the issue.

Remember, once more, that administrative work—unlike professorial duty—routinely involves weighing the pluses and minuses of compromises. In this situation, that calculus seemed strongly tilted to the positive side. We had gained large advantages of all kinds in exchange for a small and seemingly innocuous compromise. But this turned out to be a bad miscalculation, and the first hint that this might be so came soon enough. The staffer who was leading the job of seeking out minority applicants for our graduate programs began to pout about the fact that too few of them were being accepted by the departments. On average, one in three applicants was accepted into a UCSC graduate program at that time, but the figure for minority applicants was one in four. (Our graduate program was still fairly new—established graduate programs are usually able to be still more selective.) It was easy enough for me to explain the discrepancy: when you are trying to find and motivate people who might not otherwise have applied, the average applicant that results from this process will likely be not quite as strong as those who applied all by themselves. But the staffer was still despondent, because from his point of view the results of a great deal of time and effort were being met with much less than enthusiasm. This was not an unreasonable reaction; everyone tries to maximize the scope and effectiveness of his or her office, and it was perfectly understandable that he should do so too. But this was the first sign that the federal program had, in fact, planted a Trojan horse on the campus. Staff who looked for minority applications naturally took an interest in how they fared. They inquired of departments; they expressed disappointment that an applicant whom they had thought promising did not get in; and, in effect, they lobbied for them.

The mostly liberal faculty did not like to seem completely unreceptive to advocates for minority students; in any case, they, too, gradually began to respond to the fact that more money and more credibility came to people and departments that joined the bandwagon. As a result, they started to give the outreach staff a more sympathetic hearing. At the outset, our proposal to the federal program director had been quite clear about the fact that all applicants would be treated equally, but within a short time that was obviously no longer true, and it was the dynamic created by the program itself that led inexorably to that result. And once the climate began to change, the rate of that change was astonishing. Within ten years of the start of the program, one large department deliberately rejected all male applicants and admitted fifteen women. Another received ten black applicants and admitted all ten, the result being a virtually all-black first-year graduate class. So extreme did the climate become, and so quickly, that I even had two irate Marxist faculty members protest to me about their department's now mindless automatic admission of black graduate students.

With hindsight, it is possible to see how the process of deterioration worked. The initial small lobby for overriding merit-based application decisions grew slowly with each compromise that was made. With each faculty appointment and student admission made with the intent of increasing the numbers of minority members and women, the lobby for more of the same the next time around was numerically stronger—and the time after that it was stronger still, and so on. Given this process of intensification, the virtual collapse of merit-based admissions in some departments was inevitable. Still, the collapse was an amazing thing to watch. At each stage, as one's breath was quite taken away by what was happening, there was always the thought that things could not possibly get worse. But they always did: the downward trajectory simply continued until an absolute bottom was reached, one in which minorities and women were admitted for the sake of admitting minorities and women, period.

Why was it seemingly so impossible to hold affirmative-action measures to a level that was reasonable and defensible? Why did the whole thing run away with us and become a cause that overwhelmed other values? I had plenty of time to think about this after I decided to quit my deanship and return to teaching and research. And I finally understood what had happened and why it had been impossible to stop the slide to the bottom once the process had begun.

Before all this started, life in the academy was governed by the principle that all students deserve equal consideration. That does not mean that they were treated equally—their individual characteristics make that impossible—but it does mean that any inequality of treatment derived from their performance as students, not from any other considerations. Now when we decided to spend more time looking for and motivating certain kinds of students, defined not by their abilities but by their skin color or gender, we had made the decision to deviate from that principle (in a rather small way, to be sure), because we saw that deviation as serving a good cause. The crux of the matter is once we had departed from our basic principle, the question must arise: If a small deviation from the guiding principle of equal consideration is a good thing, why shouldn't a slightly bigger deviation be an even better thing? To all these demands for more, there is only one principled answer: it is wrong to treat students other than with equal consideration. *But that was the argument we gave up when we took the very first, smallest step*: it was no longer available once we had decided to take that first step. And that is why nothing can stop the slide down the slippery slope. With the first step, we had abandoned the only principled defense against being pushed into taking the next, and the next, and the next.

This realization brings with it an unambiguous judgment on the so-called "good" affirmative action: there is no such thing. When the federal government asked us to institute modest, outreach-only affirmative action, it was in effect cutting us loose from the principle that had organized our lives as university teachers, and that led inexorably to the catastrophe that was to come.

Before I left office, I was to see the full horror of what I had set in motion at the beginning of my deanship. When departments at UCSC make the decision to expel graduate students from their programs, those graduate students have the right to appeal their dismissal to the dean as a last resort. Few took that opportunity, but suddenly there were two such interviews on my schedule, both with black students whose departments had decided that their work was not such that they could ever be expected to get a PhD. The two interviews were virtually identical in character. Both students were absolutely devastated; they had been led to expect that they could attain the exalted rank of Doctor of Philosophy, only to be thrown out with nothing. They were extraordinarily bitter and hostile. They poured out their resentment at the system that had betrayed them. They charged the institution in general, and their departments in particular, with racism and bigotry, but they reserved their most bitter criticism for their faculty advisers, whom they accused of the vilest prejudice against black people. That alone told me how much damage we had done to these two, for I knew the two faculty advisers well. One was the only black man in his department, an enormously decent man who took very seriously what he regarded as his obligation to help black students as much as he could. The other was a white liberal scholar who was well known nationally both for his writings on race relations and for his advocacy of racial equality. The two students were so filled with hatred for the institution that had failed them that they were blinded to the fact that these two members of our faculty were the last ones that anyone should accuse of racial prejudice.

These two interviews were decisive for me. The human cost of what we had done was now clear. We had intervened in the normal process of people finding their own level through their own qualities—their interests, their preparation, their intelligence, their level of determination—and so distorted what should have been the result of this natural process that the outcome had been cruelly destructive for the individuals concerned. Nobody who sat through those two interviews with me could have failed to see the scale of damage of which we, with all our good intentions, were guilty. And, since that time, I have opposed affirmative action—not just the kind that gives preferences in admissions and appointments, but outreach affirmative action too, because I had now learned the hard way that the one removes any defense against the other.

A Dubious Expediency

Gail Heriot

I have no doubt that those who originally conceived of race-preferential admissions policies over fifty years ago were acting in good faith. By lowering admissions standards for African American and Hispanic students at elite colleges and universities, they hoped to increase the number of minority students on campus and ultimately to promote their integration into high-status careers.

The real conflict over race-preferential admissions policies has not been about good or bad faith or whether we should aspire to be a society in which members of racial minorities are fully integrated into the mainstream. There is no question that we should. The conflict is about the means. Should we allow the principle of color-blindness under the law to be sacrificed in the hope that, in the long run, it will help us become a society of equal opportunity?

No less a liberal icon than Justice Stanley Mosk warned of the risks associated with such temporary compromises of principle. Writing for the California Supreme Court in *Bakke v. UC Regents* (1976), he held racially discriminatory admissions policies to be unconstitutional:

> To uphold the [argument for race-preferential admissions] would

call for the sacrifice of principle for the sake of dubious expediency and would represent a retreat in the struggle to assure that
each man and woman shall be judged based on individual merit
alone, a struggle which has only lately achieved success in removing legal barriers to racial equality.[1]

Justice Mosk understood something fundamental about race
discrimination. Throughout history, the temptation to engage in
it has almost always come packaged with a justification that many
found appealing at the time.[2] When the country has succumbed
to that temptation, however, it has almost always come to regret
it. By 1976, when Mosk was writing, we owed it to ourselves to
be more skeptical.

The *Bakke* case was brought by Allan Bakke, the son of a
mailman and a schoolteacher—hardly a scion of wealth and privilege. After serving in Vietnam as a medic, he had twice applied
for admission to the University of California at Davis Medical
School. "More than anything else in the world, *I want to study
medicine*," he wrote in his statement, and his actions proved it
was true. But he was rejected both times, under circumstances
that pointed strongly to his race.[3]

At the time, UC-Davis Medical School had a two-track admissions system. The first 84 out of 100 seats in the class were given
to the most qualified applicants, regardless of their race, ethnicity, or other disadvantages. Bakke just missed making the cut.
The remaining 16 seats were reserved for the disadvantaged; but,
in practice, "disadvantaged" always meant members of racial
minorities. Bakke could have been the fatherless son of an illit-
erate washerwoman, and it wouldn't have mattered: Because he
was white, he did not qualify.

It is worth pointing out that at UC-Davis Medical School,
race was no mere tiebreaker in otherwise close cases. Bakke had
a college grade point average (GPA) of 3.46 and an undergradu-

ate science GPA of 3.44 (back before grade inflation's long march through the academy), as well as a commendable record of volunteer emergency-room service at a local hospital. He frequently worked there late into the night with victims of car accidents and street fights.[4] By contrast, the average "disadvantaged track" admittee in 1973 had a college GPA of 2.88 and an undergraduate science GPA of 2.62.

The gap in standardized test scores was also wide. Bakke's MCAT scores put him at the 97th percentile (Science), the 96th percentile (Verbal), the 94th percentile (Quantitative), and the 72nd percentile (General Information). On the other hand, the average "disadvantaged track" admittee in 1973 had MCAT scores in the 35th percentile (Science), the 46th percentile (Verbal), the 24th percentile (Quantitative), and the 33rd percentile (General Information).

Supporters of race preferences instantly denounced Mosk's decision for the California Supreme Court. Hundreds of demonstrators gathered beneath his office window to demand its reversal. Thousands rallied elsewhere. When visiting local campuses, Mosk routinely found himself greeted by picketers and hecklers.

When UC-Davis, in a conciliatory gesture, invited Mosk to give the law school commencement address in 1978, students insisted that he decline the honor. When he accepted anyway, a quarter of the graduating students walked out. But Mosk was undaunted. "Judges in California cannot be intimidated," he stated firmly. "Lawsuits are won and lost in courtrooms, not on the streets."[5]

At the time, Mosk would have probably laughed to hear his insistence on color-blindness characterized as "conservative." Up to then, he had been accused far more frequently of leaning too far to the left. But whatever his political persuasion, Mosk had been a stalwart ally of the civil rights movement from its beginning. At a time when it was not yet fashionable to do so, he had quit fraternal organizations in protest over their refusal to admit African American members. As California's attorney general, he established the office's civil rights division and banned the Professional Golfers Association from using state golf courses until it agreed to admit African American members.

Far from seeing a contradiction between his support for the civil rights movement and his opposition to the "minority friendly" admissions policies in *Bakke*, Mosk viewed them as the same. His opposition to race discrimination was a matter of principle. And he was unwilling to sacrifice that principle for what he called the "dubious" practical gains promised by supporters of race-based preferences.

Mosk's vision of civil rights did not prevail. Two years later, his opinion was superseded by the U.S. Supreme Court's decision in *Regents of the University of California v. Bakke* (1978).[6] In that fractured decision, four justices would have affirmed Mosk's decision, while four would have accorded public universities and other governmental bodies virtually unlimited power to discriminate in favor of racial groups that they perceived to be disadvantaged.

Justice Lewis Powell, Jr., whose lone opinion is now much admired by advocates of race-preferential admissions policies, purported to take a middle path. His opinion took the position that race-based preferences are permissible, but only as a method of capturing the benefits of a diverse student body for *all* students—sometimes called the "diversity rationale." At the same time, Powell's opinion decided the case for Mr. Bakke apparently on the ground that the inflexibility of the admissions policy disproved its claim to be so motivated.

In the years following *Bakke*, race-preferential admissions policies mushroomed on college and university campuses. As they grew, millions of Americans, correctly or incorrectly, came to view themselves as beneficiaries. More important, a thriving diversity and remedial education bureaucracy was established to administer the policies and deal with the consequences.[7] Rightly or wrongly, many of those so employed believe their jobs to be in jeopardy whenever race-preferential admissions policies are debated. By 2003, when the Supreme Court had the opportunity to address the issue again, it essentially adopted Powell's position.[8]

Thus, if Mosk was right that the benefits promised by race-preferential admissions were "dubious," the mistake will be difficult to correct at this late date. It isn't just the iron rule of bureaucracy at work today—that first and foremost bureaucracies work to preserve themselves. Many distinguished citizens—university presidents, philanthropists, judges, and legislators—have built their reputations on their support for race-based admissions. Their jobs may not be at stake, but their sense of accomplishment almost certainly is. Overcoming that is not easy.

But if anything can cause good-faith supporters to stop and reconsider, it is the mounting empirical research showing that race-preferential admissions policies are doing more harm than good, even for their intended beneficiaries.[9] If this research is right, we now have fewer, not more, African American physicians, scientists, and engineers than we would have had if colleges and universities had followed race-neutral policies. We have fewer college professors too, and likely fewer lawyers. Ironically, preferential treatment has made it more difficult for talented African American and Hispanic students to enter high-prestige careers.

No one should want to support race-preferential admissions policies if their effects are precisely the opposite of what was hoped for. Even if the consequences of race preferences turn out to be simply a wash—neither increasing nor decreasing the number of African American and Hispanic professionals—it is difficult to understand why anyone would wish to support them rather than adhere to the principle of race neutrality.

How can it be that affirmative action actually *reduces* the number of minority professionals graduating from colleges and universities? One of the consequences of widespread race-preferential admissions policies is that talented under-represented minority students end up distributed among colleges and universities in patterns that are very different from those of their white and Asian American counterparts. When the schools that are highest on the academic ladder relax their admissions policies in order to admit more under-represented minority students, schools one rung down must do likewise, or they will have fewer under-represented minority students than they would have had under a general color-blind admissions policy. The problem is thus passed on to the schools another rung down, which respond similarly. As a result, students from under-represented minorities today are concentrated at the bottom of the distribution of entering academic credentials at most selective colleges and universities.

The problem is not that there are no academically gifted African American or Hispanic students seeking admission to colleges and universities. The nation is fortunate to have many. But there are not enough at the very top tiers to satisfy the demand, and efforts to change that have had a pernicious effect on admissions up and down the academic pecking order, creating a serious credentials gap at every competitive level.

Unfortunately, a student whose entering academic credentials are well below those of the average student in a particular school will likely earn grades to match. And the reason is simple: Entering academic credentials matter. While some students will outperform their academic credentials, just as some students will underperform theirs, most students will perform in the range that their entering credentials suggest. Anyone who claims differently is engaging in wishful thinking at students' expense.

Hard data are difficult to come by, in part because databases that could be helpful in studying the problem are made unavailable to researchers who are not true believers. Some of the best available statistics on this point come from a few years back for law schools.[10] In 2003, UCLA law professor Richard Sander reported that at elite law schools, 51.6 percent of African American students, compared to only 5.6 percent of white students, had first-year GPAs in the bottom 10 percent of their class.[11] Nearly identical gaps existed at law schools at all levels (with the exception of historically minority schools).[12] At mid-range public law schools, the median African American student's first-year grades corresponded to the 5th percentile among white students. For mid-range private schools, the median for African American students corresponded to the 7th percentile among white students.[13]

Overall, with disappointingly few exceptions, African American students were grouped toward the bottom of their class. Moreover, contrary to popular belief, the gap in grades did not close as students continued through law school. Instead, by graduation, it became wider.[14]

I am not aware of anyone who disputes these figures. Even strong supporters of race preferences have conceded the problem is "real and serious" and that "the average black law student's grades are startlingly low."[15]

Derek Bok and William G. Bowen, authors of *The Shape of the River: Long-Term Consequences of Considering Race in College and University Admissions*, were longtime advocates of race-based admissions policies. As former presidents of Harvard and Princeton, respectively, they can fairly be said to have been among those who invented race-based admissions. Nevertheless, they have candidly admitted that the credentials gap has serious consequences: "College grades [for affirmative-action beneficiaries] present a...sobering picture," they wrote. "The grades earned by African-American students at the [elite schools we studied] often reflect their struggles to succeed academically in highly competitive academic settings."[16]

Why are poor grades a problem? Why isn't it better to get disappointing grades at a top school than good grades at a school one or two rungs down? The answer to that question is this: Everyone knows that a good student can get in over his head if he is placed in a classroom with students whose level of academic preparation is much higher than his own. He can end up learning less than he would have been capable of. Such a student has, through no fault of his own, been "mismatched."[17]

I have every confidence, for example, that I could learn basic physics, despite the fact that I have never taken a course in it and my mathematics skills are a little rusty. On the other hand, if you were to throw me into the Basic Physics course at Caltech, with many of the very best science students in the world, I would be lost and likely learn little, if anything. I would be mismatched. On a good day, I might make a few lame jokes about how law professors just aren't geeky enough to do physics; on a bad day, I might even get a little prickly about it. But it is unlikely that I would come out of that class as competent in the basic principles of physics as I would have in a less high-powered setting.[18]

That doesn't mean that putting students into separate groups according to their academic performance—"tracking," as it is sometimes called—is always beneficial.[19] In elementary schools, for example, students who are put in the less advanced class may be somewhat more likely to have behavioral problems. As a result, concentrating them together in one class can potentially make that class less effective.

But research has shown that mismatch is the problem at the college and university level. Sometimes the problem is simply that a less-than-stellar performance leads to a loss of enthusiasm for academic pursuits and causes students to put their energies into other endeavors—like athletics, social life, or campus politics. Everyone needs a niche. If, for the beneficiaries of race preferences, excelling at academics in their peer group seems out of reach, they will look to stand out in other ways. Alas, the other pathways available to them are usually less likely to lead to high-prestige careers.

Whatever the mechanism, as I will detail below, the evidence is getting extremely strong at this point: Race-preferential admissions policies as practiced today are hurting, not helping, when it comes to jump-starting the careers of preference recipients. This is not to say that all students who are given preferential treatment will have their prospects for high-prestige careers dashed. Neither is it to say that all colleges and universities that put a thumb on the scale for minority students, no matter how small, are creating serious mismatch problems.[20] But there is every reason to believe the problem is real and significant.

Let's take a look at the evidence a step at a time.

WHY MINORITY STUDENTS FLEE SCIENCE AND ENGINEERING

When Americans want to make the point that something isn't overwhelmingly difficult, we say, "Hey, this isn't rocket science." In doing so, we acknowledge that mastering real rocket science— and, by extension, other hard sciences and engineering—really is tough.[21] As one Yale University student complained to the *Wall Street Journal*, "In other classes if you do the work, you'll get an A....In science, it just doesn't work that way."[22]

Many students who start out majoring in science or engineering eventually switch to something easier. Although it is uncommon at elite schools, some drop out of school altogether, and a few may even flunk out.[23] Part of the reason may be that science and engineering are ruthlessly cumulative. A student who has difficulty with the first chapter in the calculus textbook is likely to have difficulty with later chapters and with subsequent courses in the mathematics curriculum. By contrast, an English literature student who simply fails to read the Chaucer assignment is not necessarily at a serious disadvantage when it comes to reading and understanding Virginia Woolf. Since quitting science and engineering is easy—ordinarily, all one has to do is switch majors—the attrition rate is quite high. By senior year, there are significantly fewer science and engineering majors than there were freshmen initially interested in those majors—of all races and ethnicities.[24] The pool of potential physicians, engineers, and scientists thus shrinks.

It should surprise no one that those who fail to attain their goal of a science or engineering degree are disproportionately students whose entering academic credentials put them toward the bottom of their college class.[25] Not all stereotypes about science and engineering students are accurate. But the notion that they tend to be both highly credentialed and hardworking is largely on target. They have to be.

What does surprise some, however, is this: Several unrebutted empirical studies have now demonstrated that *part of the effect is relative.* An aspiring science or engineering major who attends a school where her entering academic credentials put her in the middle or the top of her class is more likely to succeed than an otherwise identical student attending a more elite school where *those same credentials* place her toward the bottom of the class.[26] Put differently, an aspiring science or engineering major would be smart to avoid an affirmative-action preference and instead attend a school where her entering credentials compare favorably with her classmates'.

Affirmative-action beneficiaries are by no means the only ones who need to take note. This should be of serious concern to college athletes, children of alumni, and other special admittees. Still, as a nation concerned with integrating more African Americans and Hispanics into leadership positions, we need to be especially attentive to the implications for affirmative action.

A few years ago, a friend of mine took his daughter, a very talented high school senior, to visit some of the nation's top science-specialty colleges and universities—including Caltech, MIT, and Rice University. Several of these institutions tried to show off their commitment to diversity by having an attractive and personable minority student conduct the campus tour. But a pattern emerged among the tour guides: In the course of the tour, these student guides would reveal that while they had started out intending to major in science or engineering, they had switched to a softer major.

These are the schools attended by the nation's rocket scientists—both literally and figuratively. The ones who get in or almost get in—whether as affirmative-action beneficiaries or not—are all remarkable talents. But there are differences in the level of academic preparation between those who were admitted strictly on their academic credentials and those who weren't. The former, no matter what their race, often have been living and breathing science or engineering since they were in elementary school. Those who needed a preference to get in are very talented, but that frequently won't be enough to make them academically competitive with those who didn't need one.

These beneficiaries of preferential treatment nevertheless had as their first choice the study of science and engineering. That is why they chose one of these schools in the first place. All of them could have succeeded in that ambition just about anywhere else. But misguided admissions policies may cause them unwittingly to attend the only schools on the Planet Earth where they would instead come out as communications majors. This waste of scientific talent doesn't have to be.

Recent statistics show that the dearth of African Americans and Hispanics with science and engineering degrees is real. African Americans are about 14 percent of the college-age population (ages eighteen to twenty-four). But while they account for 10.4 percent of the bachelor's degrees conferred by American colleges and universities, they receive only 7.0 percent of the science and engineering bachelor's degrees and 4.6 percent of the science and engineering PhDs. Similarly, Hispanics are 22 percent of the population from eighteen to twenty-four years old and account for 14.2 percent of the bachelor's degrees conferred by American colleges and universities. But they receive only 12.1 percent of the science and engineering bachelor's degrees and 6.9 percent of the science and engineering PhDs.[27]

All other things being equal, one might expect a minority whose members are less likely to be native English speakers to major in science and engineering more commonly than native English speakers. But this does not seem to be the case with Hispanics. On the other hand, Asian American college graduates are more than four and a half times as likely to have a bachelor's degree in science or engineering and a little over seven times as likely to have a PhD in those areas as white graduates.[28]

If we were discussing fairly narrow fields—like acoustical engineering, or Russian literature, or golf—this lack of representation would be of no great moment. There is no segment of the labor force that proportionately reflects the nation's demographic profile. Physicians are disproportionately Chinese American, South Asian American, or Jewish.[29] As a result of the efforts of Hollywood actress Tippi Hedren, ethnic Vietnamese dominate the manicure business;[30] Hispanic jockeys dominate horse racing.[31] The wine industry employs more than its proportional share of Italian Americans.[32] Even within professions, disproportionality is the rule, not the exception. Among lawyers, litigators are disproportionately Irish American.[33] Among physicians, radiologists are disproportionately South Asian American.[34]

Science and engineering, however, are not narrow fields. Obtaining an initial degree in science or engineering is the gateway to a large number of respected professions and occupations—from aviation inspector to zoologist. These fields represent a significant portion of the world's most rewarding jobs, and their importance is likely to increase in the future. If African Americans and Hispanics are facing significant impediments to entering, that is a situation that calls for attention.

Lack of investment in a solution does not appear to be the problem. Concern over under-representation in science and engineering is not new. In 1992, nearly three decades ago, the popular magazine *Science* issued a special news report entitled "Minorities in Science." In it, the editors lamented:

> For 20 years, science has been wrestling with "the pipeline problem": how to keep minorities from turning off the obstacle-strewn path to careers in science, mathematics, and engineering. Thousands of programs have been started since the late 1960s to bring diversity to the scientific workforce. But their results have been dismal.[35]

By 1992, the National Science Foundation had already spent over $1.5 billion on programs designed to increase the number of minorities in science or engineering. Officials at the National Institutes of Health estimated that they had pumped an additional $675 million into the system. Uncounted state, local, foundation, and industry programs contributed much more.[36]

Nevertheless, the consensus was that much of the money had been spent unwisely. In the earliest days of affirmative action, "colleges took any person of color who wanted to become an engineer, regardless of their background," said Mary Perry Smith, a former Oakland school teacher and founder of California's Mathematics, Engineering, Science Achievement (MESA) program, which promotes minority student participation in those fields. "They tried to turn students who barely knew algebra into engineers, and it was a total failure."[37]

Things have gotten better. According to its website, MESA, founded in 1970, serves "educationally disadvantaged students" and "to the extent possible by law, emphasizes participation from groups with low rates of eligibility for four-year colleges."[38] By targeting students in high school and middle school, MESA tries to cultivate students' interest in science and engineering and make sure students get the experience they need to succeed in these disciplines in college. Programs like MESA, which require one-on-one contact with students, are expensive, but they appear to have enjoyed a measure of success.[39]

Even considering the modest success of programs like MESA, however, most of the news of the past fifty years has been disappointing. In 1992, Dr. Luther Williams, the assistant director of education and human resources at the National Science Foundation, was exasperated enough to declare, "The country cannot repeat the experiment of the last 20 years." Williams, who later went on to become provost of Tuskegee University, a historically black university with a reputation for emphasizing a science and engineering curriculum, was blunt: Those vast expenditures were "an incredible waste of financial and human resources."[40]

Williams may have sounded more pessimistic than he intended. Billions of dollars had been spent, and much of it produced nothing. But some of the programs that have encouraged members of minority groups to pursue science and engineering may well have been worth it. There is no reason to abandon successful efforts. The real question is whether we can do better, and the answer to that question is an optimistic yes. All we have to do is stop shooting ourselves in the collective foot.

First of all, the problem with the under-representation of African Americans, Hispanics, and American Indians in science and engineering is not a lack of interest on the part of the minority students. Some have assumed the opposite—that a lack of role models would cause a lack of interest among African Americans and Hispanics. Minority students are indeed less likely to have a friend or family member in science or engineering, but it doesn't seem to be the root of the problem. Study after study has found that, if anything, African American and Hispanic students are slightly more interested in pursuing science and engineering degrees than white students are.[41]

Those studies go back a long time. For example, Professors Alexander W. Astin and Helen S. Astin of UCLA's Higher Education Research Institute examined a sample of 27,065 students enrolling as freshmen at 388 four-year colleges in 1985. They found that the rate of initial interest in majoring in a biological science, a physical science, or engineering was, in descending order, 52.6 percent for Asians, 35.7 percent for Chicanos, 34.5 percent for American Indians, 34.2 percent for African Americans, and 27.3 percent for whites.[42]

Every time, it comes out the same: African Americans and other racial minorities are *more* interested in science and engineering than whites. Lack of interest among Americans in science and engineering may well be a problem. But if it is, it has been more with college-bound whites than with African Americans and Hispanics. If one wants to understand the root of the underrepresentation problem, one must look elsewhere.

Some researchers have done just that. They have shown that the problem comes a little further down the pipeline—with attrition. While African American and Hispanic students have higher rates of initial interest than white students do, they are less likely to follow through with that interest. Somewhere in college, the intention to graduate with a degree in science or engineering withers and dies. In one study of elite colleges and universities, for example, 70 percent of Asians persisted in their ambition, compared to 61 percent of whites, 55 percent of Hispanics, and 34 percent of blacks.[43]

Some observers have been inclined to ask, "What accounts for disproportionate minority attrition?" But in our age of political correctness, we have become too inclined to see every question in race-conscious terms. The right question is "What accounts for student attrition from science and engineering in general?" Once that question is answered, the question about disproportionate minority attrition essentially answers itself.

The usual culprit is lagging entering science credentials—like math SAT score, the grades received for high school courses in mathematics and science, and the number of such courses taken, all of which are strongly correlated with persistence in science.[44] The better one's entering science credentials, both in the absolute sense and in comparison to one's classmates, the more likely a student with an initial interest in science and engineering will persevere and ultimately succeed in earning a degree.

This is a double whammy for African American and Hispanic students as a group. While there are many individual students of all races with excellent entering science credentials, the average for African Americans and Hispanics as groups is below that for the nation as a whole. Until that changes, students from those groups are all but certain to have higher-than-average attrition rates from science and engineering.[45] That's unfortunate enough by itself. But as a result of race-preferential admissions policies, as well-intentioned as these policies are, those same groups are concentrated toward the bottom of selective colleges and universities. That constitutes a completely unnecessary second hit.

Improving the absolute entering science credentials of under-represented minority students is imperative, but the work is painstaking, and progress has been slow. On the other hand, improving those credentials in comparison to other students at the same school is easy. It would significantly increase the number of under-represented minority students who graduate with science and engineering degrees. All we have to do is stop encouraging students to enroll in schools at which they need a preference to be admitted.

The earliest study showing mismatch to be part of the problem, "The Role of Ethnicity in Choosing and Leaving Science in Highly Selective Institutions," was published in 1996 by a team of scholars led by Dartmouth psychologist Rogers Elliott. It found that the single most important cause for black attrition from science at the selective institutions studied was the "*relatively* low preparation of black aspirants to science in these schools."[46] The authors were careful to use the word "relatively." For successful students, it wasn't just entering credentials demonstrating highly developed ability at science that mattered, but *comparatively* high credentials. A student who attended a school at which his math SAT score put him in the top third of his class was much more likely to follow through with an ambition to earn a degree in science or engineering than was a student with the *same score* who attended a school at which that score put him in the bottom third of the class. The problem for minority students was that, as a result of affirmative action, being in the top third of the class was relatively rare.

For some, this is counterintuitive. The more prestigious the school, they believe, the more adept it should be at graduating future physicians, scientists, and engineers, no matter what their entering credentials. But instructors everywhere must pitch the material they teach at a particular level. They can pitch to the top of the class, to the middle, or to the bottom, but they can't do all three at the same time.

At elite colleges and universities, pitching to the bottom of the class is uncommon—especially in the science and engineering departments. The whole point of these institutions is to teach to the top. If these institutions were to abandon that practice and resolve to teach to the bottom of the class, there would be no good reason for them to exist.

Elliott and his coauthors cited the extraordinary record of historically black colleges and universities (HBCUs), which graduate far more than their share of black engineering and science majors, as further support for their findings. They reported that with only 20 percent of total African American enrollment, these schools had been producing 40 percent of the African American graduates with natural science degrees. Those students frequently went on to earn PhDs from non-HBCUs. According to the National Science Foundation, of the approximately 700 African Americans who earned a doctorate in science or engineering between 1986 and 1988, 29 percent earned their undergraduate degree from an HBCU. For biologists, the figure was 42 percent, and for engineers, it was 36 percent.[47] This success has continued into more recent years.[48]

There is nothing magical about HBCUs. It's just that unlike at other colleges and universities, credentials gaps are not an issue at historically black institutions. One faculty member at a historically black school—North Carolina Central University's Walter Pattillo, Jr.—told *Science* magazine in 1992: "The way we see it, the majority schools are wasting large numbers of good students. They have black students with admissions statistics [that are] very high, tops. But these students wind up majoring in sociology or recreation or get wiped out altogether."[49]

A somewhat more recent study by University of Virginia psychologists Frederick Smyth and John McArdle (now at the University of Southern California) confirmed Elliott's findings. And the effects were not subtle. In "Ethnic and Gender Differences in Science Graduation at Selective Colleges with Implications for Admission Policy and College Choice," Smyth and McArdle examined a sample of under-represented minority students at twenty-three universities who intended to major in science, mathematics, or engineering. They found that 45 percent more of the women and 35 percent more of the men would have succeeded in attaining their goals if they had attended schools where their entering credentials had been about average.[50]

Those figures, upon reflection, are stunning. If in just the time it would take a high school senior to graduate from college with a degree in science or engineering, we could add as success stories 45 percent more women and 35 percent more men coming out of these schools, that would be a breakthrough of epic proportions. Half of that would still be huge. A tenth would be a step in the right direction.

Another study—this one by UCLA law professor Richard Sander and UCLA statistician Roger Bolus—was presented to the U.S. Commission on Civil Rights early in my tenure there. It pulled data from nine University of California campuses. The authors came to a similar conclusion. "Minority attrition in science is a very real problem," they wrote, "and the evidence in this paper suggests that 'negative mismatch' probably plays a role in it." Their multiple approaches to the data yielded consistent results:

[S]tudents with credentials more than one standard deviation below their science peers at college are about half as likely to end up with science bachelor degrees, compared with similar students attending schools where their credentials are much closer to, or above, the mean credentials of their peers.[51]

All three of these studies were highlighted in a report entitled *Encouraging Minority Students to Pursue Science, Technology, Engineering and Math Careers* by the U.S. Commission on Civil Rights in 2010. The researchers' conclusions have gone largely unchallenged. Although one very recent study using a different database failed to detect a mismatch effect specific to science and engineering, the weight of the evidence continues to favor a mismatch effect, and even that study found evidence of a mismatch effect on four-year graduation rates.[52]

This body of evidence has nevertheless been ignored by colleges and universities. In *Fisher v. University of Texas*,[53] the lawsuit challenging race preferences that reached the Supreme Court in 2013 and again in 2016, the University of Texas took a position at odds with it. UT argued that it needed to use race-preferential admissions to ensure racial diversity not only in the student body as a whole but also in science classes (as well as other classes and programs). But the evidence indicates that preferential treatment for minority students aggravates, rather than alleviates, the problem of under-representation in science. The more colleges and universities engage in race preferences, the fewer African Americans and Hispanics will graduate with such degrees.

Evidence has continued to accumulate since the report of the Commission on Civil Rights. In 2012, Duke University economists Peter Arcidiacono and Esteban Aucejo and Duke University sociologist Ken Spenner found evidence supporting the mismatch thesis when researching the major choices of undergraduates enrolled at Duke. In their article "What Happens After Enrollment? An Analysis of the Time Path of Racial Differences in GPA and Major Choice," they found that black undergraduates were much less likely to persist with an entering goal of majoring in engineering, the natural sciences, or economics than white students were. The problem at Duke was not so much failing out or quitting school entirely; more often, it was giving up on science and engineering specifically. Approximately 54 percent of black males switched out of these majors, while only 8 percent of white males did.

Once again, the problem was not lack of interest in science and engineering among black students. Indeed, before starting at Duke, more black than white students indicated an initial interest in majoring in these subjects. Instead, the differences in attrition were best explained by entering academic credentials.[54]

Arcidiacono, Aucejo, and Spenner also helped dispel the common belief that affirmative-action beneficiaries catch up with their better-credentialed fellow students after their freshman year. What happens instead is that many transfer to majors in which the academic competition is less intense and grades are issued on a more lenient curve. Their GPAs tend to increase, but their standing relative to other students taking the same courses does not.

Again, the authors showed that this effect is by no means confined to affirmative-action beneficiaries. White children and grandchildren of alumni who receive legacy preferences have the same experience, earning lower grades than white non-legacies at the end of their first year. While the gap appears to narrow over time, it is only because legacy students, too, shift away from the natural sciences, engineering, and economics and toward the humanities and social sciences.

This finding helped the authors respond to the argument that under-represented minority students abandon science and engineering because they have no role models there or because they are somehow made to feel unwelcome. It is exceedingly unlikely that anti-legacy bias, lack of legacy role models on the faculty, or any other argument commonly advanced to explain racial disparities in science explains the legacies' collective drift toward softer majors. If it is the wrong explanation for legacies, it is likely to be the wrong explanation for under-represented minorities, too.

The study created a firestorm at Duke, where the administration, instead of taking the research to heart, focused on pacifying indignant students, alumni, and faculty members who felt insulted by the results. In an open letter to the campus responding to demands that the university condemn the study, Duke provost Peter Lange and other administrators stated that they "understand how the conclusions of the research paper can be interpreted in ways that reinforce negative stereotypes." They assured students that there are no easy fields of study at Duke and took the position that, insofar as the mammoth problem identified in the study exists, it could easily be solved through student counseling and a few tweaks to the science curriculum.[55]

Lange made certain that business will continue as usual at Duke. Potential affirmative-action recruits with an interest in science and engineering will continue to be told that Duke is the school for them. They will not be told that their chances of success in their chosen fields would be greater at Ohio State or, for that matter, at the University of North Carolina at Chapel Hill. Nor will they be told that if they switch majors to disciplines like African and African American studies, art history, English, sociology, and women's studies, they'll be less likely to enjoy lucrative careers or indeed to get jobs at all. In securities law, this would qualify as actionable fraud. In higher education, it is considered virtuous.

SHOULD UNIVERSITIES HAVE PREDICTED THE MISMATCH PROBLEM BACK IN THE 1960s?

Everyone seems to want to enroll in the most highly ranked college or university that will take them—with *U.S. News & World Report* as the most important, if not the sole, arbiter of rank. This kind of fierce competition for admission can, of course, be a good thing. At many institutions, it has helped create a rich intellectual climate. Even students who are ultimately denied admission to their first-choice school often benefit from the academic skills they develop in making the attempt.

In some cases, however, the competition is over the top. In 2019, a college admissions scandal involving dozens of parents, including a few Hollywood celebrities, resulted in over fifty federal indictments. Facts uncovered during the investigation—dubbed Operation Varsity Blues—showed that parents had paid more than $25 million to a facilitator who used part of the money to bribe college officials and to fraudulently inflate students' test scores.[56]

Even among law-abiding parents, things can be a bit crazy. For example, *Business Week* has reported that some are willing to fork over as much as $40,000 for advice from so-called experts on getting their son or daughter into an Ivy League school.[57]

It is unlikely that these anxious parents know about the research conducted decades ago by University of Chicago sociologist James A. Davis. Outside the field of sociology, it seems to have largely escaped notice. Published in 1966 under the title "The Campus as a Frog Pond: An Application of the Theory of Relative Deprivation to Career Decisions of College Men," it might give them reason for pause.[58] It is not clear that a student who enrolls in a school that he got into only because of some special dispensation thereby gains a career advantage.

Davis set about to study which students are most likely to enter high-prestige careers like law and medicine. More specifically, he wanted to know who is more likely to pursue a high-prestige career—the student who earns low grades at a highly competitive school or the otherwise identical student who attends a somewhat less competitive school and hence gets higher marks. Looking at data collected by the National Opinion Research Center on 35,000 students from 135 colleges and universities, Davis found that college grades were more strongly correlated with the decision to enter a high-prestige career than was the quality of the institution.

Davis was not saying that the best route to a high-prestige career is to graduate at the top of the least competitive school one can find. A local community college is unlikely to be the best option for most academically talented students. *Both* the quality of the institution a student attends *and* the grades received there are positively correlated with the likelihood that the student will enter a high-prestige career. Davis simply found that grades mattered somewhat more. All other things being equal, students were less likely to pursue a high-prestige profession if they had attended a highly competitive school at which they received low grades than if they had attended a somewhat less competitive school and received correspondingly better grades.

As Davis himself recognized, these findings tend to "challenge the notion that getting into the 'best possible' school is the most efficient route to occupational mobility." In some cases, at least, the added self-confidence one enjoys as a result of being the big frog in the small frog pond may outweigh whatever advantages an elite education in a more glamorous frog pond can offer.[59]

Whatever Davis was thinking about when he published "The Campus as a Frog Pond," it was unlikely to have been affirmative action. The year was 1966. Though there were already a few who advocated extra efforts to recruit African American students, the term "affirmative action" was not yet a household phrase, much less the euphemism for the preferential treatment for minority applicants that became so thoroughly institutionalized by the late 1970s. Still, the connection between his work and race-preferential admissions policies should have been obvious.

It is unclear why Davis's conclusions received so little attention outside the world of sociology. Perhaps it was because it was in no one's clear interest to publicize them. Top schools had every reason to ignore them. They need students to form the bottom of their class, and if some students would be discouraged from enrolling on account of hearing about Davis's frog-pond effect, these schools would just have to reach deeper into their applicant pool to find students who were not.

Schools one rung down face the same problem—on both ends of their recruitment efforts. If they tried to recruit students away from a top school by arguing the frog-pond effect, they would risk getting the word out to their potential recruits for the bottom of their class. For those students, the message would be "You'd be better off at a school somewhere on the third rung." In the end, second-rung schools would have succeeded only in making it clear that they are indeed second-rung. For the most part, only schools at the very bottom of the academic ladder have an incentive to argue the frog-pond effect, and these unselective schools (of which there are many) rarely invest heavily in recruitment. They let students come to them.

Perhaps a more important reason that colleges and universities did not draw a connection between Davis's findings and affirmative action was simply the temper of the times. It is difficult to overstate the sense of urgency that some of the earliest advocates of race-preferential affirmative-action programs felt. They did not view themselves as initiating an admissions policy that would remain in place for more than half a century. The admissions preferences they championed were a frantic response to the civil unrest that had swept through Watts in 1965; Atlanta, Baltimore, Chicago, Cleveland, and New York in 1966; Detroit and Newark in 1967; and cities across the country in 1968.

Whatever else the late 1960s might have been, they were not a time of careful and deliberate reflection. For those living through the protests and riots following the death of George Floyd in 2020, this may seem familiar.

Very early college and university affirmative-action programs focused on recruiting African American students from the inner city. Criminal records were not a barrier to admission; indeed, leadership in a street gang was sometimes considered a plus. Academic standards were not just relaxed; they were sometimes ignored altogether.[60]

In at least one documented case, a good academic record was counted *against* an African American applicant for admission. UCLA economics professor Thomas Sowell recounted a case in which a young African American woman, who had apparently just missed being admitted to Cornell University's regular program, was denied entry to Cornell on the ground that despite her humble background as the daughter of laundry workers, her academic record was *too* good for Cornell's special program. The internal report on her read:

> [H]er cultural and educational background does not indicate deprivation to the extent necessary for qualification as a disadvantaged...student. In spite of the fact that both her parents are laundry workers, she has been adequately motivated by them to a point where she has achieved academic success and some degree of cultural sophistication.[61]

At the time, many elites thought—in retrospect, too optimistically—that students from the most disadvantaged circumstances had overcome so much to get where they were that once admitted to a selective college or university, they would outperform better-credentialed students born to more prosperous parents. They were thus unlike the legacy students that Davis had been studying. Despite the lack of early emphasis on academic achievement in their lives, they would flourish in high-powered academic settings and go on to become pillars of the community—or so it was hoped.

Suffice it to say that, while these predictions of academic success were made in good faith and were not clearly and provably wrong (given what was known at the time), they turned out to be wishful thinking. That doesn't mean there weren't some success stories. There were. But the most significant consequence of this naïve form of affirmative action was to make the schools most dedicated to it—from UCLA to Cornell—even more chaotic than other American campuses of the era.[62]

A reassessment of the policy was clearly in order. But given the fanfare with which the programs had been launched, it would have already been difficult to abandon them entirely. The alternative was to reconfigure them in hopes of making them effective.

First, there was a consensus going forward that, rather than scour the inner cities looking for students who did *not* fit their usual academic profile, colleges and universities would scour the high schools for African American students who *did*. If they turned out to be from disadvantaged circumstances, that would be an added bonus. But if they turned out to be middle-class or even upper-middle-class suburbanites from Bethesda, New Rochelle, or Wilmette, so be it. The goal was no longer broadly to prevent unrest in the inner city—something that elite colleges and universities had always been ill-equipped to do. The focus was simply on the slow, deliberate expansion of the African American middle and upper-middle classes by graduating more African American students ready to enter high-status careers.

Second, there was agreement that, to make it work, minority outreach and recruitment efforts would need to be stepped up, remedial education would need to be significantly expanded, and administrators would have to be hired to oversee these efforts.

The new race-preferential admissions policies were thus not the starry-eyed policies of the late 1960s. Die-hard advocates of the more radical approach were sorely disappointed. And they were not entirely off base: When an African American son of a brain surgeon can get a preference over the Vietnamese American daughter of a dishwasher, it is hard to be sure that one is really making the world better.

At no point, however, did college and university administrators think seriously about whether their policies could be counterproductive—as Davis's "Frog Pond" research indicated. A few commentators, like Thomas Sowell and Yale law professor Clyde Summers, specifically warned them.[63] The reaction of colleges and universities to these warnings, however, was not to assess the evidence soberly, but rather to keep any evidence under wraps. Scholars couldn't study the issue if they didn't have access to data.

LAW SCHOOLS ENGAGE IN SECRECY

Secrecy has always been an important element of any race-preferential admissions policy. Consider, for example, the case of Timothy Maguire. In early 1991, this third-year law student and former Peace Corps volunteer took a job as a part-time file clerk in the Georgetown University Law Center admissions office. He likely figured it would be a good way to earn some extra money without cutting too much into his study time. He never dreamed of the trouble he was getting into. In a few weeks, he would be vilified by the Georgetown faculty, his fellow students, and the editorial pages of some of the nation's major newspapers. Over the course of the next year and a half, he would be fighting for his right to practice law.

Maguire had heard many times that affirmative action was all about putting a gentle thumb on the scale in favor of minority applicants: It was a tiebreaker, nothing more. But the admissions files he was seeing told a different story. The gap in academic credentials between white and African American admittees was stark.

He therefore decided to do a test. Taking what he regarded as a random sample of the files, he did a few back-of-the-envelope calculations. He found that the average white student accepted to the law school had an LSAT score of 43 and an undergraduate GPA of 3.7. The average accepted black student, on the other hand, had an LSAT score of 36 and an undergraduate GPA of 3.2.[64] To put those figures in perspective, an LSAT score of 43 was just a hair shy of the top 5 percent among those who took the exam. A score of 36, on the other hand, was only in the top 30 percent.[65]

To be sure, students in the top 30 percent are good students—all fully capable of becoming, in one form or another, successful lawyers. They are more typical, however, of law schools like Drexel University, the University of Louisville, and the University of

Nevada than they are of highly competitive, academically oriented schools like Georgetown, which holds itself out as a law school for outstanding students, not just good ones.[66] Rightly or wrongly, the admissions office would not have given a white student with an LSAT score of 36 and an undergraduate GPA of 3.2 a second glance: Of over 100 white admittees sampled, not a single one had an LSAT score under 39.[67]

Maguire published his findings in the student-run newspaper—the *Georgetown Law Weekly*—along with an essay critical of the school's separate and less-demanding admissions standards for African Americans. He called the credentials of white and African American admittees "dramatically unequal" and argued that Georgetown was dishonest in failing to inform its students about the gap.[68]

The failure to disclose the credentials problem made enrolling a racially diverse class seem easy, he wrote. It made it appear that if the school didn't have enough African American students, it was because the school just didn't care enough to reach out and encourage them to attend.

The campus erupted. Within days, the Black Law Students Association had filed a formal complaint demanding that Maguire be expelled.[69] The next week, six hundred Georgetown law students crammed into a lecture hall for an emotionally charged "town meeting," while others spilled over into another classroom to watch the event on closed-circuit television.[70]

Maguire had obviously touched a raw nerve. One student at the meeting called the article an attempt to chill Georgetown's "commitment to legal education for African-Americans." "The central issue is racism," said another. "I think the article is assaultive. People were injured. I think this kind of speech is outrageous."[71] With speech equated with violence, students in the last few decades have increasingly pitted themselves against free expression.

A few students defended Maguire, who had made the decision not to attend the meeting himself. One third-year student told the crowd that affirmative action had been "swept under the rug before because white people were afraid to say anything and black people felt threatened." In this student's view, Maguire was performing a service of sorts by getting the issue into the open. "Are we really going to say that because we don't like what [Maguire] said we are going to throw him out of school?" he asked.

The question may have been intended as rhetorical, but it was not treated as such. Shouts of "Yes!" rang out from some in the crowd. Tempers were flaring.[72]

All during the meeting, Georgetown dean Judith Areen blandly assured the crowd that Maguire had gotten his facts wrong. The gap was not what he suggested it was—or so she implied. She steadfastly refused, however, to provide the actual figures or to provide any details whatsoever as to Georgetown's actual affirmative-action policy. This caused even supporters some unease. "Affirmative action is a good thing," said a male first-year student. "But so much of what we're saying today is in the dark because the administration won't give us the facts."[73]

As the mainstream press picked up the story, Areen kept up her assurances that Maguire had gotten it wrong and that his "random sample" was not random at all. Maguire had evidently taken a large pile of admissions files, representing students who had been admitted, but he had no way of knowing whether that pile was really a random sample.

Following her lead, the *New York Times* editorialized that Maguire was "without the scarcest hint that he knows what a random sample is."[74] Even if true, this was harsher than necessary for the *Times* editors to make their point. This was a law student they were attacking, a law student writing in a school newspaper who was no doubt astonished to find himself suddenly thrust onto the national stage. Surely the editors of one of the world's leading newspapers could pick on someone their own size.

But the editors showed no mercy. They went on to ridicule Maguire, accusing him of writing "pretentiously" and stating that "he has learned very little" and that "he hasn't a clue about the broad purpose of a great law school." The raw nerve Maguire had touched could apparently inflict pain even in the editorial offices of the *New York Times*.[75] If anyone had ever doubted it was unsafe to talk critically about affirmative action in public, that doubt would be erased by this incident.[76]

No one should be surprised at how much harder it has gotten to talk about issues of race (or sex) in the modern world. If a law student could be attacked with that level of ferocity by the *New York Times*, anyone with name recognition could expect much worse. Interestingly, the same year Maguire was being pummeled, Congress was gearing up to pass a law that would, for the first time, make lawsuits brought pursuant to Title VII for on-the-job harassment potentially lucrative for plaintiffs. Things have never been the same.

As it turned out, Maguire was more likely understating the gap than overstating it. Shortly after the controversy exploded, an internal memorandum surfaced, the authenticity of which was confirmed to the *Washington Post* by university sources. Authored by Georgetown admissions director Andrew Cornblatt, it stated that the median LSAT score for full-time African American students at Georgetown in 1989 "increased to 33, up from 32 last year and 30 two years ago." According to the memorandum, the median score for the entering class as a whole in 1989 was 42, which would make Maguire's figure of 43 for white students in particular about on target.[77]

A score of 33 was not quite in the 56th percentile, and a score of 32 was in the 52nd percentile. Both scores were thus quite ordinary among test-takers nationally. Among actual law students, however, they were below average, since low scorers on the LSAT frequently do not attend any law school. A score of 30 was in the 41st percentile—below the average for test-takers and much below the average for actual law students.[78]

Amid the fury over his article, Maguire was charged by the school with violating confidentiality and threatened with expulsion (although he had disclosed no individual information and had published only the kind of information found in the Cornblatt memorandum and reported to the American Bar Association and *U.S. News & World Report*).[79] Fortunately for Maguire, his lawyers were able to negotiate a settlement with Georgetown. Rather than being expelled, he was issued a letter of reprimand and allowed to graduate.[80]

This did not sit well with everyone. An unhappy faculty group accused the administration of "a panicked reaction" that failed to "celebrate and vigorously defend" affirmative action. On graduation day, approximately a month and a half after the offending article was published, several students wore green ribbons to protest the settlement. A few carried placards, like the one that read "Ethics…A Meaningless Word." A group of about ten African American alumni, calling themselves the Concerned Black Law Alumni of the Georgetown University Law Center, staged their own muted protest.[81]

But unfortunately for Maguire, the story didn't end there. After graduation, Maguire took and passed the New Jersey Bar Examination. But he was found to be unfit for the practice of law by a panel of the Committee on Character. Only after protracted litigation was he able to practice the profession he had trained for.[82]

After such a story, no one can claim surprise to learn that only a small number of intrepid souls are willing to bring facts about affirmative action to public light or even to debate it. Maguire was the victim of a proto-cancel culture. As far as I have been able to determine, Maguire himself never commented again on the subject in public.

LARGE GAPS IN CREDENTIALS HAVE CONTINUED

It is common to believe that affirmative-action preferences are just a tiebreaker. This is not the case. Nor is it the case that these preferences are being slowly phased out.[83]

Consider, for example, the Supreme Court's decision in *Gratz v. Bollinger* (2003). That case was decided on the same day as *Grutter v. Bollinger* (2003)—the case that gave the green light to race-preferential admissions. *Gratz* itself was a small (but, alas, insignificant) victory for the advocates of race neutrality.

Its specific facts are interesting. Under the undergraduate admissions system used by the defendant University of Michigan in *Gratz*, 20 points were added to the academic index of each African American applicant for admission. This was the equivalent of an entire letter grade in high school GPA, all other things being equal (e.g., SAT scores, extracurricular activities). An African American applicant with a 3.0 GPA—straight Bs—would be admitted before a white or Asian student with a 3.99—just a hair shy of straight As—if their records were otherwise the same. The alternative way to look at those 20 points is in terms of SAT scores. The maximum number of points an applicant could get for SAT scores was 12. Since African American students would get 20 points just for race, an African American student could be admitted ahead of a white or an Asian American student with the same high school GPA, no matter how much better the white or Asian American student's SAT score. Race was more important than even perfect SAT scores.

By contrast, the children and grandchildren of alumni received only one point—still one point too many for a state institution, but at least a small enough advantage to make mismatch an unlikely problem. The legacy preference was thus a true tiebreaker.

This policy had an effect on performance in college. In 2003, 45 percent of African American students were on academic probation, compared to only 8 percent of white students. Only 1 percent of African American students had an honors GPA, while 10 percent of white students did.[84]

Nominally, the Supreme Court decided *Gratz* in favor of the plaintiff, Jennifer Gratz. But the Court's objection to the university's admissions policy wasn't that it was racially discriminatory. As far as the Court was concerned, race discrimination was permissible. Instead, the Court's objection was to the university's formulaic point system.

A few changes to its policy were necessary, but the university was still able to grant large preferences to under-represented minority groups. Indeed, the credentials gap grew in the aftermath of the Supreme Court's decision. We know this because the Center for Equal Opportunity (CEO), a small nonprofit organization dedicated to equal opportunity, makes it a practice to seek admissions records from colleges and universities. It deserves much credit for going after such data. At times, its staff has needed the legal equivalent of a crowbar to pry the information loose, but it is usually able to secure the data it needs.

CEO's research shows that, by 2005, the distribution of combined SAT (Math + Verbal) scores for admittees to the University of Michigan's undergraduate program was as follows:

	Blacks	Hispanics	Asians	Whites
75th percentile	1270	1360	1480	1430
50th percentile	1160	1260	1400	1350
25th percentile	1070	1180	1320	1270

For high school GPAs among admittees to the college, the distribution was as follows:

	Blacks	Hispanics	Asians	Whites
75th percentile	3.8	3.8	3.9	4.0
50th percentile	3.4	3.6	3.8	3.9
25th percentile	3.1	3.3	3.7	3.7

An analysis of the University of Michigan's admissions data showed that, in 2005, an Asian American male resident applicant (whose parents had not attended Michigan) with a GPA and SAT scores equal to the median GPA and SAT scores of black admittees stood essentially no chance of being admitted. A similar white student stood only a 1 percent chance.[85] At the 25th percentile, there was a distance of 0.6 in GPA, plus a 200-point distance in SAT scores, between black and white admittees.

CEO has found similar patterns at other colleges and universities. Using admissions data for 2016 University of Virginia matriculants, CEO found a 180-point gap in median SAT scores between black and white students. Using 2017 data, it found the College of William and Mary had a gap of 190 points. In both cases, the median high school GPA gap was smaller—about 0.15.[86] Meanwhile, at the University of Wisconsin, CEO found that at the 25th percentile, African American admittees scored 240 points lower than Asian American admittees and ranked only at the 68th percentile in their high school class, while Asian Americans ranked in the 87th percentile of theirs.[87]

Some of the best-documented evidence of race-based admissions policies is, again, at law schools, which nearly all give preferential treatment in admissions to members of under-represented minorities—in part because the schools' accreditation can depend on it.[88] Richard Sander's study of law schools, "A Systemic Analysis of Affirmative Action in American Law Schools" (discussed later in this essay), found that, on average, black students' academic index was more than two standard deviations below their white classmates'.[89]

As the CEO data indicate, this discrepancy is not confined to the most selective law schools:

- At the University of Nebraska College of Law, in 2006, a white resident with credentials like those of the average black admittee had just a 1 percent chance of admission.

By contrast, a black resident with those credentials had a 79 percent chance, and an otherwise similar black non-resident had a 35 percent chance. The probability that a Hispanic resident with the credentials of the average black admittee would be admitted was 43 percent. A similar Hispanic non-resident had a 10 percent chance. As a result, the average African American admittee had an LSAT score in the 29th percentile of test-takers nationally, with the average white admittee in the 75th percentile and the average Hispanic admittee somewhere in between.[90]

- At the University of Utah College of Law, in 2010, the median LSAT score of an African American admittee was 155.5, while the median undergraduate GPA was 3.43. The probability that an African American with these scores would be admitted was 83 percent. By contrast, a white applicant with those scores had only a 3 percent chance of admission. The median LSAT score for white students was thus 163, and the corresponding median undergraduate GPA was 3.70.[91]

Similarly, CEO studied the admissions policies of six public medical schools—the Medical College of Georgia, SUNY-Brooklyn College of Medicine, University of Michigan Medical School, Michigan State University College of Human Medicine, University of Oklahoma College of Medicine, and University of Washington School of Medicine. It found that all of them engaged in significant preferential treatment for African American students in admissions. All but the Medical College of Georgia gave preferential treatment to Hispanics, and the University of Oklahoma College of Medicine also gave preferential treatment to American Indian applicants.[92]

THE SHAPE OF MISINFORMATION

"Wait!" you might be saying. "Didn't that famous book by William G. Bowen and Derek Bok—*The Shape of the River*—disprove the mismatch hypothesis back in the 1990s?"

No, it didn't.

In September 1998, when *The Shape of the River* made it into print, race-preferential admissions policies were perceived by their supporters to be under siege. California's Proposition 209, which prohibited these policies, had passed in 1996. Washington State had a similar initiative coming up in a few weeks on the November ballot. Those who backed these initiatives hoped to bring similar initiatives to other states soon.

The Shape of the River was the Establishment's response. Generously funded by the Andrew W. Mellon Foundation and other foundations with long records of support for race-based admissions, it was authored by two former Ivy League university presidents, who viewed themselves as the cavalry arriving just in the nick of time to rescue affirmative action.

As it turned out, the Washington State initiative passed anyway. But there is a good chance *The Shape of the River* did slow the progress of initiatives like it in other states in the years that followed. Justice Sandra Day O'Connor cited the book as support for the Supreme Court's opinion in *Grutter v. Bollinger* (2003). Despite its failure to stop the Washington State initiative, it has been very influential.

Judging from the attention the book received in the media, the Mellon Foundation publicists must have been working around the clock. Few books have been published with as much fanfare.

- According to a fawning editorial in the *New York Times*, the book's "findings provide a strong rationale for opposing current efforts to demolish race-sensitive policies in colleges"; the book "flatly refutes" the arguments of opponents.[93]

- *Newsweek*'s Ellis Cose commented that the book was the "most ambitious study to date of the effects of affirmative action in higher education" and "an important corrective to conservative propaganda."[94]
- The *Atlanta Journal-Constitution*'s Cynthia Tucker, casting aside the usually prudent presumption of good faith on the part of one's fellow Americans, wrote that "the Bok-Bowen report will not convince the die-hard opponents of affirmative action—those who cling to a narrow view of 'merit' or who, for whatever reason, do not wish to see the pool of opportunity expanded." "Nevertheless," she added, "the report is a welcome antidote to those constant critics who cannot see evidence of achievement beyond mere test scores and grade point averages."[95]

Some of the commentaries were aimed specifically at the issue of mismatch. Harvard University sociologist Nathan Glazer argued in the *Washington Post* that it was now "clear" that worries over mismatch were misplaced.[96] The *Pittsburgh Post-Gazette* editorialized that the notion that race-based admissions policies have hurt African American students "is one that can be dismissed."[97] But were they right?

In some ways, the authors of *The Shape of the River* were in an enviable position. Their team of researchers had unrestricted access to the Mellon Foundation's massive "College and Beyond" database, which contains records for about 80,000 students, all of whom had enrolled at one of twenty-eight elite colleges and universities, mostly in 1976 or in 1989.[98] Any social scientist studying education issues would have considered himself lucky to have such a resource. (The Mellon Foundation denied access to Harvard University history professor Stephan Thernstrom and Abigail Thernstrom, vice chair of the U.S. Commission on Civil Rights, whose views on affirmative action were more skeptical than those of Bowen and Bok).[99] It included information about each student's academic credentials and performance as well as his or her subsequent career. It thus provided an invaluable opportunity to study many aspects of affirmative action. As a result, the book positively bristles with charts and graphs.

The database was perhaps especially useful for studying the mismatch hypothesis. Bowen and Bok were able to group the participating schools into three tiers—Tier 1 (e.g., Princeton and Yale), Tier 2 (e.g., Northwestern and Vanderbilt), and Tier 3 (e.g., Pennsylvania State and the University of North Carolina)—and attempt to draw conclusions about the effects of attending one tier as opposed to another.

Most of the book was devoted to demonstrating uncontroversial facts: The authors effectively showed that there is indeed a large gap between the academic credentials of African American and white college applicants. If the top-tier schools were to terminate race preferences for African Americans but otherwise maintain their current admissions policies, the result would be entering classes that have significantly fewer African American students.

The authors also showed that substituting class-based preferences for race-based preferences would not lead to classes of the same racial composition. Since only 17 percent of all low-income students graduating from high school who scored in the top 10 percent on standardized tests were black or Hispanic, the primary beneficiaries of class-based affirmative action would be poor Asian Americans or poor whites.[100] (This latter argument is, of course, a double-edged sword for the authors. It explains why preferences for low-income students are not a substitute for preferences for under-represented racial minority students, but it reveals that many of the beneficiaries of those preferences are higher income.)

Then they got to the more controversial parts. After conceding—as they had to—that race-based admissions policies lead to poor grades for preference beneficiaries,[101] the authors asserted that African American students who attend schools at which they are substantially mismatched are nevertheless better off with lower grades at a more elite school than they would have been with higher grades at a less elite school.

In attempting to prove this, Bowen and Bok showed that the mean earnings of black men with SAT scores of less than 1000 who had attended what they identified as a Tier 1 school were higher than those of their counterparts who had attended schools in Tiers 2 and 3.[102] It was on this basis that they claimed the right to pooh-pooh the notion that black students "pay a penalty in life after college" for having attended schools at which they were mismatched. "On the contrary," they concluded, "the black (and white) matriculants with academic credentials that were modest by the standards of these schools appear to have been well-advised to go to the most selective schools in which they were admitted."[103]

But if the authors intended to disprove the mismatch hypothesis, they made at least two serious errors in the way they conducted their study.

First, they took account only of students' SAT scores and not of other academic credentials—like high school rank.[104] One cannot assume that a student with a combined SAT score of 1200 at Princeton is the equivalent of a student with the same score at Pennsylvania State University. There is an excellent chance that the first student has a substantially better high school GPA, as well as other distinctions in his favor. That is why he is at Princeton and the other student is at Penn State.

Comparing students with the same SAT scores and finding that students at more elite schools have higher graduation rates and higher post-graduation earnings, even though they appear to be mismatched at those schools, is unfair. It is overwhelmingly likely that students attending less elite schools have, on average, less elite high school records to match.

This is not the kind of error that two former Ivy League presidents should have made. Much of their universities' public relations are built around the theme that they routinely reject applicants with perfect or near-perfect SAT scores who do not otherwise measure up to their standards. Before the publication of *The Shape of the River*, Bowen and Bok appeared genuinely to believe that students with identical SAT scores are not necessarily equivalent (and they were quite right on that).[105] Suddenly, they were asking readers to forget their earlier position.

Second, they didn't even compare students with the same SAT scores. They compared students within broad bands. While banding cannot always be avoided, it is what statisticians do when they set out to muddy the waters. And it seems to have worked in this case. The authors divided students into five categories— those with SAT scores below 1000, those with scores from 1000 to 1099, those with scores from 1100 to 1199, those with scores from 1200 to 1299, and those with scores at 1300 and above. They compared the post-graduation earnings of minority students in each of these broad bands at each of the three tiers.[106]

Such an approach has superficial appeal, until one understands that the composition of each band differs markedly depending upon which tier is being examined.

- At Princeton and Yale, students with SAT scores below 1000 are a rarity. Those that exist are not just likely to have particularly fine high school grades; they are likely to have SAT scores that are only a tiny bit below 1000. At

Penn State or the University of North Carolina, however, such students are below the median, but not so far below it as to be a rarity. Consequently, the median student in the "below 1000 band" for the Tier 1 schools will almost certainly have an SAT score quite a bit above the median student in the "below 1000" band in the Tier 3 schools.

- At the opposite end of the spectrum, the same is true. The median student in the "1300 and above" band attending a school like Princeton or Yale almost certainly has a higher SAT score than the median student in that band attending Pennsylvania State or the University of North Carolina.

- In the intermediate categories—1000 to 1099, 1100 to 1199, and 1200 to 1299—results will be skewed in one direction or another, depending on the level of selectivity of the tier being examined.

One cannot compare bands of this kind without building in a bias that makes the earnings enjoyed by the graduates of the more highly ranked schools seem more attributable to the school than they really are. It is easy for a school to have higher graduation rates and higher earnings when it simply has more academically gifted students as its raw material. If such a school didn't have higher graduation rates and earnings, it would mean something was wrong.

Given those two serious methodological flaws, *The Shape of the River*'s results seem pre-ordained. One would have to expect the data to show that the policies that these two university presidents had been following all along were justified and that mismatch was not a problem.

But lo and behold, even given these flaws, evidence of mismatch comes peeking out from behind the charts. For example, while Bowen and Bok were careful not to draw attention to it, their own figures showed that one category of black men—those with SAT scores between 1000 and 1099—earned more if they had attended Tier 2 schools rather than Tier 1. Similarly, their figures showed that black women with SAT scores between 1100 and 1199 earned more if they had stayed away from Tier 1 schools and attended Tier 2 instead. These results showed just the opposite of what Bowen and Bok claimed to prove.

Meanwhile, buried in the appendices is a bombshell that the authors appear to have been oblivious to. The charts there contain a more sophisticated analysis that is barely mentioned in the text. These charts attempt to tease out how various factors influence the subsequent earnings of African Americans who attended one of the twenty-eight colleges or universities in the Mellon Foundation database. Included among the factors are several pre-college considerations: the socioeconomic status of the student's family, SAT scores, and whether the student was in the top 10 percent of his high school class. Also included are several factors from his college days: the selectivity of the college or university he attended, his major, whether his grades put him in the top third, middle third, or bottom third of the class, and whether he went on to earn a graduate or professional degree. The effect of each of these factors was measured.[107]

The authors purported to show that, on average, attending a Tier 1 school rather than a Tier 3 school contributes to the income levels of both African American men and African American women. But something important appears just a few rows down: *College grades generally contribute more.* Again and again, through the different permutations of the analysis they conducted, their own figures show it.

Imagine two African American men with the same SAT scores; both were in the top 10 percent of their high school classes, and both come from middle-class families. Only their colleges are different. Bowen and Bok convincingly demonstrated that if the two have the same major in college and similar grades, the one who attended a Tier 1 school will earn about $17,365 more than the one who attended a Tier 3 school.

But what if they don't have similar college grades? Bowen and Bok also showed that if one of those students was in the top third of his college class and the other was in the bottom third, the former will earn an average of $34,089 more. By the authors' own calculations, therefore, it is better to graduate from Penn State in the top third of the class than to graduate from Princeton in the bottom third. The increased earnings the former will get from high grades are worth almost twice the increased earnings the latter will get from attending a Tier 1 school. And there's more: The boost in earnings the former will get for majoring in natural science as opposed to the humanities is a whopping $49,537.

If one's class rank and major were unrelated to the level of selectivity of one's college, then it might be perfectly sensible for Bowen and Bok to celebrate the finding that, on average, black male students got an earnings boost from attending a Tier 1 instead of a Tier 3 school. But they are not unrelated. For students who would not have been admitted but for race preferences, the chances of earning grades that will place them in the top third of the class are exceedingly remote. And the chances of graduating with a degree in natural science are greatly reduced.

The only question is whether an African American student who attends a Tier 1 school and winds up in the bottom third of the graduating class would have likely been in the top third at a Tier 3 school. And the answer to that question, at least in many cases, is yes.

Consider, for example, an African American male student with SAT scores of 1300 who just missed being in the top 10 percent of his high school class. He is a talented student by any ordinary measure. If he attends Pennsylvania State University, his SAT scores will put him exactly at the 75th percentile in the entering class of 2011, according to *U.S. News & World Report*. That will give him a strong shot at earning grades in the top third.[108] If he starts out intending to major in a natural science, there is an excellent chance he will stick to it. If he enrolls at Princeton instead, his SAT scores will put him ninety points below the 25th percentile for that school, making it more likely his grades will be in the bottom third, possibly even the bottom third of the bottom third.[109]

Similarly, figures in Appendix D.5.5 predict that the average African American woman with a combined SAT score of 1400 will earn upward of $3,800 more by attending the University of North Carolina (if, as her SAT scores predict she could, she graduates in the top third of her class) instead of Yale University (if, as her scores predict, she runs the risk of graduating in the bottom third).[110] As a bonus, if she has a desire to major in engineering, graduating with such a degree will earn her, on average, an additional $17,894, according to Bowen and Bok's calculations. And she is more likely to do that at UNC than at Yale.

Have Bowen and Bok, by themselves, proven that mismatch is hurting minority students? No, they have not, but they have gone further in that direction than they have in proving that it is not hurting minority students. When one combines their results with those of other researchers, a picture begins to emerge.[111]

Note that the choice of major almost certainly plays a large role in the result found in Bowen and Bok's appendices. Science and engineering degrees lead to more financially rewarding careers than do humanities degrees, and students who have received preferences are less likely to stick to science and engineering majors than their identically credentialed peers who attend schools that better match those credentials. Bowen and Bok's results are thus broadly consistent with Elliott; Smyth and McArdle; Sander and Bolus; and Arcidiacono. Whether race-preferential admissions policies are having a negative effect on graduation rates at the elite schools studied by Bowen and Bok and, if so, how great an effect is less clear (but still likely).[112] In part, this is because, at the very top of the academic pecking order, graduation rates are very high for all groups, including preference beneficiaries. Whether they graduate with a marketable degree (including, as the next section will describe, whether they go on to graduate school to get that degree) is more clear.

ANOTHER MELLON FOUNDATION PROJECT FINDS THAT AFFIRMATIVE ACTION-INDUCED LOW GRADES HURT MINORITIES

In 2003, five years after *The Shape of the River*, another project of the Andrew W. Mellon Foundation came to fruition. This one, however, was not released with the same fanfare. In fact, the Mellon Foundation did everything but disown it.

The book was called *Increasing Faculty Diversity: The Occupational Choices of High-Achieving Minority Students*, and it was authored by Stephen Cole, professor of sociology at State University of New York at Stony Brook, and Elinor Barber, a research associate in the provost's office at Columbia University. Its purpose was to advise Ivy League and other colleges and universities on how to increase the racial and ethnic diversity of their faculties. The original research for the project—which consisted of individual interviews with students, focus groups, and many thousands of questionnaires—was heavily underwritten by Mellon.

Cole and Barber's study easily could have become just one more of the large number of reports on diversity funded by some hapless foundation with more money than it knows how to spend. It could have recited the usual clichés: *Colleges and universities should make greater efforts to make minority members feel welcome; they should celebrate diversity; they should go the extra mile.* Universities could wallpaper their administrative offices with such reports.

Instead, the authors tried to answer the question of why so few high-achieving African Americans and Hispanics choose to go to graduate school with an eye to becoming college and university professors. Unlike many of their predecessors who had weighed in on that question, they declined to ignore the problem of affirmative action–induced low grades. As the authors put it:

> [Many of the best prepared African American students] are admitted to schools where, on average, white students' scores are substantially higher, exceeding those of African Americans by about 200 points or more. Not surprisingly, in this kind of competitive situation, African Americans get relatively low grades. It is a fact that in virtually all selective schools (colleges, law schools, medical schools, etc.) where racial preferences in admission is practiced, the majority of African American students end up in the lower quarter of their class.[113]

As Cole and Barber acknowledged, that leads to problems:

> It is not at all surprising that academic performance in college should turn out to be an important influence on the decision to select academia as a career. If a student is not academically successful and has not received rewards for his or her academic performance, it would make little sense for that student to think of spending the rest of his or her life in a job where "being good in school" is a prerequisite.[114]

No surprise there: Young people tend to go into fields that they perceive they will be good at. Weak swimmers do not sign up for training as lifeguards. And the kind of person who perpetually burns the toast doesn't seek the training necessary to become a professional chef. At college, students get a sense of how good they would likely be as college professors from their grades. Students who are not toward the top of the class are less likely to think of academia as the best place to apply their talents. Cole and Barber, unlike their predecessors, were willing to say so.

One approach to that problem might be to try to tell minority students not to worry about their lackluster grades—that colleges and universities will rush to hire them anyway. But telling students, "We don't really care how good you will be at this job; we want you anyway" is not a good hiring strategy. Few with the long term in mind want to enter careers in which their comparative advantage is their skin color.

Cole and Barber put the matter more delicately, but they agreed. They cautioned against "highly visible affirmative action programs" that "may send a positive message" that "elite colleges and universities care strongly about having a diverse student body" but that also may telegraph to minority students "that they were admitted to a selective school because of affirmative action programs and that they 'don't really belong.'"[115]

Rather than recommend staying the course on affirmative action, Cole and Barber argued for a change in direction. Finding that "African American students who attend less selective schools are more likely than those who attend selective schools to persist with a freshman interest in academia," they advised:

> Instead of recommending that minority students go to the most prestigious school they can get into, high school guidance counselors should recommend that each student go to a school where he or she is likely to do well academically. An HBCU may be such a school. Guidance counselors, in short, should try to reduce some of the lack of fit between the level of academic preparation of minority students and the schools where they enroll.[116]

In some ways, *The Shape of the River* and *Increasing Faculty Diversity* are twins. They both contain a wealth of data, and in both books, the data showed that affirmative action–induced low grades were creating a serious obstacle to minority students' achievement. The difference is that Cole and Barber understood what they had uncovered and reported it in the text of the book forthrightly. In *The Shape of the River*, the data were ignored or misinterpreted.

Unlike *The Shape of the River*, *Increasing Faculty Diversity* was barely mentioned in the press. The hardworking publicists for the Mellon Foundation were apparently on holiday. An exception to the media blackout was an article entitled "The Unintended Consequences of Affirmative Action" in the *Chronicle of Higher Education*, which reported on the efforts of the Mellon Foundation to distance itself from Stephen Cole (Dr. Barber had passed away while the book was in preparation).[117]

"Researchers report the findings as they see them, and they may not be consistent with what we'd like to see or what we think are there," Harriet Zuckerman, senior vice president of the Mellon Foundation, told the *Chronicle*. "The Mellon imprimatur is not on this, just as it is not on other research we support." Readers should be "cautious about putting much weight on certain findings," she added.

Jeffrey H. Orleans, the executive director of the Council for Ivy Group Presidents, which had furnished seed money for the project before the Mellon Foundation stepped in with major funding, reacted similarly. "There are a whole lot of data in here, and if one started out with an ideological position—whatever it was—you could find a whole lot to support that."

Cole was obviously furious with the treatment he received. He told the *Chronicle* that he "wouldn't get up and make a blanket statement that I'm opposed to affirmative action. But if you're looking at this issue, affirmative action is contributing to the number of minority students getting lower grades, which seems to contribute to them selecting non-high achievement careers." As for comments like Zuckerman's and Orleans's, he said, "I was trained at a time before social science became so politicized.... I believe that social science should be objective and value-free, and you should design a study to answer a question and what the answer is, that's what it is."

According to the *Chronicle*, Cole figured "that there is 'no chance' he'll receive money again from the Mellon Foundation. 'And I don't care.'"

Cole died in 2012. *Increasing Faculty Diversity* never got the attention it deserved.

WHERE ARE THE MISSING BLACK LAWYERS?

In 2004, UCLA law professor Richard Sander published his first study of mismatch (prior to beginning his science and engineering study discussed above). Unlike his work in science and engineering, his work concerning law schools received quite a lot of attention, in part because the student editors of the *Stanford Law Review*, which published the piece, solicited responses.

Evidently anticipating that some of the same accusations of racial bias hurled at Stanley Mosk, Timothy Maguire, and others might be thrown at him, Sander took the unusual (and somewhat awkward) step of including biographical information in his otherwise dry and scholarly article:

> No writer can come to the subject of affirmative action without any biases, so let me disclose my own peculiar mix. I am white and I grew up in the conservative rural Midwest. But much of my adult career has revolved around issues of racial justice. Immediately after college, I worked as a community organizer on Chicago's South Side. As a graduate student, I studied housing segregation and concluded that selective race-conscious strategies were critical, in most cities, to breaking up patterns of housing resegregation. In the 1990s, I cofounded a civil rights group that evolved into

the principal enforcer (through litigation) of fair housing rights in Southern California. My son is bi-racial, part black and part white, and so the question of how nonwhites are treated and how they fare in higher education gives rise in me all the doubt and worries of a parent. As a young member of the UCLA School of Law faculty, I was deeply impressed by the remarkable diversity and sense of community the school fostered, and one of my first research efforts was an extensive and sympathetic analysis of academic support as a method of helping the beneficiaries of affirmative action succeed in law school.[118]

Of course, even if Sander had been a lifelong opponent of race-based admissions, it is not clear why that fact would in itself be sufficient to dismiss his findings out of hand. As president of Princeton University from 1972 to 1988, William G. Bowen, along with Derek Bok, who presided over Harvard from 1971 to 1991, were pioneers in formulating affirmative-action policies. They had every motivation to want to find those policies to have been successful. While this is useful to know in evaluating their strongly pro-preference *The Shape of the River*, it is not by itself reason to ignore them. Ultimately, their findings must be addressed on their own terms. Unfortunately, however, Sander turned out to be right that he would be viewed suspiciously for his work.[119]

Sander's work brought to public attention two undisputed facts:

1. During the period for which data were available, the average African American law student had an academic index that was more than two standard deviations below that of his average white classmate.
2. A majority of African American law students during that period were in the bottom 10 percent of their class.

More important, Sander demonstrated that this disappointing law school performance was almost entirely the result of race-preferential admissions. When African American and white law students with similar entering credentials competed against each other, they performed very close to identically.[120] Race-based admissions, therefore, were creating the illusion that African American students were destined to do poorly in law schools at every level. The real problem was far less daunting: Fewer African American students than anyone would prefer had the entering academic credentials necessary for admission on a color-blind basis to the most elite law schools, but there were many more who would likely do well at schools a little further down the pecking order—if they were attending those schools.

Just like supporters of race-based admissions at the undergraduate level, supporters of race-based admissions in law school often asserted that, despite the increased likelihood of poor grades, minority students were better off accepting the benefit of a preference and graduating from the most prestigious law school willing to take them. Someone had to be at the bottom of every class; there was no real harm in its being minority students.

Up until Bowen and Bok's misdirected effort in *The Shape of the River*, few advocates of race-preferential admissions at the undergraduate level made any effort to demonstrate that preference beneficiaries were, in fact, better off than they would have been had they attended a school in which their entering credentials matched those of their peers. It was largely taken on faith. That's why the Sander study was so important. Unfortunately, the news he was able to provide bore out the fear that mismatch is likely hurting African American law students' career prospects.

Sander noted two important effects of race-based admissions policies.

First, African American students attending law schools failed or dropped out at much higher rates than white students: 19.3 percent versus 8.2 percent.[121] Overwhelmingly, this phenomenon was associated with poor performance and not financial hardship.[122] Since many of these students who left law school would likely have performed better at a less competitive law school, they were, in a very real sense, victims of race-preferential admissions.

Second, among African Americans who graduated and took the bar, the proportion who passed on the first attempt was not just lower than that for whites, it was lower even when one controlled for academic index (a combination of LSAT score and college GPA). For example, 71 percent of African Americans with an index of 400 to 460 failed the bar on their first effort, while only 52 percent of whites did. Similarly, 26 percent of African Americans with an index between 640 and 700 failed their first time, while only 13 percent of whites did.[123]

Ultimately, only 45 percent of African Americans who entered law school passed the bar on their first attempt, as opposed to over 78 percent of whites. Even after multiple attempts, only 57 percent of African Americans succeeded. The gap was thus never closed.[124]

Something was clearly wrong. When African American and white law students with similar academic credentials competed against each other at the same school, they earned about the same grades. And when African American and white students with the same grades from schools at the same tier took the bar examination, they passed at the same rate. Yet African American students, as a whole, had dramatically lower bar passage rates than white students with similar credentials. What could explain this?

As Sander pointed out, the most plausible answer was that they were not attending the same law schools. The white and Asian American students were likely to be attending a school that takes things a little more slowly and spends more time on matters that are covered on the bar exam.[125] They were learning—while their minority peers were struggling at more elite schools, where the bar exam and indeed legal doctrine are often mocked as things of little importance by faculty members.

Sander calculated that if law schools were to use color-blind admissions policies, fewer African American law students would be admitted to law schools (3,182 vs. 3,706). But he further calculated that, since those who were admitted would be attending schools where they had a substantial likelihood of doing well, fewer would fail or drop out (403 vs. 672). In the end, more would pass the bar on their first try (1,859 vs. 1,567), and more would eventually pass the bar (2,150 vs. 1,981) than under the current system of race-based admissions.[126]

Sander's findings had to be deeply troubling to any fair-minded supporter of race-preferential admissions. But unlike the mismatch literature in science and engineering, this was just a single study, using a single database. And there were doubters—some of whom were able to raise legitimate questions.[127] The database Sander was working from was not ideal for testing the mismatch hypothesis. For that reason, the U.S. Commission on Civil Rights, while impressed with the study, recommended in its 2007 report, entitled *Affirmative Action in American Law Schools*, that more research be undertaken.

The stakes were obviously high. If Sander was right or even partly right, it may fairly be said that decades of race-preferential admissions at law schools were for nothing—or worse than nothing. Just as Justice Mosk had warned, the principle of nondiscrimination would have been sacrificed "for the sake of a dubious expediency"—a practical gain that never materialized.[128]

It would have been nice if someone besides Sander had set out to find a database that would allow a second look at the issue of law school mismatch. But given the treatment that Sander and Timothy Maguire before him received, it is not surprising researchers did not at first step forward. So Sander took the lead. What he was looking for was a state bar that kept extensive records on the characteristics of each person who had sat for the bar examination. At a minimum, he needed the test-taker's race,

LSAT score, college GPA, and law school. He also needed to know how well each test-taker had performed on the bar examination. Finally, the state would need to be a large one, with a wide range of law schools.

Sander found such a state in California. Alone among the fifty states, California had all the data he would need to retest the mismatch theory.

In 2006, Sander assembled a team of researchers with diverse opinions about the mismatch issue and approached the State Bar of California for permission to examine the records. In a better world, this request might have been pro forma. The whole purpose of keeping such records is to allow useful research to be conducted upon them, and the State Bar of California had allowed them to be used for education research in the past. The privacy of individuals would have to be protected, but that was hardly an insurmountable obstacle. Sander and his colleagues were not interested in identifying individuals. They just needed to work out a way to turn over the data that would ensure that everyone's needs were accommodated.

At first, it seemed more than likely Sander and his team would have the state bar's cooperation. The professional staff with whom Sander was dealing seemed to understand the importance of the project and appeared prepared to recommend to the Board of Bar Examiners of the State Bar, whose final approval would be necessary, that the project be undertaken.

Then, slowly, a door began to close.

The first sign of trouble came on January 15, 2007, from the Long Island–based Society of American Law Teachers (SALT).[129] Calling itself "the largest membership organization of law teachers in the United States," SALT sent a letter urging the State Bar of California not to cooperate with Sander.

SALT's self-description was a bit misleading. In fact, the only reason SALT can claim to be the largest membership organization of law professors in the country is that there is no general-interest association of law professors. The Association of American Law Schools, which functions in effect as the largest association of law professors, is in fact, as its name implies, an association of law schools. By contrast, SALT is a much smaller activist group that leans so far to the left that it is in danger of falling over on its side. It is in no way representative of law professors, who, while tending very much toward the left side of the political spectrum, are not usually in SALT territory.

The SALT letter subtly threatened the State Bar of California with litigation if it turned over the data.[130] It was clear that not all of Sander's critics had an interest in ensuring that he had access to newer data with which to test the mismatch theory.

Another letter came from an individual who had complained in the past that the Sander study should be discounted because it relied on a dataset that was several years old. Now he was seeking to prevent Sander and his co-investigators from getting newer data, arguing, among other things, that bar examination scores are a poor "proxy for 'student learning'" and that their disclosure "risks stigmatizing African-American attorneys regardless of how successful they may be in legal practice."[131] (Sander, of course, had not requested names or any information that would allow him to identify particular persons.)

Then the law school deans started weighing in. They had heard—presumably from SALT—that research into mismatch was going to take place and that it could make them look bad.

Sander enlisted Gerald Reynolds, chair of the U.S. Commission on Civil Rights, to fly to San Francisco and plead with the Committee of Bar Examiners on behalf of the project. He also got letters from several of the nation's more iconoclastic former law school deans who happened to reside in California. But these efforts were unavailing.

It is something of an honor to be appointed to the Committee of Bar Examiners of the State Bar of California. It is not something lawyers undertake because they are looking to do battle with activist organizations like SALT or with law school deans. I find it unlikely that too many committee members were out to protect affirmative action even at the expense of its supposed beneficiaries. But perhaps it reached a point where cooperating with Sander would have been unpleasant for them, and it was certainly easier to say no than to say yes. So that's what they did.

Sander therefore requested the records pursuant to the California Public Records Act, California's version of the Freedom of Information Act. When they were not forthcoming, he sued in California state courts. The litigation was protracted. It looked as if he might prevail when, in 2013, the California Supreme Court issued an opinion that broadly construed the state bar's duty to disclose and remanded the case to the lower courts for further action.[132] Ultimately, however, relief was denied, and Sander's efforts in court came to naught.[133]

Fortunately, Sander was not completely stymied during the litigation. While the litigation was pending, he was able to conduct research into law school mismatch more obliquely. In "The Secret of My Success: How Status, Eliteness, and School Performance Shape Legal Careers," he and coauthor Jane Bambauer found that, among lawyers, one's grades in law school were a better predictor of success in the legal profession than was the eliteness of the law school one attends. This is not to say that it is not "better" for one's future to attend, say, Harvard Law School, as opposed to a less prestigious law school, all other things being equal. But if the choice is between disappointing grades at Harvard or good grades at a somewhat less prestigious law school, the student who chooses good grades is more likely to go on to a successful career.[134] Meanwhile, research conducted by economist E. Douglas Williams provided further support for Sander's law school mismatch thesis.[135]

Significantly, in 2016, two economists on opposite sides of the affirmative-action debate—Peter Arcidiacono and Cornell University's Michael Lovenheim—published a review of the mismatch literature to that date. They wrote:

> We find the evidence suggesting that shifting African-Americans to less-selective schools would increase bar passage rates, particularly for first-time passage, to be fairly convincing. This is especially the case since the low quality of that data would tend to bias estimates away from finding mismatch. On the other hand, an argument could be made that the data are too noisy and provide sufficiently imprecise information on actual law-school quality that they preclude one from drawing any concrete conclusions regarding mismatch. Regardless, the law-school debate makes clear that this is a question that merits further attention, where more definitive answers could be answered with better data. Our hope is that better datasets soon will become available.[136]

Maybe Arcidiacono and Lovenheim have had that hope fulfilled. Preliminary indications are that one better dataset has indeed become available. In a yet unpublished study, Sander and coauthor Robert Steinbuch take fine-grained data from three law schools—one very elite, one not quite as elite, and one less elite. Two of these law schools are in California, and one is in Arkansas. A 2019 draft of the resulting article found evidence of a strong mismatch effect on bar passage—perhaps stronger than anyone anticipated. The authors state:

> In the three schools we examine, greater levels of mismatch are strongly associated with weaker first-time performance on state bar exams. Indeed, our analyses suggest that one's relative position in one's law school class (in terms of credentials) matters more than the absolute level of one's credentials. To put it differently,

the improved measure of mismatch we are able to create with this data suggests that the harmful effect of law school mismatch upon bar passage rates is larger than earlier research...documented.

...Our results imply that African-American and Hispanic bar performance could improve dramatically if student levels of mismatch were reduced or the effects were otherwise successfully addressed.

A final version of the paper is awaited.[137]

WHAT HAS HAPPENED IN STATES IN WHICH RACE-PREFERENTIAL ADMISSIONS HAVE BEEN SIMPLY OUTLAWED?

We already have a good idea about what happens when race-preferential admissions are outlawed, since several jurisdictions, beginning with California in 1996, have adopted popular initiatives doing exactly that. The operative clause of California's Proposition 209, which amended the state constitution, reads:

> The State shall not discriminate against, or grant preferential treatment to, any individual or group on the basis of race, sex, color, ethnicity, or national origin.[138]

Similarly worded initiatives have been passed in Washington State (in 1998), Michigan (in 2006), Nebraska (in 2008), Arizona (in 2010), and Oklahoma (in 2012). In 2014, the U.S. Supreme Court, in the curiously titled *Schuette v. Coalition to Defend Affirmative Action, Integration and Immigrant Rights and Fight for Equality by Any Means Necessary*, held these initiatives to be constitutional—a point that never should have been subject to doubt.[139]

In California, the state for which we have the most data, Proposition 209 has led to more under-represented minority honor students and fewer under-represented minority students with unacceptably low grades. It also has led to higher graduation rates for under-represented minority students.

Consider the case of the University of California at San Diego—a highly selective institution, but not quite as selective as the University of California's flagship campus at Berkeley. In 1997, prior to Proposition 209's implementation, only one African American student at UC-San Diego had a freshman-year GPA of 3.5 or better—a single African American honor student in a freshman class of 3,268. By contrast, 20 percent of the white students on campus had such a GPA.

Failure rates were similarly skewed. Fully 15 percent of African American students and 17 percent of American Indian students at UC-San Diego were in academic jeopardy (defined as having a GPA of less than 2.0), while only 4 percent of white students were. Other under-represented minority students hovered close to the line. Since UC-San Diego didn't keep separate statistics for those minority students who needed a preference in order to be admitted and those who would have been admitted regardless, it is impossible to say exactly how high the failure rate was for preference beneficiaries in particular. Suffice it to say it was high.[140]

This was not because there were no other African American students capable of doing honors work at UC-San Diego. The problem was that such students were often at Harvard, Stanford, or Berkeley, where often they were not receiving honors. Similarly, white and Asian American students were not magically immune from failure. Those at high risk of failure, however, had not been admitted in the first place. Instead, they were at less competitive UC campuses—Davis, Irvine, Santa Cruz, or Riverside—where their performance was more likely to be acceptable or even better than acceptable.

Being toward the bottom of the class can be demoralizing for anyone, just as being toward the top of the class can be uplifting. But bad grades created by preferential admissions policies can be especially troubling. When a class consists of students with roughly the same level of academic preparation, the student at the bottom of the class will ordinarily be the one who didn't try hard enough. At the end of the term, he may decide to change his priorities and study more. Or, wisely or foolishly, he may decide that his priorities were right and that he is better off excelling at football, working part-time, or spending time with his friends and family rather than trying to improve his academic performance.

In contrast, when the reason a student is having difficulty is not that she isn't trying, but rather because her academic credentials are significantly lower than those of her classmates, the lesson learned is that hard work doesn't pay off. You can knock yourself out, but even when you do, you may only eke by. Sometimes students in that position find themselves dependent on the kindness of a teacher to allow them to get by—another unfortunate lesson in a nation that prizes self-reliance and an independent spirit.

Race-preferential admissions policies add an additional wrinkle. If an individual student is doing poorly at a selective college, that doesn't mean that her siblings or cousins are likely to be doing poorly too. It doesn't necessarily mean her friends at church are doing poorly. But it is one thing for an individual student to find herself toward the bottom of the class. It is quite another for an African American student to find herself toward the bottom of the class and to find half her African American friends and acquaintances there too.

It is easy to develop a "sour grapes" attitude under those circumstances: "It's all politics," or "Getting good grades isn't really a black thing." Culture comes from shared experiences. Up to 1996, affirmative action had been giving too many California minority students the shared experience of feeling unsuccessful at academic pursuits.

Then came Proposition 209. Although initially tied up in litigation, it went into effect in time to affect the undergraduate admissions decisions for the entering class of 1998.

The media coverage of the implementation seemed calculated to create the impression of an educational crisis. "Acceptance of Blacks, Latinos to UC Plunges," one *Los Angeles Times* headline bellowed.[141] For a few days, UC's color-blind admissions policies—which had caused the share of Berkeley's offers of admission to African Americans, Hispanics, and American Indians to go from 23.1 percent of the total offers to 10.4 percent—permeated the national airwaves.[142]

The claim that Berkeley had become "lily white" was unfounded. In 1997, 58.6 percent of its freshman admissions went to students who had checked minority boxes—primarily blacks, American Indians, Asian Americans, and Hispanics. When Proposition 209 went into effect, the figure declined to 48.7 percent. Only a bare majority of seats went to whites. Asian Americans accounted for about 38 percent of the total.[143]

Moreover, the non-Asian minority students who would have attended Berkeley in the past had not simply vanished. They had been accepted to somewhat less highly ranked campuses—often UCLA and UC-San Diego—based on their own academic record rather than their skin color. In turn, students who previously would have been admitted to UCLA or UC-San Diego on a preference were now being admitted to UC campuses like Davis, Irvine, Santa Cruz, and Riverside—somewhat less competitive, but nevertheless part of the prestigious UC system, which (in theory at least) caters only to the top 12.5 percent of California's high school graduates.

In fact, UC-Riverside and UC-Santa Cruz both posted impressive gains in minority admissions. At Riverside, for example, black and Latino student admissions shot up by 42 percent and 31 percent, respectively. Santa Cruz's increases were less dazzling but nevertheless notable. UC-San Diego reported mixed results. Black enrollment there was down 19 percent, but the enrollment of two other "under-represented" groups, Filipinos and Latinos, was up by 10 percent and 23 percent.[144]

At UC-San Diego, the performance of black students improved dramatically. No longer were African American honor students a rarity. Instead, a full 20 percent of the African American freshmen were able to boast a GPA of 3.5 or better after their first year. That was higher than the rate for Asians (16 percent) and extremely close to the rate for whites in the same year (22 percent). Suddenly African American students at UC-San Diego found themselves on a campus where achieving academic success could be considered normal. By contrast to the experience of African American students in other places, nobody could accuse them of "acting white" or "acting Asian." Academic excellence had lost any hint of association with race.[145]

The sudden collapse in the minority failure rate was perhaps even more impressive. Once race preferences were eliminated, the difference between racial groups all but evaporated at UC-San Diego, with the black and American Indian failure rate falling to 6 percent.

UC-San Diego's internal academic performance report announced that, while overall performance had remained static, "under-represented students admitted to UCSD in 1998 substantially outperformed their 1997 counterparts" and "the majority/minority performance gap observed in past studies was narrowed considerably." But "narrowed" was an understatement. The report found that for the first time, there were "no substantial GPA differences based on race/ethnicity." A discreet footnote makes it clear that the report's author knew exactly how this happened: 1998 was the first year of color-blind admissions.[146]

Granted, UC-San Diego had twelve fewer African American freshmen in the first year of Proposition 209's implementation, forced as it was to reject students who did not meet the academic standards of the rest of the class. But it also had seven fewer African American students in academic jeopardy at the end of the first year. Meanwhile, those twelve students probably attended a school where their chances of success were greater.[147]

The next few years were good ones. Proposition 209's critics have been loath to admit it, but the big news following its implementation was skyrocketing minority graduation rates. As Richard Sander and Stuart Taylor, Jr., reported in their 2012 book *Mismatch: How Affirmative Action Hurts Students It's Intended to Help, and Why Universities Won't Admit It*:

> Minority graduation rates rose rapidly in the years after Prop 209, and on-time (four-year) graduation rates rose even faster. For the six classes of black freshmen who entered UC schools in the years before race-neutrality (i.e., the freshman classes of 1992 through 1997), the overall four-year graduation rate was 22 percent. For the six years after Prop 209's implementation, the black four-year graduation rate was 38 percent. Thus, even though the number of black freshmen in the UC system fell almost 20 percent from 1997 to 1998, the number of black freshmen who obtained their degrees in four years barely dipped for this class, and the entering class of 2000, four years later, produced a record number of blacks graduating on time. The increase in black six-year graduation was less dramatic (63 percent before and 71 percent after Prop 209) but still substantial.[148]

Not all of this astonishing increase can be traced to Proposition 209. But Duke University researchers have found that almost 20 percent of the overall increases in graduation rates of UC minority students can be.[149] If Proposition 209 had been implemented with greater rigor, it would likely have contributed even more. In a world in which steps forward in education, when they occur at all, are rare and incremental, that is a stunning victory.

Moreover, the gains have not been limited to grade point averages and graduation rates. Between 1997 and 2003, the number of African American and Hispanic students graduating with a degree in science or engineering rose by about 50 percent. Not unrelatedly, the number of African American and Hispanic students majoring in ethnic studies and communications fell by 20 percent. Academic self-confidence was growing among minority students.

Note the Triple Crown: (1) college GPAs of under-represented minority students and (2) graduation rates of such students were improving at the same time that (3) they were increasingly majoring in science and engineering. Ordinarily, these three goals would be difficult to achieve all at once. For example, grading curves are traditionally lower in science and engineering departments than they are in the rest of the university, so it is remarkable that GPAs would be going up alongside increases in the number of science and engineering majors.

Now combine those victories with an increase in graduation rates. When graduation rates increase, it is generally because some weaker students, who might have dropped out in an earlier day, are managing to make it to the end. One would thus expect increasing graduation rates to have a depressive effect on GPAs and/or on the proportion of students majoring in science and engineering. Instead, improvements were made in all three areas. It is as if Ford had come up with an automobile that was both more luxurious and better on gasoline mileage—and cheaper too.

Sadly, the effect may not be as strong as it was in the years immediately following Proposition 209's implementation. Over the years, the University of California at Berkeley has developed techniques that allow it to get around Proposition 209 to the greatest extent possible while still enabling it to argue publicly that it is in compliance. Some of these techniques are more legally defensible than others. As a result, the performance gap may have begun to return.

One thing we can be fairly sure of: Proposition 209 and similarly worded initiatives in other states continue to have an effect. If that were not the case, there wouldn't be so much effort being put into repealing them. Washington State voters just barely defeated their legislature's repeal effort in 2019. Then in 2020, California's deep-blue legislature attempted the same: In the midst of the COVID-19 pandemic, it voted to repeal. Because Proposition 209 is part of the state constitution, however, this required submitting the issue to a vote of the people. The repeal referendum was known as Proposition 16.

A few weeks before the California mail-in vote was set to begin, the *New York Times* heralded a new, unpublished study by a UC-Berkeley graduate student, which had not yet been peer-reviewed and which relied in large part on data that the student claimed he could not release to other scholars.[150] The study purported to find that under-represented minority students had been rendered worse off by Proposition 209.[151]

The story received a great deal of media attention in the Golden State. Almost needless to add, the peer-reviewed studies cited in this essay by full-fledged faculty members using data available to those skeptical of their conclusions never received that kind of attention. Shortly after the *New York Times* piece ran, Richard Sander published a devastating rebuttal, pointing out, among other things, that the study gets many basic statistics about the University of California's minority enrollment wrong.[152]

On November 3, 2020, California voters sensibly voted to stick with Proposition 209 and reject the repeal effort.[153]

THE ROAD NOT TAKEN

I began this essay with California Supreme Court Justice Stanley Mosk. When asked to abandon the principle of color-blindness in exchange for "dubious expediency," he declined. The indications are that his doubts were prescient.

Mosk was never forgiven—not even in death—for his deviation from what had become liberal orthodoxy. In his 2001 *New York Times* obituary, he was accused of having a knack for anticipating and bending with political currents.[154] For good or ill, nothing could be further from the truth. When it came to standing up for what he believed, the man was unbendable.

Despite Mosk's history of support for civil rights, it was Justice Lewis Powell, a mild-mannered Nixon appointee, who ended up beloved by the civil rights establishment. Unlike the irascible Mosk, the gentlemanly and accommodating Powell was an unlikely civil rights hero. As the Richmond School Board chairman between 1953 and 1961 and a member of the Virginia Board of Education between 1961 and 1969—the crucial years following the Supreme Court's decision in *Brown v. Board of Education* (1954)—he was in a position to take a leading role in dismantling Jim Crow. But Powell, who later went on to be ABA president, did not distinguish himself as an advocate of desegregation "with all deliberate speed."[155] As Berkeley sociologist Jerome Karabel put it:

> His own carefully worded assessment of his service in these positions was that it had taken place when the pace of desegregation had been "necessarily more measured than civil rights leaders would have liked." But this was a rather generous interpretation of his role in the years after the *Brown* decision, for when Powell stepped down as chairman of the Richmond School Board in 1961, after eight years of service, only 2 of the city's 23,000 black

children attended school with white children. And during his two terms with the state Board of Education, Powell's sympathetic but fair-minded biographer reports that "he never did any more than was necessary to facilitate desegregation... [and] never spoke out against foot dragging and gradualism."[156]

I mean no disrespect to Powell, who I believe was, on balance, a good jurist.[157] But when the right thing to do was stand on principle in the face of demands for expedience, Mosk was the one to call on and not Powell.[158] Powell's reputation as a resolute supporter of civil rights is undeserved. A former ABA president, he could be described as a conciliator. Or he could be described as a man who was disinclined to rock the boat. But the two descriptions of Powell's temperament are one and the same. It is a virtue or vice, depending upon the situation.

History does not disclose its alternatives. But it is difficult not to wonder what might have been if Stanley Mosk, instead of Lewis Powell, had sat on the U.S. Supreme Court.[†]

[†]An earlier version of this essay was published by the Heritage Foundation.

Diversity's Descent

Peter W. Wood

Diversity is a word of astonishing versatility. It gives ballast to Supreme Court decisions that would otherwise float away like dandelion fluff in the breeze. It writes paychecks to thousands of superfluous personnel with titles such as "Global Diversity Officer."[1] It casts Broadway plays, doles out highway improvement contracts, and hires football coaches. Ministers and priests invoke its godlike blessings. Politicians court it as eagerly as they do millionaire campaign contributors. The books we read, the movies we watch, and even the food we eat are weighed and sifted on *diversity* scales.

For anyone born after 1978, this appears to be the natural state of things. A couple of generations of Americans have been born into a society in which *diversity* is treated as an unquestionable good and perhaps the preeminent value.[2] It belongs to a class of words such as *freedom, fairness, justice,* and *equality* that name principles that Americans hold in high regard but that only now and then require us to grope for exactly what they mean.

KEY CONCEPTS

This essay offers a short course on how *diversity* found its place among the key concepts through which we Americans think about our society. It then considers how the American left has grown disenchanted with what was once its favorite conceit.

Diversity is never just one thing. It names several things at once: the ideal of a harmonious social order made of different groups, the apportionment of social goods in relation to the size of an ethnic group's population, a shorthand for "black under-representation," an exploitative trick played by white suprema-cists, and more. To explicate the concept of *diversity* requires an eye and ear for how the word changes meaning depending on the speaker and the context. We could say the same about those other key words. "Freedom" (or "liberty") is also a layered word, the meanings of which are as divergent as the Bill of Rights from *Bobby McGee* ("Freedom's just another word for nothin' left to lose.") But *diversity* comes especially fraught with contradictory impulses.

SUPREME COURT RULINGS

In that company of luminous words such as "freedom," "fair-ness," "justice," and "equality," *diversity* is the newcomer. It was invented, more or less, on June 28, 1978: the date that the U.S. Supreme Court handed down its decision in *Regents of the University of California v. Bakke.*[3]

The word "diversity," of course, existed long before 1978, but a justification for race preferences was never among its uses. And the idea that people benefit from proximity or connection to others unlike themselves had also been around for a long time, but it had never crystallized as either the legal doctrine or the cultural ideal of *diversity.*

The *Bakke* case famously involved Allan Bakke, a white appli-cant to a University of California medical school who was refused admission to make room for a less qualified black applicant. The University of California tried to justify Bakke's exclusion as part of a remedy for America's long history of race discrimination. But by a 5-4 vote, the Supreme Court rejected the university's position and said that Bakke had to be admitted to the medical school after all. He went on to become a successful anesthesiologist.

The swing vote in the Court's decision came from Lewis Powell, who offered something to both sides. He agreed with the four conservatives that Bakke had been unfairly treated on the basis of race. Bakke, intoned Powell, had been denied the equal protection of the law. But Powell also agreed with the four liberals that "race may be taken into account as a factor in an admissions program." That is, Powell refused to close the door on race preferences, even though he rejected the way the University of California had applied them in the case of Allan Bakke.

This left hanging the question: *What sort of race preferences in college admissions **would** be acceptable?* Powell proposed an answer, though none of the other eight justices endorsed it. His answer was *diversity.* Or, more specifically, Powell said that *if* the University of California could defend its decision to prefer a less qualified black student to a more qualified white student on the ground that it was trying to achieve the educational benefits that would accrue to all students from participating in a more racially diverse cohort of students, he, Powell, would have decided the case differently. Powell thought the university's feint in the direction of a "diversity" argument was merely a rationalization cooked up after the fact.

Powell's opinion in *Bakke* was plainly not the first time anyone had thought of this argument. Not only had the University of California mentioned it as a minor consideration in its legal pleadings, but it had featured prominently in an amicus brief submitted by Harvard and several other universities. But the *diversity* rationale for race preferences had stirred little interest in the courts or in popular opinion before the *Bakke* decision. Powell gave opinion leaders something new to chew on. The straightforward pro-preference argument that universities ought to engage in race preferences to make up for past discrimination was left dead and buried by the *Bakke* decision, but Powell had conjured the possibility that future litigation might vindicate the *diversity* rationale.

That litigation eventually came, most decisively in the 2003 case of *Grutter v. Bollinger*,[4] in which Justice Sandra Day O'Connor, writing for the majority, finally turned Powell's speculation about *diversity* as a possible rationale for race preferences in college admissions into a constitutional principle. It is a principle hedged with more conditions and qualifiers than the typical international arms control agreement, but in essence it said that colleges and universities can get away with discriminating in favor of minorities in their admissions so long as they *say* that such discrimination serves the higher purpose of advancing the educational benefit of *diversity*.

How is anyone to know whether an act of race discrimination by a university was the result of this supposedly wholesome motive and not an effort to dodge the restriction of race preferences for their own sake? The basic answer delivered by the Supreme Court came in a pair of cases, *Fisher v. University of Texas (Fisher I and II)*, in 2013[5] and 2016.[6] And the answer turned out to be that the Court would simply trust the word of the university. If the university said it acted on the basis of *diversity*, that would satisfy the Court. Technically, universities must meet a "strict scrutiny" standard that requires that a racial classification serve a "compelling public interest" and that there be no other, less invasive way to advance that interest. But "strict scrutiny" is like the costume of a burlesque dancer: it simply disappears as the show heats up, and the Court doesn't complain.

This is a highly simplified account of a tortuously complicated history of judicial interventions, but it will suffice because *diversity* in common parlance has almost nothing to do with what the courts say it means. Court decisions over the course of forty-some years have invested the word "diversity" with potent authority, but in practical application the pursuit of *diversity* has become a euphemism for thrusting race preferences into any and all decisions about how social goods—jobs, contracts, public funding, parades, TV shows, gigs, awards, political offices, and so on—should be distributed.

CULTURALIZING THE CONCEPT

Long before the 2003 *Grutter* decision, *diversity* escaped the narrow context of who gets admitted to competitive undergraduate and graduate academic programs. It had become, like *freedom*, *fairness*, and *equality*, a pliable concept, and its pliability lay in how it could be invoked to stake a claim for minority race preferences in almost any situation. It had also become the duct tape of racial rhetoric: a handy and instant repair to the fractures, tears, and splinters of ethnic rivalry.

This background lies both outside and inside the story of what happened to diversity in higher education. It is outside in that the pursuit of *diversity* in society at large is divorced from the Supreme Court's airy pronouncements on "educational benefits." When PepsiCo retired Aunt Jemima brand pancake mix and syrup, it was not in the least thinking about how adjacently seated individuals of different races in a law school classroom might enhance one another's appreciation of Blackstone. PepsiCo may have been thinking, instead, of the stones that could be thrown through the windows of its corporate headquarters in Purchase, New York. Mass marketing responds to cultural trends, and the headwinds now are blowing strongly against imagery that links to slavery or the antebellum past. And we have learned to talk about marketing (and almost everything else) as either enhancing or diminishing *diversity*.

The pursuit of *diversity* in corporate America and virtually every other social context has a logic of its own, grounded in fear of friction with blacks and other minority groups, a good-willed desire to advance positive racial relations, and a sense of moral indebtedness that entails reparations of some sort.

These are cultural imperatives that cut across all contexts in our society, including the special context of higher education. But higher education also must also deal with the narrower concept of *diversity* handed down by successive Supreme Court decisions and now embedded in university policies. Colleges and universities present a picture that is confusing for outsiders, one in which these separate and often contradictory doctrines are in play at the same time. We can begin to clarify the picture by considering *diversity* in relation to three other key terms: equity, multiculturalism, and inclusion.

EQUITY AND *DIVERSITY*

First, the idea of *racial equity* has a powerful grip on the imagination of progressive academics and students. This is the radicalized version of *diversity* as understood in American society at large. *Racial equity* as I use it here is the idea that social goods should be distributed in exact proportion to the size of a racial group to the general population. If 14 percent of the population is black, then 14 percent of a college class should be black; 14 percent of the faculty should be black; and perhaps 14 percent of the books assigned should be written by black authors. The racial equity principle can be extended indefinitely. It has no natural limits, which leads some equity arguments in higher education over the cliff into such absurdities as demanding the hiring of people who simply don't exist in the numbers the equity principle specifies, such as black mathematics professors.

An equity argument doesn't logically depend on the *diversity* rationale. The racial equity concept is grounded, instead, in an idea of fairness coupled with ethnic-group solidarity. It is at odds with American ideals of individuals choosing their own paths, markets emerging from millions of independent decisions, and opportunities awarded on the basis of merit. But there is a sympathetic vibration between racial equity arguments and *diversity* arguments. Both regard America as a racial spoils system in which, to advance, a minority group must find a way to channel opportunities to its own members. Equity arguments go straight to demands for set-asides and quotas. *Diversity* arguments detour through other considerations, such as the need for a "critical mass" of students in a particular ethnic group and the need for "holistic" assessments of students. *Diversity* leads onward to strange formulations such as "inclusive standards" (i.e., different benchmarks for measuring accomplishment, depending on affiliation with a racial or other identity group). Racial equity arguments need not bother with such subterfuges.

MULTICULTURALISM AND *DIVERSITY*

Second, multiculturalism emerged in the 1960s and '70s from some of the same cultural discontents that eventually gave rise to the *diversity* concept. Both were born out of dissatisfaction with the rigidities of mid-century higher education, with its emphases on the Western Civilization survey courses as the spine of the undergraduate curriculum, the post-Sputnik concentration on the hard sciences, and a strong commitment to liberal ideals of meritocracy. One of the rallying cries of campus protesters in the 1960s, "Open it up or close it down!" was a demand both to dismantle the supposedly ossified curriculum of the university and to remake the institution into something better suited to the needs of students from minority groups and from impoverished families. Student radicals, organized primarily through Students for a Democratic Society (SDS), offered an alternative vision of higher education as an engine to transform American society by altering the attitudes and motivations of college students, conceived as ready to cast off bourgeois values if offered an attractive alternative. SDS's *Port Huron Statement* laid out this plan explicitly.

The Western Civilization survey course fell quickly. In 1964, it was common among elite colleges and universities as a two-semester general education requirement and nearly universal as a requirement for history majors. By 1989, only one prominent university—Georgetown—retained the general education requirement in anything like its original form. (Columbia University maintained a core program of classic Western texts but not a historical Western Civilization course.) Western Civilization had generally slipped to the status of an elective, even for history majors.[7] The demise of the Western Civilization survey course was accompanied by the rise of its antithesis: the multiculturalism survey course. The substitution took place in full view of academe in 1987, when Stanford University responded to the demand to eliminate its already weakened Western Civilization course (at that point called "Western Culture") and replaced it with a multiculturalism requirement. Stanley Kurtz, in *The Lost History of Western Civilization*, provides a finely detailed account of how this played out at Stanford and how quickly other colleges and universities followed suit.[8]

Multiculturalism is an ideology, not just an isolated course or a curriculum centered on such a course. As an ideology, it depicts Western civilization as uniquely exploitative and oppressive but all other "cultures" as having both inherent worth and the potential to teach Westerners important ethical, aesthetic, and experiential lessons. Multiculturalists argue on principle that "cultures" (excepting the West) are equal and to be equally valued. This principle, however, often dissolves into mere declaration.

The concept of a "culture" as a discrete entity that can be pluralized (e.g., "humans have many cultures") was a 19th-century German contribution to anthropology, anglicized by Franz Boas in the 1880s and popularized in the United States by Boas's students Margaret Mead and Ruth Benedict in the 1930s. Anthropologists have struggled with its conceptual complications ever since. Culture is supposed to be a matter of shared assumptions, beliefs, norms, and customs that cohere as a whole, but these seldom fit together as a neat package. Communities are almost everywhere riven by disagreements, contending ideals, and sometimes violent disputes. Often they are fractured by language, dominated by aristocracies, chiefs, or priestly classes. The unity invoked in the idea of culture is often no more than the rationalization offered by a privileged faction. Moreover, cultures often lack the sort of boundaries that would allow one to say "This culture ends here and that culture begins there." People can feel at home in more than one culture, or they can feel alienated from their own culture.

These would be considerable problems for multiculturalists if they were interested in actual cultural difference. They would have to confront the messy reality that to talk about culture is to talk about dominance, oppression, extirpation, and war as much as it is to talk about favorite foods, colorful ceremonies, and ethnic pride. Multiculturalism in the American university has more in common with Disneyland's theme park *It's a Small World* boat ride than it does with any serious reckoning with how humanity roils in the antagonisms of large and small differences.

But the aim of multiculturalists is primarily to elevate the status of non-white ethnic groups in the United States. The interest in cultures around the world is superficial and merely instrumental. If ethnic pride among some segments of America can be stirred by invoking Ashanti legends or Polynesian voyages, multiculturalism cheers. If the Ashanti role in the West African slave trade or internecine warfare in Polynesian Hawai'i comes up, the multiculturalist falls awkwardly silent or summons the principle of non-judgmentalism: Who are we to stand in judgment? To judge is to be ethnocentric, which to a multiculturalist is the final verdict on the merits of an observation.

Multiculturalism is mainly about the curriculum, while *diversity* is mainly about student admissions and faculty hiring, but fundamentally the two words name the same subject and entail the same psychology. They are about four things: conferring benefits on favored racial or ethnic groups; derogating Western and, more specifically, American culture; fostering grievance-based solidarity among "oppressed" identity groups; and projecting an image of benevolent intent, as though the exacerbating of ethnic hostility is a righteous and wholesome undertaking. Multiculturalism, like *diversity*, has developed its own library of books that celebrate its achievements and explore its frontiers, as well as a more modest library of books by skeptics of the doctrine.

Multiculturalism and *diversity* also converge in the realm of fantasy. Both summon images of a utopian future in which racism has at last vanished from the whole world in favor of some sort of sustained era of peace and justice. The outlines of this utopia are necessarily vague. Banished will be human hierarchy, patriarchy, invidious distinctions among cultures, capitalism, and all forms of human exploitation. The ills that infest the world will be shoved back into Pandora's box for good. The interests of other advocacy groups will be integrated too. Alternative-energy-loving sustainatopians will be at the perpetual party. The queer activists and gender-on-demand transsexuals will also be accommodated.

The warrant for combining all these often conflicting interests is "intersectionality," which is the theory that all forms of oppression are linked and that resistance to oppression in one area creates a common interest with those resisting other forms of oppression.

Advocates of multiculturalism and *diversity*, however, tend to shy away from depicting the longer-term future. Their battles are in the present.

INCLUSION AND *DIVERSITY*

Third, the idea of "inclusion" was born in debates in the 1980s over how colleges and universities should deal with disparities in academic performance, mainly between black students as a category and all other students. Any explanation that pointed to average differences in ability, especially as measured by standardized tests, were deemed outrageous and insulting. Explanations that focused on the inadequacy of earlier academic preparation were more bearable but still carried the implication that black students as a whole were not capable of performing at the level of other students. The socially acceptable explanation that emerged was that the black students were victims of multiple forms of racism. American society had short-rationed their schools; college teachers treated them as racially inferior; racist assumptions were built into everyday life in America; and universities were "structurally racist."

This last is the bridge to the conception of "inclusion." Inclusion means recognizing that black students must be recognized as possessing their own cultural standards of expression, achievement, and excellence. Judging them by "white standards" is racist—structurally racist. A non-racist college or university would accommodate black students by judging them by black standards.

The connection to multiculturalism is evident. Inclusion, as a doctrine, incorporates the idea that black students have a separate culture, the norms of which must be respected. Eradicating all the "white assumptions" that pervade the university, however, is no small task. It requires a deep dismantling, the name for which is "Anti-Racism." We get to "inclusion" by identifying and removing anything that might make black students feel disrespected or that might cast their academic performance in unflattering contrast to the average performance of other students.

Once we start down the path of such "inclusion," as the path of "equity," there are no natural limits. Does the SAT include sections in which black students, on average, perform less well than members of other ethnic groups? Out goes the verbal analogy section. Do test scores still lag? Out go standardized tests altogether. Do the names of campus buildings honor historic figures who have some connection to slavery? Rename the buildings. But if the remaining buildings are named after white people, doesn't the problem remain?

Inclusion creates its own paradox, for ultimately the only way for an ethnic group to experience the world entirely on its own terms is to separate itself from the prevailing culture. To be "included," it may have to exclude itself, or at least put its relations to other groups and to the institution as a whole on an exclusive basis.

Dion Pierre and I traced this process in two studies published in 2019, *Neo-Segregation at Yale* and *Neo-Segregation at Wesleyan*. In both instances, the origins of racial self-segregation lay in how black students who were recruited in significant numbers to these elite colleges in the mid-1960s responded to the pressures of undergraduate life, which included some contemptuous treatment from white students. More than half the black students dropped out at Yale. Those who remained formed an isolated enclave, Black Students at Yale (BSAY), that began to make demands on the administration to be allowed more and more freedom to self-isolate. One of BSAY's demands was the creation of Black Studies—the first department of its kind in the United States.[9]

The Yale administration accommodated most, if not all, such demands, largely in the hope that these arrangements would gradually give way to real racial integration. The exact opposite occurred. BSAY's members, feeling empowered, only began to increase their demands for greater autonomy; soon, other ethnic-based solidarities, starting with the Puerto Rican students, emulated the tactics.

Eventually, almost everything at Yale that could be segregated—with the exception of residence halls—was segregated. Black students are recruited separately, attend separate orientations, have separate academic counselors, enjoy an exclusive cultural center, engage in a wide range of racially segregated social activities, can choose a de facto racially segregated academic program, attend a racially segregated graduation, and are enlisted in a racially segregated alumni society. While on campus, they enjoy a high level of immunity from the rules that other students must follow. In effect, they have become a privileged caste.

This is what "inclusion" looks like at Yale and at hundreds of other colleges and universities. It is, in principle, voluntary. Black students have the option of refusing the comforts of self-segregation and instead engaging Yale (or whatever their college may be) in wholehearted embrace, but to do so means resisting a great deal of peer pressure. Inclusion is not just an option that students can take or leave, like a fruit salad on the dining-hall menu. It is an expectation, backed up both by fellow students and by college administrations.

Inclusion of this sort runs counter to *diversity* as it is usually presented. The *diversity* doctrine rests on the idea that education is enhanced for everyone by the opportunities to learn from people unlike ourselves. It doesn't reckon with the possibility that those who aren't like us might prefer their own company.

This has given the institutional pursuit of *diversity* a double character from the start. *Diversity* is marketed to white students as a life-enhancing and educationally enriching encounter with students of other races and ethnicities. But when colleges speak of *diversity* to minority students, that integrationist rhetoric and imagery disappears and is replaced by strong assurances that the university has an abundance of students in their own racial group and lots of well-funded opportunities to bond with people *just like you.*

Same word, two starkly different realities. *Diversity* means cross-cultural connection and, at the same time, in-group exclusivity. Anyone who points out this contradiction is on a short path to being canceled as a racist. Seeking to overcome racial barriers is, on today's campuses, considered not part of *diversity*, but an exercise in *white privilege*. That's because white students are seen as merely tourists in the land of *real diversity*. They can leave and go home, while black students have to live in *diversity*-land 24/7.

Inclusion would mean the black students could pull up the drawbridge, or perhaps move to Wakanda, the make-believe world of black super-accomplishment pictured in the *Black Panther* comic books and blockbuster Hollywood movie. The only role left for whites is the role of "allies," which requires an attitude of humble submission to black demands and repentance for the crimes of white supremacy.

DIVERSITY DISCONTENTS

The concept of *diversity* still, somehow, retains an aura of goodwill and fellowship, even in an era of radicalized anti-white protest. While the protests and riots have moved to city streets across the country (at least as I am writing in the summer of 2020), they are fueled by the doctrines that colleges and universities have been teaching for the last thirty-some years. At the heart of these doctrines is disdain for American culture. America in particular and the West in general are pictured as uniquely terrible. They are the original source of brutality, oppression, and injustice. It would be inaccurate to say that this reflexive hatred of our culture stems mainly from the *diversity* doctrine. *Diversity* plays a significant part in softening students for the more poisonous messages that follow. But *diversity* is not itself the distilled cultural self-loathing. *Diversity*, after all, encodes a goodwill and a desire to be friends with people who presumably have dissimilar experiences and beliefs. Diversity welcomes these as an exciting challenge, not a grim duty. We are enjoined (endlessly) to "Celebrate Diversity!" not merely endure it.

On the far side of *diversity*, however, lie discontents that *diversity* itself can never salve. Why does the dancing world of *diversity* quilts and happy unicorns never emerge, despite all the ardent *diversity* campaigns? The suspicion lurks that someone is undermining the effort, perhaps cold-hearted people who are indifferent to the lovely community waiting to be born—or, worse, hidden racists who seek to pit groups against one another.

Sooner or later in the life of every eager diversiphile, the suspicion ripens into anger. And anger fastens on enemies. The *diversity* doctrine is primarily about race relations, but it has never settled exclusively on race. The pursuit of *diversity* is also a rhetorical position for some feminists, gay and transgender activists, illegal immigrants, the handicapped, and many others who see a way of leveraging their demands for social approval through the image of society as a great coalition of those who have unjustly suffered discrimination. *Diversity* is a compensatory tool for all who can mount an identity-group-based grievance.

But it is a better tool for some than others, because it is strictly hierarchical. Blacks are the victim group *par excellence* and, in that sense, have primary ownership of *diversity* claims. All the other identity groups emulate and attempt to trade on black grievance.

This has propelled Black Lives Matter to the forefront of grievance politics, at a considerable cost to the *diversity* establishment. BLM has little interest in the "nice" side of diversity. It doesn't seek to make whites feel better about themselves or optimistic about a racially harmonious society just on the other side of the hill. Rather, it aims to exacerbate racial animosity as the only way to surface deeper injustices. Its target is "systemic racism," which becomes the obsession of diversiphiles after they are disillusioned with the fairy-tale version of cultural progress they had indulged.

Black Lives Matter, however, is only one of the sharks in the pool. Higher education has made itself home for a slew of anti-American and anti-Western ideologies, each vying to be more radical than the next in its defining hatred. The climate change movement depicts the whole world created by the 18th-century industrial revolution and the harnessing of fossil fuels as putting the planet on the path of existential peril. That trumps the peril of racism, if you can convince people to believe it is true. Climate change hysteria is a strong rival to the *diversity* doctrine, and it appeals primarily to white students. Denied the precious status of victimhood under the *diversity* rubric, the climate activists can, instead, claim to be victims of Big Oil and heedless capitalism. *Diversity* also faces other rivals, in the form of anarchist groups such as Antifa, that ostentatiously reject the vision of peace and racial accord that *diversity*, in its better mood, attempts to parlay into power.

But perhaps the biggest threat to *diversity* as a movement is the rise of *intersectionality*, the doctrine that all victim groups have a deep commonality by virtue of their oppression. *Diversity* had already created an oppression sweepstakes, in which victimhood had become a status marker. Intersectionality amplifies these claims to the point of no return. It is congenial to the Black Lives Matter leadership (black, Lesbian, and militantly anti-heterosexual male), and it leaves no room at all for the conciliatory message of *diversity* that has so long enamored college admissions directors and corporate marketing departments. Intersectionality is too hard-edged for that.

It leads, instead, to what is now called Anti-Racism—a term

that seems perfectly designed to be misunderstood by everyone but its initiates. Anti-Racism is a concentrated form of the idea that American society is, in every molecule, a racist enterprise and that white people are the profound embodiment of racism. To be an Anti-Racist is to accept a lifelong sentence of penitence, along with the premise that no white person can ever fully understand the pain and degradation inflicted on blacks by white supremacy.

One might have thought this fringe cult lay beyond the capacity of even the most eager-to-appease college administrators—a level of abasement that even Kingman Brewster at Yale never reached. But not so. After the death of George Floyd in Minneapolis and the riots that swept American cities, hundreds of American college presidents issued statements proclaiming their institutions were now committed to Anti-Racism.

DIVERSITY HANGS ON

I would not go so far as to say this means the end of the *diversity* movement. *Diversity* still provides the legal rationale for colleges and universities to engage in otherwise statutorily and constitutionally prohibited race discrimination. That game will continue. But *diversity* has lost much of its cachet as an exciting idea about how to manage the racial spoils system in America. The effort to keep it alive goes by the name EDI—equity, diversity, and inclusion. The creation of a sandwich with *diversity* in the middle is a sign of weakness in the doctrine, not strength. Equity and inclusion are essentially rival concepts, and the effort to make them three tines on the same pitchfork of racial resentment illustrates the waning confidence of academic and corporate America in their continuing efforts to find a way out of America's long descent into antagonistic identity-group politics.

On the other hand, the idea of a harmonious, multicultural, and inclusive community is the official destination of nearly all colleges and universities. Racial equity and racial harmony are starkly opposed as ideals and as practical goals—though, as typically happens when a community is riven by a fundamental contradiction in its values, higher education denies it. Instead, our college and university leaders issue fervent proclamations insisting that they can have it both ways at once. They can wave the Black Lives Matter banner while declaring, "All Lives Matter." They can insist that America is a fundamentally racist nation that inevitably denies blacks and other ethnic minorities their fair share of the nation's wealth while they champion the claim that education transcends racial division. One side of this division intensifies racial grievance, while the other side attempts to mollify it.

The dynamic on campus is a fitful combination of accelerant and fire extinguisher. The university hires diversity deans and provosts whose job is, in large part, to stoke group resentment.

PARTICULARS

The fly-over view of *diversity* that I have just provided has said nothing about the burgeoning genre of books on the subject. Nor have I touched on the stream, now torrent, of journal articles, conferences, and policy statements that are the routine work-product of the many thousands of professional diversicrats. Likewise, I've skipped over the prominent place that *diversity* occupies in the news as a major concern of the business community, the arts, sports, and so on. Lastly, I've alluded to only some of the landmark events in the still-unfolding history of this concept.

I'm not an innocent party to any of this. My 2003 book, *Diversity: The Invention of a Concept*, which preceded the *Grutter* decision by four months, provided a close reading of how *diversity* had gained so much ground in its first twenty-five years. In the fall of 2019, I published *Diversity Rules*, which attempted a synopsis of the developments since the *Grutter* decision in 2003. I refer the reader who seeks an account of the ground war—the assaults on the garrison, the hills gained, the cities lost, the partisans who continue to fight after the army has slumped home in defeat—to those books. Or to others, such as Heather Mac Donald's coruscating volume, *The Diversity Delusion* (2018).[10]

Mac Donald and I are among those who critique the *diversity* doctrine as divisive, wasteful, ill-founded, and rife with abuse. But *diversity* has also long attracted critics of another sort, who fault it as a superficial medicine for deeper ailments, inadequate to its own professed goals, and too readily co-opted by those who have faint interest in more profound forms of social change. Among the examples of this sort of critique is Pamela Newkirk's *Diversity, Inc.: The Failed Promise of a Billion-Dollar Business* (2019). Newkirk is a journalist and professor of journalism at New York University. Her book opens by expressing her disappointment that the newspaper industry is "disproportionately White," as are academia and "other influential fields—from the arts, advertising, and fashion, to law, technology, and investment banking." Affirmative action, and then the pursuit of *diversity*, were supposed to change all of that, but they failed. Why?

> Given the sturdy foundation of White domination on which America rests, it has perhaps been naive of many diversity advocates to expect even those viewed as progressive allies to relinquish hardwired attitudes and centuries-old customs, no matter how ignobly attained.[11]

Newkirk, in other words, attacks the progressive left's commitment to *diversity* as hypocritical and ranges herself with the supporters of the idea that America is essentially a racial hierarchy based on white exploitation of blacks and other minorities. Corporate *diversity* statements, commitments, officers, and consultants are merely window dressing.

This view had been gestating for a while among black intellectuals. The idea that America is founded on racism (as opposed to liberty, justice, equality, or several other possibilities) gained a powerful work of advocacy in Ibram X. Kendi's *Stamped from the Beginning*, modestly subtitled *The Definitive History of Racist Ideas in America* (2016). Kendi, a professor of history at Boston University and head of a newly established Center for Antiracist Research, does not waste a word on the *diversity* doctrine. His only mention of "diversity" is the diversity of people called "black" who are really to be "differentiated by gender, class, ethnicity, sexuality, culture, skin color, profession, and nationality—among a series of other identifiers." Of course, almost any word can be splintered this way. Kendi's purpose is to render even the elementary distinctions embedded in American ideas of race—and *diversity*—inoperative. Everything comes down to power and subordination, and no amount of intervention in the name of *diversity* can touch that. What's needed, according to Kendi, are "Americans committed to antiracist policies seizing and maintaining power over institutions, neighborhoods, counties, states, nations—the world." He offers no democratic path to this "seizing." It will be a revolutionary act.[12] Kendi followed this book with a still more bristling manifesto, *How to Be an Antiracist* (2019).[13]

Yet another sour view of *diversity* from the left comes from Matthew Johnson, a professor of history at Texas Tech, who offers an account of racial politics at the University of Michigan, *Undermining Racial Justice: How One University Embraced Inclusion and Inequality* (2020). The title, which sounds confusing, gives voice to Johnson's idea that university administrators manipulated the pliable minds of black student activists into working to advance trivial institutional goals instead of real "racial justice." The administrators believed that *diversity* was still the golden ticket to gaining broad support for race preferences at the University of Michigan but "added tepid statements about social justice" to win the support of the Black Student Union and other activists. This pitch fell short. Johnson cites the university's Association of Black Professionals and Administrators, who responded, "Diversity and pluralism are terms that obscure the ethical and moral issues that underlie the causes of social inequality." Their preferred goals were "justice" and "equality."[14]

Cyndi Kernahan's *Teaching about Race and Racism in the College Classroom: Notes from a White Professor* (2019) touches a different chord of leftist disenchantment with *diversity*. According to Kernahan, a professor of psychology at the University of Wisconsin–River Falls, *diversity* training fails to alter the attitudes of whites. In her book, she describes how one form of training, aimed at making whites "understand what it feels like to be a person of color, to feel the sting of oppression," backfired. It "created so much stress in the participants that they simply avoided learning more about race after the training." Kernahan seems to believe that "teaching about race" is better than *diversity* training, which "is usually about compelling some employees to behave better," rather than a deep transformation of attitudes. She cites other studies to the effect that "interventions to reduce bias can often induce backlash, increasing rather than decreasing prejudice." Kernahan's own approach involves leading white students to "feel as if racism is important in their lives," which requires "finding ways to talk about Whiteness as one part of the overall system of racism."[15]

Diversity has still other harsh critics. Daniel Markovits, a professor of law at Yale, thunders in *The Meritocracy Trap: How America's Foundational Myth Feeds Inequality, Dismantles the Middle Class, and Devours the Elite* (2019) that "The elites' intense concern for diversity and inclusion also carries an odor of self-dealing." Meritocracy, he says, opposes prejudice "in order to shore up inequalities it seeks to legitimate against their increasing size and instability." Support for *diversity*, in Markovits's analysis, is just another mask worn by the privileged to ensure their own domination:

> A genuine embrace of diversity and inclusion allows an elite institution to tell black, female, or gay students that while its culture is not perfect, it is committed to welcoming them on their own terms and supporting their authentic selves.

He notes that this show of generosity to some groups is paralleled by imposition on middle-class students to "overwrite" their "original identities" with the meritocratic ideals of the institution.[16] These are but a few examples of how deeply out of favor the *diversity* doctrine has fallen with the stewards of progressive opinion in the United States. Even a recent book aimed at a comprehensive historical summing up of America's efforts to advance racial parity gives *diversity* short shrift. Virginia Commonwealth University emeritus historian Melvin I. Urofsky, in *The Affirmative Action Puzzle: A Living History from Reconstruction to Today* (2020), consigns *diversity* to the role of a dysfunctional work-around, saying that it confuses and demoralizes students:

> Asian Americans feel that they are being held to a higher standard; white students feel similarly penalized; and people of color complain the system is so opaque that if they do get into a good school, it must be because of their color, a marker that will trail them well after graduation.[17]

WHY UNIVERSITIES CLING

But the left's intellectual discontent with the concept doesn't mean *diversity* will be retired from higher education's armory any time soon. The pursuit of race preferences by colleges and universities must still pass the Supreme Court's rubric in which all such racial impositions have to be justified as the pursuit of *diversity*. And universities now have very large bodies of administrators—most of them meagerly qualified members of minority groups—who owe their positions to the *diversity* doctrine. Any institutional retreat would set off massive protests and accusations of racism.

Many universities also are employing the *diversity* doctrine as a way of prying open academic appointments in departments that have fought fiercely to maintain their disciplinary standards. This is especially true in the hard sciences. The University of California, for example, is now using *diversity* statements in STEM faculty hiring, actively weeding out the most qualified applicants in order to create opportunities for far less qualified minority applicants.[18] The chair of the Mathematics Department at the University of California at Davis, Abigail Thompson, published a widely noted complaint about this new diversity initiative in a 2019 essay in *Notices of the American Mathematical Society*, which added to a growing chorus of such complaints.[19]

A STAKE THROUGH ITS HEART

The *diversity* doctrine will thus abide with us for some time, but it would not do to conclude this essay without mention of how out-of-joint diversity is with the racial animus of the 1619 Project—the attack on the foundational ideals of America launched by the *New York Times* in August 2019. The 1619 Project purports to be "history," though it has provoked mostly scorn from real historians across the political spectrum. It is, rather, a slickly packaged anti-white, anti-American, and anti-Western mythology that advances a narrative of the nation as a "slavocracy," from its earliest colonial days to the present. I've elsewhere offered my own detailed account of what the 1619 Project is and what it means, so here I will only add that it is a stake through the heart of *diversity*.[20]

Charles Kesler, a professor of government at Claremont McKenna College, addressed the violent summer 2020 urban protests in a newspaper column titled, "Call Them the 1619 Riots." Kesler traced the attack on supposed "systemic racism" in America to "the most prominent proponent" of that idea, the primary author and face of the 1619 Project, Nikole Hannah-Jones.[21] Hannah-Jones tweeted a response that "It would be an honor" to accept that responsibility.[22]

The summoning of racial hatred and urban rebellion as the means to pursue "Anti-Racism" is about as far from the soft counsels of *diversity* for the good of all that we can possibly get. Yet somehow, in the perplexing world of higher education, we have a plentitude of college presidents and faculty members who believe that they can pursue both policies at once.

If there is any summing up, it is that not only is *diversity* a word of astonishing versatility, it is also a concept of astonishing incoherence. Our national willingness to treat it as an honorary member of our founding ideals of freedom, fairness, justice, and equality would puzzle our forebears. It is a measure of our cultural descent that we take it so easily in stride.

Segregation Now

Peter N. Kirsanow

When I attended Cornell in the 1970s, racially separate programs were just getting started. A scant few years earlier, the focus had been on integration. But by the time I showed up at Cornell in 1972, racially separate programs, racially separate dorms, and race preferences in admissions were sprouting on campuses like mushrooms after the rain.

I chose not to join the racially separate program at Cornell. I knew it was not for me.

This essay will describe several programs, some at Cornell and some at other universities. Some of these programs are residential, and others are racially themed student centers and the like. This essay is not intended to be exhaustive as to the existence of these programs generally, the number at a particular institution, or the history and activities of any particular program. The amount of information available about the purpose, history, staff, and students of these programs varies; therefore, so do the length and detail of the program profiles in this essay.

These are merely sketches to give the reader an idea of what these programs do, how they are developed, and what I consider to be their pernicious effects.

RACIALLY FOCUSED PROGRAMS AT PRIVATE UNIVERSITIES

Ujamaa Residential College at Cornell

Ujamaa House was founded in 1972, shortly before I arrived at Cornell.[1] Ujamaa House was created in the racial ferment on Cornell's campus that reached its highest point in the take-over of Willard Straight Hall.[2] Ujamaa House's official website explains, "The term 'Ujamaa' is Kiswahili, roughly meaning collective economics. The name affirms our commitment as a community to pool resources and be participants in each other's fulfillment."[3]

Ujamaa had a higher concentration of "political" (or, in today's terminology, "woke") black students than other residence halls. Although it was not uncommon for black students of the era to sport Afros, they were nearly ubiquitous (and more impressive) among Ujamaa residents, both male and female. Cornrows and ostensibly African attire and effects also were more prevalent among Ujamaa residents. Dorm-room walls sported African-themed posters and art extolling the virtues of all things African and black; the overall effect was an uncanny preview of the imagery contained in the *Black Panther* film released nearly fifty years later.

There was a greater insularity among Ujamaa residents than the rest of the black students on campus. The tendency to self-segregate while dining, partying, and studying persisted from matriculation through graduation.

A vague sense of militancy hung over the dorm; allegations, rumors, and protests of disparate treatment seemed dispropor-tionately to emanate from Ujamaa relative to black students in other residence halls.

Today, Ujamaa Residential College is a residential complex that "celebrates the rich and diverse heritage of Black people in the United States, Africa, the Caribbean, and other regions of the world."[4] Prospective residents are assured, "Understand that we, the Ujamaa residential team foster individuals defining their Blackness and living in their truth."[5]

Jalissa Elias, who is currently the residence hall director for Ujamaa, wrote in her official profile, "My passion is developing ways for students who hold marginalized identities to have positive experiences in higher education."[6]

Elias's goal sounds innocuous enough. But what exactly are "marginalized identities"? Presumably skin color, given that this residence is dedicated to the experience of black people. Exactly why skin color is supposed to be a great commonality among people from across very different regions is left unexplained. Is it cultural similarity? Why would a black kid from Cleveland have more in common with a black kid from Nigeria than with a white kid from Cleveland? Is it the experience of being a minority? Well, if you are a black person from Africa, you're in the racial majority on that continent. How are you the possessor of a "marginalized identity"?

At least during my time at Cornell, denizens of Ujamaa House had, quite possibly, experienced invidious race discrimination. After all, the Civil Rights Act of 1964 wasn't passed until I was in elementary school. It appears that today, however, programming at Ujamaa House encourages students to magnify slights and cultivate resentment against whites. A November 2019 article in the *Cornell Daily Sun* reported on an Ujamaa House event entitled "For Colored Boys: Why Education Fails Black Men."[7] At this event, students discussed complaints such as: a fourth-grade teacher didn't believe I, a black student, could read more than was assigned, but believed a white student could; and how attending "a predominantly white high school...came at the expense of exposure to her own culture."

Asian and Asian American Center at Cornell

Since I graduated from Cornell in 1976, programs promoting racial separatism (and other forms of identity separatism) have not decreased. In fact, they have proliferated. The Cornell Asian and Asian American Center is an example of how even a well-intentioned effort to solve a serious problem disproportionately affecting students of a particular race or ethnicity can be hijacked to advance an agenda of racial separatism.

The Cornell Asian and Asian American Center declares, "The Asian & Asian American Center is a second home for Asian, Asian American, Pacific Islander, and bi/multiracial undergraduate and graduate/professional students, allies, families, and friends."[8] Among its stated purposes are "Advocacy: Serve as an advocate for students. Advise on issues that affect the community and offer guidance on specific issues as they arise" and "Identity: Foster space for students to explore their multiple and intersecting identities."[9]

The roots of A3C, as it is called, stretch back almost twenty years to when a serious problem came to the attention of Cornell administrators and faculty. Asian and Asian American students make up such a large portion of the student body that they can't seriously be considered to experience "racial isolation." However, Asian and Asian American students were a disproportionate percentage of Cornell students who committed suicide. Thirteen Cornell students committed suicide between 1996 and November 2002.[10] Six of those students were Asian and male. By 2006, the total number of suicides had increased to twenty-one, of whom thirteen were Asian or Asian American.[11] Cornell responded by bringing in an alumnus, now a psychiatrist at NYU, who specialized in Asian American mental health issues, to talk to students and staff.[12] The university also formulated strategies for reaching out to Asian and Asian American students who might be in need of mental health or other counseling. So far, so good: The university identified a particular group of students who were at heightened risk of doing serious harm to themselves, likely due to specific cultural pressures from their parents and communities, and was trying to respond.[13] Completely reasonable.

How, then, did "Let's have a 'special mental health-oriented Asian and Asian American Campus Climate Task Force to address the causes behind the high number of suicides'"[14] turn into "space for students to explore their multiple and intersecting identities"?

According to Cornell's class profile, Asian American students accounted for 20.1 percent of the class of 2023.[15] This made them the second-largest racial/ethnic group in the class, behind only white students.[16] The profile of the class of 2023 lumps all international students into one group and does not break them down by nationality, but it seems likely that a significant portion of international students are from Asian countries. It seems unlikely that a racial group that makes up approximately a quarter of the student body experiences alienation and racial isolation that necessitates a special student center. Nevertheless, since 2009, A3C has had its own dedicated space.[17]

A separate student center for Asian American and Asian students makes sense, though, when you realize that the bureaucracies at many universities wish to reinforce racial and ethnic identity. If you are part of a racial group that is one-quarter of the student body, and the only larger racial group is about a third of the student body, there is nothing unusual about you. You are as ordinary as anyone else on campus, as far as race goes. As my friends at the National Association of Scholars illustrated in their report on racial separatism at Yale, however, the point really isn't whether anyone is experiencing "racial isolation."

A blog post written by the co-chair of the A3C Committee, Caroline Hugh, illustrates how a laudable effort to ensure that mental health resources were available to Asian students turned into a racially separate student center. Hugh, responding to an editorial by an Asian American student opposing the creation of a separate student center, wrote:

By the way, if Cornell administrators say they support program housing, it's about time they speak up on this issue—publicly—and why they support it. While the A3C will not be a program house, program houses and the A3C (as well as the Lesbian, Gay, Bisexual, Transgender Resource Center) are safe spaces for oppressed groups to gather and have resources devoted to their needs.[18]

Exactly how the second-largest racial group on campus is "oppressed" is left unexplained. What is clear is that, as the National Association of Scholars has documented in its report, "Neo-Segregation at Yale," A3C is another example of how "colleges promote ethnic enclaves, stoke racial resentment, and build organizational structures on the basis of group grievance."[19] A blog run by students who led the effort to force Cornell to establish A3C stated:

> The committee aims to create an AAA [Asian and Asian American] center on campus, a hub that would offer space for community-building, cultural celebration, *and the development of an AAA consciousness*—similar to what spaces such as the Africana Studies and Research Center, the Latino Studies Program, and the Lesbian, Gay, Bisexual, and Transgender Resource Center currently do for other marginalized populations on campus. [emphasis added][20]

Although there are occasional references to the mental health needs of Asian and Asian American students on the student blog, it appears that the student activists mainly wanted to establish A3C to have a separate racial enclave. These separate racial centers and programs also encourage students (whether deliberately or not) to view themselves as an allied block of non-white (and LGBT) students. The Cornell administration was hesitant to expend money on A3C (or any other construction project) during the worst economic downturn in a generation. To increase pressure on the administration, the student activists pushing for A3C suggested holding "Info sessions to all people of color organizations to (1) get them informed and (2) get their support in the A3C effort."[21] There is no particular reason why Asian American, black, or Latino students together should view their interests as separate from those of white students. There is surely no reason why the interests of Asian American, black, and Latino students are necessarily aligned. If students are going to view their interests as aligned (or not aligned) with those of other racial groups, it would make just as much sense for Asian American students to view their interests as more closely aligned with those of white students. Unless, of course, the goal of the student activists (many individual students likely do not care at all) is to nudge students into viewing themselves as a "people of color" block with an adversarial posture toward whites.

A3C also helps students acquire experience in racial and left-wing activism that they can carry beyond their college years. Essentially, A3C trains missionaries to carry the faith of intersectionality into the world beyond the Cornell campus. These students are also paid for the time they spend learning to be activists. A3C runs the "A3C Internship Program." The blurb on the website informs potential interns:

> Interested in identity-based work, social justice, community building? Potentially looking at a career in multicultural/diversity affairs or higher education? This internship could be for you. The A3C selects a group of undergraduate interns to help organize and run the center's activities. This is a paid position and interns are supported by our A3C Graduate Interns and Professional Staff (Director and assistant Director).[22]

Graduate students are not completely shut out of this exciting opportunity, as A3C "hires one or two paid student staff each year" who "work on a variety of identity, social justice, and educational-based programs and assist with daily center operations, outreach, mentorship, and new initiatives."

There is an aspect of many diversity programs that is simply a good old-fashioned racket. People who are interested in having a career in "identity-based work" and "social justice" come up against an unwelcome reality. That reality is that outside human resource departments (whose influence, alas, is growing), there are not a great many remunerative positions for those whose interests are "identity-based work" and "social justice." Leave aside the usual conservative grumbling about "those kids should have learned plumbing/gotten an engineering degree/learned how to change a tire." Not even the federal government is interested in hiring a recent college graduate whose primary qualifications are "social justice" and "community building." (If you don't believe me, take a quick look at postings on USAjobs.gov.)

Where students whose primary qualification is a racial chip on their shoulder *can* find employment is academia. An expansive reading of Title IX spawned an entire bureaucracy devoted to defending that expansive reading and justifying its own existence.[23] Likewise, the more demand multicultural student centers can drum up for their services, the more jobs will be created for students who want careers in "identity-based work" and "social justice," and the more secure the jobs of the diversity bureaucrats will be.

Ujamaa House at Stanford

Ujamaa at Stanford, like Ujamaa House at Cornell, is a residential facility dedicated to the "African Diaspora."[24] It was established in 1970. According to Stanford, "this African-American themed dorm has expanded its intellectual focus to include the entire African Diaspora."[25] Approximately half of Ujamaa residents belong to the "Black Diaspora" (Stanford's term, not mine) and the other half belong to the rest of the human race.[26]

Using the term "diaspora" imposes a sort of unity on the group that does not really exist. When originally used to refer to Jews scattered throughout the nations of the world, the term did refer to people who shared a common religious background. Members of the "Irish Diaspora" came from the same small geographic area and generally shared the same religion. Literally the only thing shared by the "African Diaspora" is that people come from the same gigantic continent. Even their ancestors did not come from the same parts of Africa, have the same culture, or worship the same gods. Yet, somehow, Ujamaa and other multicultural centers suggest that there is some sort of pan-African unity between the son of a Jamaican Anglican clergyman, the Detroit-born daughter of Nation of Islam members, and a young man from Ethiopia whose family has been Ethiopian Orthodox for millennia. If "diaspora" means anything in this context, we might as well refer to the "human diaspora."

As we have seen in the context of other racially themed dorms, Ujamaa is premised on the assumption that non-white students are disproportionately subject to suffering on campus. Individuals who wish to be considered for staff positions at Ujamaa are informed that "Empathy is key for connecting with our residents, many of whom may go through great strife on campus, racial or otherwise."[27] This year (2020) marks the fiftieth anniversary of Ujamaa's establishment on Stanford's campus. If the official commitment to elevating and furthering the black community that Ujamaa represents has not improved things beyond the point that black students can expect to experience racial strife on Stanford's campus, it may be time to admit this effort has failed. If Stanford's official view is that black students can expect to face racial strife on campus, why should we expect another fifty years of Ujamaa and similar initiatives to produce any better results? And, for that matter, why are the most privileged students in the world, of whatever color, encountering "great strife" on Stanford's campus, period?

Students who hope to join Ujamaa must submit an "Ujamaa Scholars Theme Proposal," which is a proposal for a lecture or discussion that the student would lead during weekly gatherings at Ujamaa to discuss issues pertaining to black identity.[28] Ujamaa provides a sample proposal to guide applicants, which apparently was submitted by a real student (as the name and other identifying information are blacked out). The sample proposal is entitled "#BlackTransLivesMatter: Black transgender incarceration and activism."[29] The "desired learning outcomes" include that participants "Can define 'transgender' and 'gender non-conforming'"; "Can articulate the challenges trans (and specifically black trans) people face in regard to policing and the prison industrial complex"; and "Understand how centering the experiences of black trans people, and other trans people of color, can contribute to activist movements for collective liberation."[30]

Casa Zapata at Stanford

Casa Zapata is Stanford's "Latinx" residence hall.[31] It was founded in 1972.[32] Stanford's residential website describes Casa Zapata thus:

> Casa Zapata is a four-class house focusing on the Chicanx and Latinx experience through educational and cultural programs. Zapata residents are engaged in a wide range of activities—staging plays for Zoot Suit week, planning film series, and sharing poetry and music at regular dorm gatherings. Zapata has been a source of inspiration, creativity, and community for over three decades. Decorated with vibrant murals by renowned Latino artists throughout the common areas, Casa Zapata is also a hub for community events such as Floricanto, Posadas, and Chicanx/Latinx Reunion Homecoming, as well as host to performing groups

such as El Mariachi Cardenal, Ballet Folklorico, a cappella groups, and service organizations. Zapata provides students with the opportunity to share a distinct cultural experience, form strong friendships across all undergraduate classes, and still experience the enthusiasm and spirit that is usually reserved for freshman dorms....

Casa Zapata's ethnic-focused theme creates a common bond for all residents—Latino and non-Latino alike—that fosters cross-cultural understanding and creates outstanding learning opportunities. Dorm life is full of many different activities and programs, some of which focus on Chicanx/Latinx history, art and culture, while others address issues that are defined by residents and the greater Stanford community. And it has been our experience that this environment creates unparalleled opportunities to pursue your passions and to explore new ones. We hope to foster an environment that encourages exploration, fosters honest and open dialogue about difficult issues, and values diversity.[33]

According to a 2010 *Stanford Daily* article (although this is not stated on Stanford's residential services website), all ethnically themed dorms at Stanford, except for the Native American–themed dorm, require 50 percent of residents to identify as a member of the ethnic group that is the dorm's theme.[34] Students who seek to be assigned to Casa Zapata are required to participate in various ethnically themed dorm activities, such as presenting on a theme project and volunteering in "Zapata-Wide Educational and Cultural Programs."[35]

As of 2018, the most recent year for which information is available, Elvira Prieto was the "Resident Fellow" at Casa Zapata.[36] Prieto explained to incoming students that her role was to serve as "the educational leader of the house" and to "support you and create engaging educational programming to help you feel at home in our beautiful community, learn more about yourself and others, and explore Zapata's Latinx culture theme."[37] Prieto has since been promoted to associate dean of students, but it is unclear whether she left her position as resident fellow upon receiving the promotion.[38] Prieto's career has been focused on higher education administration, although she has also published a book of memoirs and poetry.[39]

In addition to Resident Fellow Prieto, Zapata had a "Graduate Theme Coordinator" in 2018.[40] The graduate theme coordinator "will promote and support our theme programming in addition to sharing her own scholarship, intellectual and community focused pursuits with our Zapata familia."[41] The graduate theme coordinator for 2018 was Luz Jimenez Ruvalcaba, a PhD student in "Modern Thought and Literature."[42] According to her departmental profile, her academic interests are as follows:

At the intersection of literary study, critical race studies, and feminist studies, Luz's research investigates the cultural and historical preconditions that foster intimate violence. Specifically, in her dissertation project, she studies the ways in which domestic violence is represented—how it originates, develops, and is manifested—in 20th and 21st century Latinx literature. In broader terms, Luz returns to experiences and conceptions of violence whose hermeneutic devastation has been normalized. What happens, then, when we attend to forms of everyday violence we dismiss because we have resigned ourselves to them? What happens when we care for the less visible and more quiet expressions of loss? With an emphasis on the literary skill of close reading, she thinks about forms of violence that might not always be readily perceived as such. Her attention is often with absence and the absented/disappeared, as well as with desperation and proleptic mourning. Ultimately, her research stresses the humanity of those [Frantz] Fanon termed the *damnés* of the earth who, as marginalized bodies, are nevertheless active subjects of radical hope. Ultimately, Luz hopes to offer literature as a touch stone that might help us further understand ourselves as members of a society founded upon the inherent violences of racial and gendered hierarchies.[43]

Ethnically themed dorms have not been without controversy at Stanford, as evidenced by a small, but consistent, smattering of articles published in the *Stanford Review* over the years. Most of these articles defend the existence of the ethnically themed houses, which suggests that some students are opposed to these dorms. In a 2017 article, student Sam Wolfe defends ethnically themed houses, saying they serve as:

> [T]he backdrops for profound personal development.... One wonders why they would be so over-subscribed if prospective students didn't feel that a common understanding of the experience of being black, Asian, Native American, or Hispanic in America (or, indeed, in general) could ignite enduring communal bonds.[44]

Sierra Garcia made a similar point in an op-ed defending the themed dorms, arguing that ethnically themed dorms expose students to diverse life experiences and views:

> [I]t is absurd to imagine that a student from an upper class Haitian family, another from inner city Detroit and another from an LA suburb would be in an entirely familiar and unchallenged environment living together. In the Review's simplistic argument, these students would be doing a disservice to their liberal arts education by living together in Ujamaa, *even though every other aspect of their life at Stanford includes interactions with the whole student body.* Some students who did not grow up in communities of their same ethnicity will gravitate towards an ethnic theme dorm for the exact opposite reason that the Review's article suggests: not because they want to be comfortable surrounded by people just like them, but because they have never been around others

of their own ethnicity in their home community or high school.
[emphasis in original][45]

Statements by other students suggest that the residents of
ethnically themed dorms may not be as interested in interacting
with the rest of the community as Garcia suggests and that their
existence encourages students primarily to interact with members
of their own race. In 2010, student Joe Gettinger wrote:

> It's unexpected, but inevitable. A recurring anachronism every
> year in Lakeside Dining: segregated seating. In the main hall, you
> could draw a line separating a large body of black students from
> tables of mixed students.
>
> Although on the surface, this split may seem racial, in fact dining
> is not split black and white. On one side of the divide are the West
> Lag dorms, and on the other side is Ujamaa, the African-themed
> dorm (one of Stanford's four ethnic themed houses). Each sits on
> its own side, simply as a matter of convenience.[46]

A contretemps on campus involving the Stanford College
Republicans and Casa Zapata also illustrates that the ethnically
themed dorms can operate as "safe spaces" where ideas opposed by
the most vocal members of the minority group are not permitted.
In October 2019, the Stanford College Republicans (SCRs) sought
to post flyers in dorms, including Casa Zapata, to advertise an
upcoming Ben Shapiro lecture.[47] There are competing versions
of events, but both sides agree that the SCRs sought to enter
Casa Zapata to post their flyers and were not permitted to do so.
The defenders of Casa Zapata claim that the SCRs were denied
entry because "Casa Zapata has a strict visitor policy created
after repeated racist acts of vandalism targeting the dorm in the
past few years."[48] Given that this op-ed is entitled "SCR: Your
Hate Speech Is Not Welcome Here," which apparently means

that posters advertising a Ben Shapiro lecture are hate speech, perhaps this account of events should be taken with a grain of salt. (No actual examples of hate speech by SCR are cited in the article, as they undoubtedly would be had any such hate speech occurred.) The Casa Zapata visitor policy apparently requires that any visitor from outside the dorm be admitted by a friend within the dorm. The Casa Zapata student staffers who wrote this article say, "The fact that not a single individual in the dorm was willing to vouch for SCR and let them in, and that community members reported feeling unsafe in the presence of members of SCR, is a perfect indicator of the damage this group has already done in the community."[49]

On the other hand, Stephen Sills, the president of SCR, gave the following account of his experience to Young America's Foundation:

"A jeering mob assembled to block us from entering the dorm [Casa Zapata]," Stephen Sills, the president of the conservative group, told YAF. "We were turned away from the door exclusively because we were postering for the Ben Shapiro lecture. When I asked to see if there was a way I could speak to the Resident Fellow of the dorm, I was told by one of the residents to go 's*ck a d*ck.'"

Sills described that after leaving and heading over to another dorm to poster, they had been followed by a group of 8 students. "They shouted obscenities, heckling us and keeping us from entering the other dorms," Sill said. "Never before have I ever feared as much for my safety on campus as I did then."[50]

Everyone involved agrees that (1) the SCR students were prevented from entering Casa Zapata and (2) the SCR students were not allowed to post their flyers[51] (one student reported that he was able to slip into the dorm but was prevented from posting his flyers).[52] It is clear that many of the residents of Casa Zapata are at the very least left-leaning, with mindsets that would stand out even on a very progressive campus. It seems likely that the ethnic theme of the dorm contributes to this sense of grievance and radicalism, given the statements of the residents themselves, who claim that they initiated their restrictive visitor policy after phrases such as "Build the Wall" and "#MAGA" were (allegedly) written on dorm whiteboards by Stanford students from other dorms.[53]

Wolfe also defends the ethnically themed houses as a safe place for minority students from ethnically homogeneous communities to "speak in your accustomed vernacular or language" or "openly engage in cultural practices," saying that they also "preserve the culture" of the students who live there. As student John Rice Cameron points out, however, keeping students from ethnically homogeneous communities in dorms dominated by members of their own ethnic group hardly prepares them for life in a diverse society (which, as Cameron did not point out, the admissions folks at universities constantly assure us is the reason we must have racially preferential admissions).[54] As Gettinger pointed out in his article, this leads to less interaction between minority students and non-minority students on campus as a whole, as most friend groups are formed in the freshman dorms. A system in which a substantial percentage of minority students self-segregate necessarily means less contact and fewer friendships between members of different racial groups.

On the other hand, Wolfe says that "These bastions of culture also allow students who previously have not had an opportunity to meaningfully explore their identities to do so." In a 2010 article on the ethnically themed houses, residents of the houses applauded their existence for just this reason. "For Alexzandra Scully '13, a resident in Muwekma-Ta-Ruk [the Native American–themed house] and 20 percent Choctaw Indian, living in a cross-cultural dorm has given her the strong exposure to other natives that she did not receive while growing up in the Virgin Islands."[55] Jackson Dartez, an Ujamaa resident, stated that the African American–themed house was valuable to the residents because many of them had been raised in predominantly white communities or attended predominantly white prep schools.

There are common themes in these rationales for the existence of racially separate housing. First, no matter your cultural differences or life experiences, having the same skin color is the most important commonality, and it is one that is worth cultivating. As Sierra Garcia said, what do a student from an upper-class Haitian family, a student from inner-city Detroit, and a student from the LA suburbs have in common? Apparently, if the answer is "skin color," that is enough. But another theme is that some ethnic minorities feel they are *too* assimilated. It's odd that "lack of exposure to their culture" is considered a strong reason for living in an ethnically themed dorm, because of necessity, these kids were raised by their parents…all of whom, except for the occasional adoptive parent, shared their ethnicity. This suggests that some—perhaps many—of these students were raised by parents who generally embraced the color-blind ideals of an older America but that their children are prioritizing their racial identities instead.

Chocolate City @ MIT

Yes, that is the real name of a residence hall at MIT. The mission statement on the residence hall's website states:

> Chocolate City is a brotherhood of MIT students and alumni who identify with urban culture and share common backgrounds, interests, ethnicities, and/or experiences. By cultivating a tradition of social, intellectual, character, and leadership development, the Brothers of Chocolate City exemplify a high standard of excellence which is founded on continual growth. We seek to enrich the MIT

and greater global communities by embodying the principles of our brotherhood.[56]

As Roy Haygood, one of the founders of Chocolate City, explained in giving the history of the residence hall:

> Forgotten, is the fact that the Institute approached MIT students, seeking groups of students willing to leave their existing living arrangements and venture into New House 1. New House officially opened to students Fall of 1975. We co-founders did not boldly demand a Black living group. We were among several groups rightfully vying for the top three (3) floors of New House 1! Fortunately, in the Spring of 1975, Glenn A. Graham '77 pulled the lucky number from out of a hat, as I recall, in the Bush Room. Also note that CC was not the only Black living group during my 1974-78 era. Black folk congregated at MIT East Campus 3rd West, women on the fifth floor McCormick and who can forget the brothers in G-Entry at McGregor. So, at the time, we didn't view ourselves as revolutionaries. Just some young lads who had formed friendships and sought to move into New House 1 together.[57]

Thus, as we have seen elsewhere, barely two decades after the Supreme Court prohibited segregated education in *Brown v. Board of Education*, college students were re-segregating themselves. Although Haygood states that he and his friends "didn't view ourselves as revolutionaries," his reminiscences of the other "Black living groups" makes clear that many black students desired predominantly black living areas. It is only natural that college students would want to live among their friends. It is sad, though, that these students' friendships seemed to be bounded by race. Even if they had white friends, they wanted to *live* among other black students.

If this had remained merely voluntary clustering in particular parts of dorms—groups of friends all bidding to be in the same wing of a certain dorm, as college students have done for decades—it would not be troubling. Just as governments should not engage in racial bean-counting to decree there are "too many" people of one race in a particular area when that is the result of housing choices, so universities should not engage in racial balancing of residence halls. But neither should universities allow certain residence halls to be officially designated "Chocolate City" and therefore give the official imprimatur to racial separatism.

When one looks at the public biographies of residents of Chocolate City, what jumps out from some of them is what some Americans would consider indices of privilege. Kelvin Green II, '21, writes in his biography, "I am originally from Round Rock, TX but have lived in Exeter, N.H.; Beijing, China; and most recently Richmond, VA."[58] In addition to chairing the Political Action Committee of the MIT Black Students Union, Green writes, "I care about liberating people who are under oppressive systems and believe in the necessity of decolonizing minds." So having spent his high school years at Phillips Exeter Academy (verified by checking his LinkedIn page),[59] living in Beijing for a year, and now attending MIT, Green maintains that minds need to be "decolonized." On the other hand, freshman Ronald Vaughan II states that he has rarely left Detroit and that Massachusetts is the farthest he has ever traveled, but "I haven't experienced racism before (that I know of), and my knowledge of it has been limited to the media, academic knowledge, and the occasional story from those around me."[60]

Overall, however, Chocolate City seems far less interested in racial identity *per se* than other racially segregated residence halls; the "Three Pillars" of Chocolate City are "Social, Academic, and Professional." Unlike Stanford's Ujamaa House, it does not appear that Chocolate City residents are required to present on a racial topic (e.g., #BlackTransLivesMatter) to their fellow students. Probably MIT students are busy enough with academic coursework that they do not have time or inclination for fluff. Given the number of residents who list music, dancing, and sports among their interests in their biographies, it seems likely that a large part of the draw is also non-political shared interests (in a video interview with current residents, one resident said he was first attracted to Chocolate City because the residents were playing Jamaican music at an outdoor dance party called "Jukebox").[61]

Asian, Pacific Islander, Desi American Leadership Community at the University of Southern California

The University of Southern California also has racially segregated housing. The APIDA [Asian, Pacific Islander, Desi American] Leaders Community is located within the Birnkrant Residential College.[62] The racially separate residential floor was only recently established; the first year it was in operation was 2017. However, APIDA is a project of USC's Asian Pacific American Student Services (APASS), which was created in 1982.[63]

According to an account by Jeff Murakami, who had been active in the Asian American community as a USC student and later served as APASS director for seventeen years, the creation of APASS was prompted by meetings with Asian American students in the early 1980s.

> The students were doing well academically and seemed to be increasingly more engaged socially through the emergence of various ethnic organizations, but what they seemed to lack was a sense that the University recognized them, appreciated their diverse cultural experiences and sought to provide relevant services to them.
>
> These students, many of whom were the leadership of a newly-formed student organization, the Asian Pacific Student Outreach

(APSO), began to strategize ways to get the University to recognize them and their concerns. The students, led by Michael Matsuda, Scott Lee, Karen Wong, and advised by USC staff psychologist Dr. Sarah Miyahira organized a series of meetings with university administrators, including the new university president Dr. James Zumberge, and public "demonstrations" (sometimes with as many as 200 students gathered). Together with Black and Latino student groups, a coalition emerged to advocate for a viable Ethnic Studies program and for APA student services.[64]

Much like the black student programs and housing first established in the 1970s, the long existence of APASS and the recent establishment of racially separate housing for Asian American students makes one question how successful APASS has been in its mission. The establishment of racially separate housing for Asian students at USC, twenty-five years after the establishment of APASS, suggests that Asian American students feel no less estranged from non-Asian members of the student body than they did in 1982. In fact, this demand for more racial segregation, rather than less, suggests that perhaps they feel *more* estranged from the rest of the student body than they did in the past.[65]

Asian American students at USC—the second-largest American racial group there—were, in many cases, raised in California, as were many of the white students.[66] If cultural differences between Asian students born and raised in the Los Angeles area are so dramatically different from white students born and raised in the Los Angeles area that cross-cultural educational programming is necessary for the two groups to understand each other, we, as a country, have serious problems.

APASS does not seem especially interested in simply helping Asian American students find their place at the university and, perhaps, in American society. It appears focused on building an identity for political purposes that transcend the university. There is no particular reason why a Japanese American student and a Chinese American one should be expected to embrace the same ethnic identity. However, if your goal is to weld disparate ethnic identities together to wield political power, this makes some sense. It does not make sense if you want Asian American students to embrace a primarily American identity and not see themselves as perpetual outsiders or in a defensive stance vis-à-vis the rest of American society.

It makes even less sense for APASS to conceive of its mission as fostering an identity that "continues to grow in the transnational sphere." This strongly suggests that, for example, APASS tries to encourage Chinese American students to prioritize their Chinese racial identity across national lines, rather than to prioritize their identity as American citizens. This can easily lead to Asian American students feeling more alienated from American society.

RACIALLY FOCUSED PROGRAMS AT PUBLIC UNIVERSITIES

ScHOLA²Rs House at UConn

At this point, you might be tempted to think that racially separate housing is confined to private schools. "A solid state school," you might be saying to yourself, "has no truck with such efforts." You would be wrong.

Throughout this essay, I have tried to convey that the push for voluntary racial segregation and the consequences of such segregation are not limited to university campuses. Nor is the impulse for racial segregation limited to elite or private colleges. Nor has the desire to create segregated living spaces declined as the days of *de jure* segregation recede further and further into the past.

In 2016, the University of Connecticut created a "learning community" called "ScHOLA²Rs House." It is worth noting that ScHOLA²Rs House received $300,000 in seed capital from the

Booth Ferris Foundation.[67] Support for racial separatism is not limited to higher education. It apparently extends to the philanthropic world as well.

The UConn residential life website describes ScHOLA²Rs House as follows:

> ScHOLA²Rs House is a Learning Community designed to support the scholastic efforts of male students who identify as African American/Black through academic and social/emotional support, access to research opportunities, and professional development. The intent of this Learning Community is to increase the retention and persistence of students using educational and social experiences to enhance their academic success at UConn and beyond in graduate and professional school placement. ScHOLA²Rs House will encourage involvement with the larger university community to foster peer and mentor relationships and will actively engage students in inclusion efforts at UConn.[68]

The observant reader may note that 2016 was sixty-two years after *Brown*. When this news broke, I, along with Gail Heriot, one of the editors of this volume, wrote a letter to UConn's president, advising against the creation of this "learning community."[69] When UConn received our letter, the official response was "the misconception was that the house would be separate or segregated from the rest of the school" and that "although African-American males are given preference, all races are invited to apply."[70] I note that as of this writing, this is the official mission of ScHOLA²Rs House on UConn's website:

> Mission: ScHOLA²Rs House is designed to support the scholastic efforts of male students who identify as African American/Black through academic and social/emotional support, access to research opportunities, and professional development.[71]

UConn buys itself some wiggle room by providing that any male student can apply who is "interested in engaging in topics related to the experience of black males in higher education."[72] Still, although anyone is permitted to apply, the university makes no bones about whom this program is intended to benefit.

In a UConn TV news report on the newly opened ScHOL-A²Rs House, Dr. Erik Hines, who first led the learning community, said that the impetus for creating the learning community was "the graduation rate—currently our graduation rate is at 55 percent."[73] In the next breath, the student journalist reports that a university spokeswoman says that "despite African-American males' low graduation rates, they are meeting high academic standards." Something here does not compute. It is far more likely that the African American male students at UConn are victims of academic mismatch, which is discussed elsewhere in this volume.

Multicultural Student Center at UVA

UConn is far from the only public university that deliberately fosters heightened racial identity. The University of Virginia recently had an embarrassing incident in which an angry student publicly declared the purpose of these identity-focused spaces.

In February 2020, a black student at the University of Virginia harangued her fellow students in the Multicultural Student Center. She said in her filmed tirade:

> Excuse me, if y'all didn't know, this a [Multicultural Student Center] and frankly there's just too many white people in here and this a space for people of color.... So just be really cognizant of the space that you're taking up because it does make some of us POCs uncomfortable when we see too many white people in here.[74]

UVA's embarrassed administration immediately issued a statement clarifying that the Multicultural Student Center is open to students of all races.[75] However, this merely illustrates one of the many problems with having particular programs and buildings dedicated to the use of people of a particular race or races. Even if the program or space is officially open to students of all races, the mere name and mission statement proclaim who it is "meant" for. The Multicultural Student Center website states, "We aim to facilitate a student-centered, collaborative space that supports underrepresented and marginalized communities while cultivating the holistic empowerment of all students."[76]

The Multicultural Consciousness Series is one of the "signature" events of the MSC and is described as "[including] lectures, debates, panel discussions, films, videos, performances, and other events.... The series features topics in diversity and multiculturalism within the University context and within the nation and world."[77] The events for spring 2019 and fall 2019 were the following:

- Black Music and Black Histories
- Gentrification & Classism in [Charlottesville]
- Mixed Matched: Multiculturalism & Bone Marrow Donations
- #RaceAnd Series: Race & Gender: Intersectionality of Black Womanhood
- #RaceAnd Series: Race & Sex: Let's Talk about Sex!
- #RaceAnd Series: Race & Mental Health

Nothing about this list suggests, for example, any interest in exploring cultural differences between, say, French-Canadians and Anglo Canadians, or between early-20th-century German immigrants to America and the older English stock. The only thing the Multicultural Consciousness Series seems interested in is the non-white experience in contemporary America. This strengthens the sense that the Multicultural Student Center and its programming exist for the benefit of non-white students (although perhaps the occasional white student will attend the Multicultural Consciousness Series to have her consciousness raised). This encourages minority students, like the young woman discussed above, to police the boundaries of "their" space.

Munk-skukum Indigenous Living-Learning Community and Native American Longhouse Eena Haws at Oregon State University

Decades have passed since the 1964 Civil Rights Act, which included Title VI and its ban on race discrimination in federally funded education.[78] As we saw with A3C at Cornell, however, the passage of time has not dimmed the enthusiasm for racial separatism on campus. This fall (2020), Oregon State University plans to open a new "living-learning community" that caters to Native American students. Oregon State explains on its website:

> The munk-skukum Indigenous Living Learning Community offers a residential space for students to find community, explore cultural identity and learn more about the lands on which they will be residing. This community offers connections to other students with a shared interest in centering Indigenous people, to cultural events on campus and to resources to help support students while they are at Oregon State University. munk-skukum means "to strengthen" in chinuk wawa (the local trade language), and we believe a strong community is central to your time at Oregon State.
>
> Oregon State University is located on Kalapuya land and as such, we give thanks and respect to the Grand Ronde and Siletz Tribes they are now a part of.[79]

Munk-skukum will be located on the first floor of an existing residential hall. Although the website states that the living-learning community is for "students of shared or similar interest in Indigenous, Native American and Pacific Islander communities,"[80] it is clear that it is focused on housing and building community among Native American students. The same page of the website includes a section on "Campus Community":

> There are many ways to be involved in community on campus. The Native American Longhouse Eena Haws serves as a hub of Indigenous-based activities at Oregon State. Events are offered throughout the year like the annual Salmon Bake and Klatowa Eena Pow-Wow. We also host open beading every Friday.
>
> You can also learn more about student organizations there as well, including the Native American Student Association, RAD Indigenous Queer & Two-Spirit Student Alliance, Pacific Islander Club, multicultural Greek letter organizations and more.[81]

Note that everything listed in this "campus community" section is based on racial or sexual identity. No "intramural athletics," or "Intervarsity," or "outdoors club." Even if students do not consciously wish to primarily associate with fellow Native American students to the exclusion of students of other ethnicities, the proffered list of extracurricular activities funnels them into doing so. Statements made by a former student staffer, Tyler Hogan, as part of an oral history project illustrate this point:

> NF [Natalia Fernandez]: And how would you describe the impact of the Longhouse on native students?
>
> TH: I would say, we always say we're a home away from home but we really are. You start to develop a family after you've been here long enough, these people become such close friends that

when you don't see them for a day you're like "oh wait, where is so and so? Why are they not here right now and I know they don't have class right, [they're] supposed to be in here" and so it's really cool building that sense of community, especially because most of our communities are relatively small, often times it's just, you know, a family, an extended family or whatever. And you get to build that while you are here on campus, only you do it with the friends that will become your kind of native OSU family. I think that's pretty cool.[82]

It becomes clear that this is likely a deliberate choice when examining the website of the Native American Longhouse Eena Haws (henceforth "NAL Eena Haws"), which is essentially the parent organization of munk-skukum. NAL Eena Haws, established in its current location in 1972, emerged from the demands for racially separate spaces that swept the country in the 1960s and 1970s.[83] An Oregon State University news article about Luhui Whitebear, the assistant director of NAL Eena Haws, notes that she and the rest of the staff are from various tribes around the country.[84] (Although Whitebear's title is "Assistant Director," that refers to her position in the larger Diversity and Cultural Engagement Department. Whitebear is the head of Eena Haws.[85]) In an interview Whitebear gave when she was a PhD student at Oregon State, the author wrote:

> Whitebear wants to recenter the stories about Indigenous activist circles to focus on Indigenous women and LGBTQ2S+ people, "…to help reclaim not only positions within activist circles but within our communities because of the way that settler colonialism has really strove to erase those stories and those roles," she said.[86]

Later, in response to the question "Would you describe yourself as an activist? Do you have that side to your personality?" Whitebear replied:

Activism is not just in the streets. The book *"Life as Activism"* by June Jordan really helped me think about the different moments in our lives that are themselves activism as well. That helped shape how I think about our very existence as being activism because settler colonialism in this area is dependent on the continued erasure of the Indigenous people on these lands and just our very existence already is a form of resistance.

I don't know how to separate activism from who I am. Some people don't even like the term activist, but if we look at the definition of the term it is movement for change. *That is why I like the term because I do not like this current system that we live in. But I don't really think we live in it, I think it lives on top of us as Indigenous people.* [emphasis added][87]

The NAL Eena Haws mission statement is no less radical.

We strive to deconstruct colonial borders' impact on indigenous identities while also honoring the sovereignty of tribes. While protecting and preserving the rights of Indigenous people, we provide a sense of home/community for Indigenous students that helps preserve their Indigenous identities while in college. The NAL provides a source of support honoring the cultures of the first people of these lands. We also provide educational opportunities to educate all about the region's tribes.[88]

There are several aspects of the attitude promoted by NAL Eena Haws as an organization that are particularly troubling in regard to Native American students. First, Native American students who were raised on reservations may, indeed, be particularly homesick or have trouble adjusting to life outside the reservation.[89] It seems questionable, though, whether emphasizing "Indigenous identity," rather than trying to help students adjust to mainstream American society and reconcile that with their tribal culture, will prepare them for future social and career success.

The problem here is that many of these students already have a well-formed Native American identity, but stressing further immersion in Native American culture seems unlikely to help them integrate into society.

Another problem with laying such stress on Native American identity is that Native Americans are very likely to be descended from multiple racial groups. More than half of Native Americans marry someone who is not Native American.[90] Most of those interracial marriages are to a white person.[91] Yet Whitebear refers to European languages as "colonizer languages" and to the presence of non–Native American people as "settler colonialism."[92] In its mission statement, NAL Eena Haws speaks of preserving students' indigenous identities.[93] Where does this leave students who have white parents or grandparents? Are they to view their own loved ones as "settlers" and "colonizers" who are interlopers on Native land? Add in the reality that, although intermarriage is extremely widespread among Native Americans, it is a source of tension and sometimes openly discouraged, and this oppositional view of Native American identity becomes even more troubling.[94]

A third problem with putting such stress on Native American identity is that many students, particularly those who are "urban Indians" and did not grow up on reservations, are already assimilated into American life. Stressing Native American identity encourages them to change their view of themselves from someone who is as American as anyone else to someone who is somehow an outsider. For example, as Tyler Hogan stated above, one of the strengths of NAL Eena Haws is that it encourages students to develop a sense of Native American community, because "most of our communities are relatively small, often times it's just, you know, a family, an extended family or whatever."

Much as with Asian student centers and black student centers, there is no particular reason why students with Native American heritage who hail from completely different tribes should be assumed to have more in common with each other than with students of other races. Like every other racial group, different Native American tribes have different cultures and histories. Tyler Hogan alluded to this difficulty in his oral history interview, explaining, "It's difficult because we all have different traditions; we all have different cultures, so trying to find a way to get a unified message out of our 500 tribes is difficult."[95]

CONCLUSION

This year, 2020, has witnessed an explosion in racial identity politics. "Politics" is too mild a word for the rioting, looting, and vandalism that has swept this country in the wake of George Floyd's death. "Black Lives Matter" is the approved rallying cry; "All Lives Matter" may get the unwary employee fired.[96] "BIPOC"—black, indigenous, people of color—has become the new buzzword, to be juxtaposed against "white"—people who have no color but are merely a homogenous mass of oppressors. These attitudes and ideas are first inculcated in many students at colleges and universities, not least by the ethnic dorms and ethnic centers that teach non-white students that they must unite together against whites. For their part, white students learn that they must ally themselves with the BIPOC and fight against everything that supposedly contributes to the oppression of non-whites—notably the United States, Western civilization, and Christianity. These students, white and BIPOC, go forth from their universities to spread this poison into workplaces, churches, government, and society at large. Racially themed dorms and student centers are not the only contributors, but they certainly play a part. End them.

Breaking the STEM

Heather Mac Donald

In March 2020, as scientists raced to discover a vaccine for the novel coronavirus, the National Science Foundation, America's premier funding source for basic research, posted a grant solicitation for its ADVANCE program. ADVANCE is one of many programs underwritten by the National Science Foundation to boost the number of women and members of underrepresented minorities in STEM (sciences, technology, engineering, and math).[1] The NSF claims that progress in science requires a "diverse STEM workforce." Accordingly, ADVANCE seeks "organizational change for gender equity in STEM." Successful applications, whether in molecular bioscience or mechanical engineering, would apply "intersectional approaches" to institutional change, recognizing that "gender, race, and ethnicity do not exist in isolation from each other and from other categories of social identity."[2]

Intersectionality (the increased oppression allegedly experienced by individuals who can check off several categories of victimhood—e.g., being female, black, and trans) would seem marginal to such pressing matters as decoding a virus's DNA or designing easily manufactured hospital equipment to protect medical personnel. Yet the NSF doles out tens of millions of taxpayer dollars a year to fight alleged heteronormativity and the microaggressions that the agency believes cause the lack of race and gender proportionality in research labs. Despite this massive federal expenditure, most of the scientists involved in the multi-pronged attack on the novel coronavirus have been male. Should that matter? If you believe diversity bureaucrats, government officials, and many academic deans, the answer is yes.

In June 2019, Francis Collins, director of the National Institutes of Health, announced that he would no longer participate in scientific conferences that showed insufficient "attention to inclusiveness," code for the absence of a critical mass of female, black, and Hispanic participants.[3] Dr. Collins challenged his colleagues in the biomedical field to join his boycott of "manels" (predominantly male scientific panels). Never mind if the most cutting-edge researchers working on a problem might happen to be white (or Asian) males. On January 30, 2020, cable news channel CNN blasted President Donald Trump's coronavirus task force for being too white and too male. Would Dr. Collins have turned down an invitation to participate on that team unless Dr. Anthony Fauci, head of the National Institute of Allergy and Infectious Diseases and the most prominent member of the White House coronavirus task force, were replaced by a Native American epidemiologist? His challenge would suggest so.

Identity politics has engulfed the humanities and social sciences on American campuses; now it is taking over the hard sciences. The pressure to increase the representation of women, blacks, and Hispanics is changing how science is taught and how scientific qualifications are evaluated. The results will be disastrous for scientific innovation and for American competitiveness.

A UCLA scientist reports: "All across the country the big question now in STEM is: how can we promote more women and minorities by 'changing' (i.e., lowering) the requirements we had previously set for graduate level study?"[4] Mathematical problem-solving is being deemphasized in favor of more qualitative group projects; the pace of undergraduate physics education is being slowed down so that no one gets left behind.

Besides ADVANCE, the National Science Foundation bankrolls the tortuously named "Inclusion across the Nation of Communities of Learners of Underrepresented Discoverers in Engineering and Science" (INCLUDES) program.[5] INCLUDES purports to further "fundamental research in the science of broadening participation." There is no such "science," just an enormous expenditure of resources that ducks the fundamental problems of basic skills and attitudes toward academic achievement. A typical INCLUDES grant from October 2017 directed $300,000 toward increasing Native American math involvement by incorporating "indigenous knowledge systems" into Navajo Nation Math Circles. Indigenous knowledge systems are not going to help design low-cost ventilators or antibody tests. In July 2017, the NSF awarded $1 million to the University of New Hampshire and two other institutions to develop an implicit "bias awareness intervention tool." Another $2 million that same month went to the Department of Aerospace Engineering at Texas A&M University to "remediate microaggressions and implicit biases" in engineering classrooms.

The INCLUDES initiative has already generated its own parasitic endeavor, Early-concept Grants for Exploratory Research (EAGER). The purpose of EAGER funding is to evaluate INCLUDES grants and to pressure actual science grantees to incorporate diversity considerations into their research. The ultimate goal of such programs is to change the culture of STEM so that "inclusion and equity" are at its very core.

Somehow, NSF-backed scientists managed to rack up more than two hundred Nobel Prizes before the agency realized that scientific progress depends on "diversity." Those "un-diverse" scientists discovered the fundamental particles of matter and unlocked the genetics of viruses. Now that academic victimology has established a beachhead at the agency, however, it remains to be seen whether the pace of such breakthroughs will continue. The NSF is conducting a half-million-dollar study of intersectionality in the STEM fields. Two sociologists are polling more than 10,000 scientists and engineers in nine professional organizations about the "social and cultural variables" that produce "disadvantage and marginalization" in STEM workplaces.

One of the study's directors, Erin Cech, is a University of Michigan sociologist specializing in gender and sexuality. Cech has received multiple NSF grants; one of her recent publications is "Rugged Meritocratists: The Role of Overt Bias and the Meritocratic Ideology in Trump Supporters' Opposition to Social Justice Efforts."[6] The other lead researcher, Tom Waidzunas, is a sociologist at Temple University; he studies the "dynamics of gender and sexuality" within STEM, as well as how "scientists come to know, and hence constitute, sexuality and sexual desire." Such politically constituted social-justice research was not likely envisioned by Congress in 1950 when it created the NSF to "promote the progress of science."

Francis Collins's National Institutes of Health are another diversity-obsessed federal science funder. Medical schools receive NIH training grants to support postdoctoral education for physicians pursuing a research career in such fields as oncology and cardiology. The NIH threatens to yank any training grant when it comes up for renewal if it has not supported a sufficient number of members of underrepresented minorities (URM). One problem: there are often no black or Hispanic MDs to evaluate for inclusion in the training grant. If there *is* a potential URM candidate, the principal investigators will pore over his file multiple times in the hope of persuading themselves that he is adequately qualified. Meanwhile, the patently qualified Indian doctor goes to the bottom of the candidate pile. For now, medical schools can claim Argentinians and the sons of Ghanaian plantation owners as members of underrepresented minorities, but if NIH bean-counters become more scrupulous in their "diversity metrics," this aspect of biomedical research will reach an impasse.

The diversity mania also determines the way medical research is carried out. The NIH has onerous requirements that government-sponsored clinical trials include the same proportion of female and minority patients as is found in the medical school's "catchment area" (its geographic zone of study). If some of these populations drop out of medical trials at disproportionate rates or are difficult to recruit, too bad. If these URM and female enrollment quotas are not met, the medical school must "invest the appropriate effort to correct under-accrual," in the words of the NIH guidelines.[7]

The "appropriate effort" can cost a fortune. Schools such as the Mayo Clinic, located in overwhelmingly white areas, must still meet a diversity quota, which they can fulfill by partnering with a medical school in Tennessee, say. Lung cancer and coronary-artery disease afflict adults. If a particular immigrant group in a research trial's catchment area contains a disproportionate share of young people compared with the aging white population, that immigrant group will be less susceptible to those adult-onset diseases. Nevertheless, cancer and heart-disease drug researchers must recruit from that community in numbers proportionate to its share of the overall population.

Accrediting bodies reinforce the diversity compulsion. The Accreditation Council for Graduate Medical Education requires that medical schools maintain detailed diversity metrics on their efforts to interview and hire URM faculty. Medical school search committees go through lengthy implicit-bias training sessions and expend enormous amounts of effort looking for something that they often know a priori doesn't exist: qualified URM faculty candidates. The very definition of "diversity" used by academic review panels is becoming ever more exacting. A 2015 panel assessing the academic strength of San Diego State University's biology department complained that the faculty, though relatively representative of traditional "underserved groups," nevertheless failed to mirror the "diversity of peoples in Southern California."[8] The use of a school's immediate surroundings as a demographic benchmark for its faculty is a significant escalation of the war between the diversocrats and academic standards. Naturally, the accrediting panel made no effort to ascertain whether those Southern California peoples—including Hmong, Salvadorans, and Somalis—are netting PhDs in biology and are applying to SDSU's biology department in numbers proportional to their population in Southern California.

Many private foundations fund only gender- and race-exclusive science training; others that do fund basic research, such as the Howard Hughes Medical Institute, nevertheless divert considerable resources to diversity. The major scientific societies push the idea that implicit bias is impeding the careers of otherwise competitive scientists. In February 2018, Erin Cech presented preliminary findings from the NSF intersectionality study at the American Association for the Advancement of Science (AAAS) annual meeting; naturally, those results showed "systemic anti-LGBTQ bias within STEM industry and academia."[9] Another AAAS session addressed how the "hierarchical nature" of science exacerbates gender bias and stereotypes and called for the "equal representation of women" across STEM.

STEM departments are creating their own internal diversity enforcers. The engineering school at the University of California, Los Angeles, minted its first associate dean of diversity and inclusion in 2017, despite already being subject to enormous pressures from the Vice Chancellor for Equity, Diversity and Inclusion and other deans. "One of my jobs," the new engineering diversocrat,

Scott Brandenberg, told UCLA's student newspaper, is "to avoid implicit bias in the hiring process."[10]

The science diversity charade wastes extraordinary amounts of time and money that could be going into basic research and its real-world application. If that were its only consequence, the cost would be high enough. But identity politics are now altering the standards for scientific competence and the way future scientists are trained. "Diversity" is now often an explicit job qualification in the STEM fields. An August 2020 job listing for a lecturer in environmental conservation at the University of Massachusetts–Amherst announces that "all applicants must submit a statement of Contributions to Diversity, Equity and Inclusion, identifying past experiences and future goals."[11] The University of Georgia recently sought a lecturer in biochemistry and molecular biology who will be "expected to support the college's goals of creating and sustaining a diverse and inclusive learning environment."[12]

In February 2020, Harvard's dean of sciences announced that he would be hiring two junior faculty in STEM based on their ability to "strengthen diversity, inclusion, and belonging" in the Sciences Division.

Mandatory diversity statements are now ubiquitous in STEM hiring. An Alzheimer's researcher, say, seeking a position in a neurology lab, must document his contributions to diversity, equity, and inclusion. Showing sufficient diversity zeal is a threshold requirement for being considered at all at many schools. At the University of California, Berkeley, the Life Sciences Department rejected 76 percent of the applications it received in the 2018–2019 academic year because the applicants' diversity, equity, and inclusion statement was not sufficiently effusive. The hiring committee did not even look at the failed applicants' research records. Were the remaining 214 contenders the best scientists in their field? It doesn't matter. What they *were* good at was discussing "distinctions and connections between diversity, equity, and inclusion" during their job talk, in the words of the University of California's diversity guidance. The rejected applicants, by contrast, would have shown little knowledge of the "dimensions of diversity that result from different identities, especially URMs [underrepresented minorities, i.e., blacks and Hispanics]." They might even have been so rash as to suggest that racial and sex quotas in STEM hiring are antithetical to the university's research mission. The diversity culling continued throughout the process, resulting in a 75 percent drop in white scientists from the original hiring pool to the final contenders, while the percentage of Hispanic applicants in the final short list rose 450 percent and the percentage of black applicants rose 325 percent from their initial share of the hiring pool.[13]

Few of Berkeley's Nobel laureates in medicine, physics, and chemistry would be hired today under the Diversity-Equity-Inclusion test. It is hard to imagine that Ernest Lawrence, inventor of the cyclotron, would have "provided evidence" of having informed himself about the "personal challenges that URMs face at academic research institutions." Lamentably, Mr. Lawrence would probably have been too focused on understanding the behavior of nuclear particles.

It's impossible to overstate the extent to which the diversity ideology has encroached upon UC's collective psyche and mission. No administrator, no regent, no academic dean or chair can open his mouth for long without professing fealty to diversity. It is the one constant in every university endeavor; it impinges on hiring, distorts the curriculum, and sucks up vast amounts of faculty time and taxpayer resources.

Thus it was that UC San Diego's electrical and computer engineering department found itself facing a mandate from campus administrators to hire a fourth female professor. The possibility of a new hire had opened up—a rare opportunity in that budget climate—and after winnowing down hundreds of applicants, the department put forward its top candidates for on-campus interviews. Scandalously, all were male. Word came down from on high that a female applicant who hadn't even been close to making the initial cut must be interviewed. She was duly brought to campus for an interview, but she got mediocre reviews. The powers-that-be then spoke again: her candidacy must be brought to a departmental vote. In an unprecedented assertion of secrecy, the department chair refused to disclose the vote's outcome and insisted on a second ballot. After that second vote, the authorities finally gave up and dropped her candidacy. Both vote counts remained secret.

An electrical and computer engineering professor explained what was at stake. "We pride ourselves on being the best," he said. "The faculty know that absolute ranking is critical. No one had ever considered this woman a star."[14] You would think that UC's administrators would value this fierce desire for excellence. Thanks to its commitment to hiring only "the best," San Diego's electrical and computer engineering department has made leading contributions to circuit design, digital coding, and information theory.

Maria Herrera Sobek, UC Santa Barbara's associate vice chancellor for diversity, equity, and academic policy and a professor of Chicana and Chicano studies, provided a window into how the diversity bureaucracy thinks about its mission: If a faculty hiring committee selects only white male finalists for an opening, Sobek said, the dean will suggest "bringing in some women to look them over." These female candidates, she noted, "may be borderline, but they are all qualified." And what do you know! "It turns out [the people on the hiring committee] really like the candidates and hire them, even if they may not have looked so good on paper."[15] This process has "energized" the faculty to hire more women, Sobek explained. She added that diversity interventions get "more positive responses" from humanities and social-sciences professors than from scientists.

Leave aside Sobek's amusing suggestion that the faculty just happen to discover that they "really like" the diversity candidate whom the administration has forced on them. More disturbing is the subversion of the usual hiring standard from "most qualified" to "borderline but qualified." The diversity bureaucracy sets the hiring bar low enough to scoop in some female or minority candidates and then declares that anyone above that bar is qualified enough to trump the most qualified candidate, if that candidate is a white or an Asian man. This is a formula for mediocrity.

Sometimes, the diversity bureaucracy can't manage to lower hiring standards enough to scoop in a "diverse" candidate. In that case, it simply creates a special hiring category outside the normal channels. In September 2012, after the meritocratic revolt in UC San Diego's electrical and computer engineering department, the engineering school announced that it would hire an "excellence" candidate, the school's Orwellian term for faculty who, it claims, will contribute to diversity and who, by some odd coincidence, always happen to be female or members of an underrepresented minority.

Entry requirements for graduate education are being revised. The American Astronomical Society has recommended that PhD programs in astronomy eliminate the requirement that applicants take the Graduate Record Exam (GRE) in physics, since it has a disparate impact on women and members of underrepresented minorities and allegedly does not predict future research output. Harvard and other departments have complied, even though an objective test like the GRE can spotlight talent from less prestigious schools. The National Science Foundation's Graduate Research Fellowship Program has dropped all science GREs for applicants in all fields.

Expectations are changing at the undergraduate level, as well. Cornell University gets about two and a half times as many male as female applicants to its undergraduate engineering program. Females enjoy a 300 percent admissions advantage, however, resulting in an admitted class that is 50-50 male-female. That rebalancing does not reflect female students' superior math qualifications; in fact, female students have lower math scores than male students.

In 2018, Oxford University extended the time limit on its undergraduate math and computer science exams, hoping to increase the number of female high-scorers; results were modest. Expect test-time extensions, nevertheless, to spread to the United States.

Medical school administrators urge admissions committees to look beyond the Medical College Admission Test scores of black and Hispanic student applicants and employ "holistic review" in order to engineer a diverse class. The result is a vast gap in entering qualifications. This achievement gap does not close over the course of medical school, but the URM students who do complete their medical training will be fanatically sought after anyway. Adding to medical schools' diversity woes is the fact that the number of male URM student applicants has been declining in recent years, making it even harder to find qualified candidates.

Race preferences in med school programs are sometimes justified on the basis that minorities want doctors who "look like them." Arguably, however, minority patients with serious illnesses want the same thing as anyone else: subject mastery.

The push for gender proportionality in medical education and research is not quite as quixotic as the crusade for URM proportionality, but it, too, distorts decision-making. Two-thirds of the applicants for oncology fellowships at a prestigious medical school are male. Half of the oncology department's fellowship picks are female, however, even though females do not cluster at the top of the applicant pool.

A network of so-called teaching and learning centers at universities across the country is seeking to make science classrooms more "inclusive" by changing pedagogy and expectations for student learning. The STEM faculty is too white, male, and heteronormative, according to these centers, making it hard for female, black, Hispanic, and LGBTQ students to learn. Lecturing and objective exams should be deemphasized in favor of "culturally sensitive pedagogies that pay close attention to students' social identities," in the words of the Association of American Colleges and Universities. STEM teaching should be more "open- than closed-ended," more "reflective than prescriptive," according to the association. At the University of Michigan, the Women in Science and Engineering program (WISE) collaborates with the Center for Learning and Teaching to develop "deliberately inclusive and equitable approaches to syllabus design, writing assignments, grading, and discussion." Yale has created a special undergraduate laboratory course, with funding from the Howard Hughes Medical Institute, that aims to enhance URM students' "feelings of identifying as a scientist." It does so by being "nonprescriptive" in what students research; they develop their own research questions. But "feelings" are only going to get you so far without mastery of the building blocks of scientific knowledge.[16]

Mastering those building blocks involves the memorization of facts, among other skills. Assessing students' knowledge of those facts can produce disparate results. The solution is to change the test or, ideally, eliminate it. A professor at an Ivy League medical school told me that he was reprimanded for giving an exam in pharmacology that was too fact-based. Presumably, however, the ability to quickly grasp facts about the interaction between a cell's immunity mechanisms and drugs is an important skill to have in the fight against infectious diseases such as COVID-19.

Grading on a curve is another vilified practice for those interested in building "inclusive" STEM classrooms. The only surprising aspect of that vilification is that it acknowledges one of the most self-defeating aspects of black and Hispanic culture: the stigma against "acting white." Underrepresented minorities may "reject competitiveness as an academic motivator," explains a 2015 UCLA report on the undergraduate academic-achievement gap.[17] Instead, underrepresented minorities "draw strength in peer acceptance, nurturance, and cooperation." Translation: instead of pulling all-nighters studying for a linear algebra exam, they may be inclined to hang out in the Afro-Am or Latinx center. This rejection of academic competitiveness is a "coping mechanism," says the UCLA report, one that allows individuals to "devalue" things that threaten their sense of well-being, such as high academic expectations. A grading curve contributes to academic competition by objectively ranking students. As a result, URM students will be further alienated and further withhold their academic efforts. The solution, according to diversity proponents, is to throw out the curve and to grade students on whether they have achieved the expected learning outcomes. This sounds unobjectionable, but in practice a curve is the only reliable defense against raging grade inflation.

An introductory chemistry course at UC Berkeley exemplifies "culturally sensitive pedagogy." Its creators described the course in a January 2018 webinar for STEM teachers, sponsored by the University of California's STEM Faculty Learning Community.[18] A primary goal of the course, according to teachers Erin Palmer and Sabriya Rosemund, is to disrupt the "racialized and gendered construct of scientific brilliance," which defines "good science" as getting all the right answers. The course maintains, instead, that "all students are scientifically brilliant." Science is a practice of collective sense-making that calls forth "inclusive ways" of being brilliant. In practice, these principles mean that students work in groups arranging data cards in the proper sequence to represent chemical processes, among other tasks. Chemical terms of art are avoided wherever possible, to accommodate students' different academic backgrounds. The instructors hold the teams "accountable to group thinking"; a team can't question an instructor unless it has arrived collectively at the question and poses it in "we" language.

Progressive pedagogy has long embraced the idea that students should work exclusively in groups as a way to model collectivist democracy. This political agenda is simply a pretext for masking individual differences in achievement that might reinforce group stereotypes. Here, the rationale for group organization is that students are modeling "collective chemical practice." The group design "makes space for students to recognize themselves as competent thinkers and doers of chemistry." *Are* they competent thinkers and doers of chemistry? It's hard to say. The course's grading is idiosyncratic and thus not comparable with other intro-chemistry courses. The final grade is based on homework (notoriously easy to crib), a final exam (which the teachers no doubt wish they could ditch), and an informal presentation to friends or family about the chemistry of compounds. Use of slang or a language other than English in this presentation is encouraged. One such effort featured a photo of the character Joey from the TV sitcom *Friends* dressed in several layers of unmatched clothes to suggest the relationship between positive and negative charges. The teachers have done no follow-up evaluation to see how students performed in their subsequent courses, nor have they determined whether the attrition rate of URM students is lower than in traditional chemistry classes. What they do know is that students showed a positive shift in *believing* that they were good at science. Scientific self-esteem is, apparently, now an academic goal.

When it comes to members of underrepresented minorities,

math deficits show up at the earliest ages. It is only there where the achievement gap can be overcome—through more rigorous, structured classrooms and through a change in family culture to put a high premium on academic achievement. The institutional response to the achievement gap, however, is race preferences. College freshmen are brought into elite academic environments for which they are unprepared, especially in STEM fields, in order to satisfy administrators' desire to look out upon a "diverse" student body. Those inaptly named preference "beneficiaries" drop out of their STEM studies at high rates. Students who are admitted to schools for which they are unprepared learn less, in fact, than they would in a student body that matches their own academic level. A controversy at Duke University demonstrated, however, that such pesky details may have no effect on the preference regime.

Duke admits black students with SAT scores on average over one standard deviation below those of its white and Asian students (at Duke, black students' combined math and verbal SAT scores are 1274; white students' are 1416; and Asian students', 1457). Not surprisingly, black students' grades in their first semester are significantly lower than those of other students, but by senior year, the difference between black and white students' grades has shrunk almost 50 percent.[19] This convergence in GPA might seem to validate preferential admissions by suggesting that Duke identifies minority students with untapped academic potential who, over their college careers, will narrow the gap with their white and Asian peers.

Three Duke researchers demonstrated in 2012 that such catching-up is illusory. Black students improve their GPAs because they switch disproportionately out of more demanding science and economics majors into the humanities and soft social sciences, which grade much more liberally and require less work. If black students stayed in the sciences at the same rate as white students, there would be no convergence in GPAs. And even after their exodus from the sciences, black students don't improve their class standing in their four years of college.

This study, by economics professor Peter Arcidiacono, sociology professor Ken Spenner, and economics graduate student Esteban Aucejo (now a professor at Arizona State University), has major implications for the nationwide effort to increase the number of minority scientists.[20] The federal government alone has spent billions of taxpayer dollars trying to boost minority participation in science; race preferences play a key role in almost all college science initiatives. The Arcidiacono paper suggests that admitting aspiring minority scientists to schools where they are less prepared than their peers is counterproductive.

The most surprising finding of the study is that, of incoming students who reported a major, more than 76 percent of black male freshmen at Duke intended to major in the hard sciences or economics, higher even than the percentage of white male freshmen who anticipated such majors. But more than half of those would-be black science majors switched track in the course of their studies, while less than 8 percent of white male science majors did—so that, by senior year, only 35 percent of black males graduated with a science or economics degree, while more than 63 percent of white males did. Had those minority students who gave up their scientific aspirations taken introductory chemistry among students with similar levels of academic preparation, they would more likely have continued with their original course of study, as the record of historically black colleges in graduating science majors suggests. Instead, finding themselves in classrooms pitched at a more advanced level of math or science than they have yet mastered, preference recipients may conclude that they are not cut out for quantitative fields—or, equally likely, that the classroom "climate" is racist—whereas the problem may just be that they have not yet laid the foundations for more advanced work.

Attrition from a hard science major was wholly accounted for in the paper's statistical models by a freshman's level of academic qualifications; race was irrelevant. While science majors had SAT scores that were fifty points higher than those of students in the humanities in general, students who had started out in science and then switched had SAT scores that were seventy points lower than those of science majors. Any student in a class that assumes knowledge of advanced calculus is likely to drop out if he has not yet mastered basic calculus.

This experience of academic failure only exacerbates the anti-acting-white syndrome acknowledged in the 2015 UCLA study discussed above. You can read through report after report on achieving diversity in STEM, however, without coming across any acknowledgement of the academic skills gap.

Predictably, a number of black students, alumni, and professors portrayed Arcidiacono and his coauthors' research, whose methodology was watertight, as a personal assault. Members of Duke's Black Student Alliance (BSA) held a silent vigil outside the school's Martin Luther King Day celebration in protest of the paper and handed out flyers titled "Duke: A Hostile Environment for Its Black Students?" In an email to the state's NAACP chapter, the BSA called the paper "hurtful and alienating" and accused its authors of lacking "a genuine concern for proactively furthering the well-being of the black community."

Members of the Duke faculty claimed that the study "lacked academic rigor," "re-opens old racial wounds,"[21] and was a "political tract disguised as scholarly inquiry," representing a "crusade to reduce the numbers of black students at elite institutions."[22] A group of recent black graduates called on the study's authors to "stop their attack on students of color."

To the extent these critics tried to address the paper's arguments, they missed its gist entirely. The Duke alumni alleged that black students "shy away" from "so-called 'difficult' majors" because they've been told all their lives that they are "inferior"—overlooking the fact that Duke's black students "shied away" from the sciences only *after* starting out in those fields.

The study's critics also asserted that the intellectual demands of humanities and science majors are indistinguishable. Here, too, the protestors ignored the paper's empirical evidence: Duke seniors in the hard sciences have lower grades than freshmen in the humanities and social sciences, even though the SAT scores of science majors are, on average, higher than those of humanities majors. For black students, the disparity in grading is even greater. Black freshmen at Duke get higher grades in the humanities and social sciences than white students do in the hard sciences, though black students' test scores and overall grades are significantly lower than other students'.

In a different world, the Duke administration might have tried to dispel the critics' distortions of the Arcidiacono paper, given the authors' patent lack of invidious intent and the rigor of their work. Instead, Duke's top bureaucrats let the authors twist in the wind. In an open letter to the campus, provost Peter Lange and a passel of deanlings declared: "We understand how the conclusions of the research paper can be interpreted in ways that reinforce negative stereotypes."[23] It is hard to imagine a more hypocritical utterance. To the extent that the paper reinforced "negative stereotypes," it did so by describing the effects of Duke's policy of admitting black students with lower academic qualifications than white and Asian students. It is Duke's predilection for treating black students as a group whose race trumps their individual academic records that constitutes "stereotyping," not the authors' analysis of the consequences of that groupthinking.

But perhaps a concession to black anger had to be made in order to clear some space for a defense of the Arcidiacono paper? Not a chance. The deanlets and provosts followed their invocation of "negative stereotypes" with an anodyne general-ization about academic freedom: "At the same time, our goal of academic success for all should not inhibit research and discussion to clarify important issues of academic choice and achievement." In other words, don't blame us for what those wacky professors might say.

As for women, they, too, are the target of constant efforts to boost their representation in STEM environments. Yet we are to believe that highly educated heads of research teams are so benighted that they refuse to hire or promote scientists whose superior qualifications would increase the lab's chance of a sci-entific breakthrough, just because those scientists are female. The diversity crusade rests on the belief that absent discrimination, every scientific field would show gender parity. That belief is ungrounded. Men outperform women at the highest reaches of mathematical reasoning (and are overrepresented at the lowest level of mathematical incompetence). Differences in math pre-cocity between boys and girls show up as early as kindergarten. For decades, male students in every ethnic group have scored higher than female students in their same ethnic group on the math portion of the SAT. In 2016, the percentage of male students scoring above 700 (on an 800-point scale) was nearly twice as large as the percentage of female students in that range. In the United States, among those in the top 0.01 percent of math abil-ity, there are 2.5 males for every female, according to a February 2018 paper in the journal *Intelligence*.[24] But female high-scorers are more likely than male high-scorers to possess strong verbal skills as well, according to authors Jonathan Wai, Jaret Hodges, and Matthew Makel, giving them a greater range of career options. Traditionally, individuals who score well in both the math and verbal domains are less likely to pursue a STEM career. Moreover, on average, females are more interested in people-centered rather than abstract work, which helps explain why women account for

75 percent of health-care-related workers but only 14 percent of engineering workers and 25 percent of computer workers. Nearly 82 percent of obstetrics and gynecology medical residents in 2016 were female. Is gynecology biased against men, or are women selecting where they want to work?

STEM industry leaders are fully on board the diversity juggernaut, having absorbed academic identity politics. The giant Silicon Valley companies offer gender- and race-exclusive mentoring programs and give special consideration to women and URM members in hiring and promotions. Managers go through the same costly implicit-bias training as faculty committees. The experience of James Damore, a computer engineer fired by Google in August 2017, illustrates how the "commitment to diversity" may not be questioned within Silicon Valley.

After attending a diversity training session, Damore wrote a ten-page memo titled "Google's Ideological Echo Chamber." He observed that "differences in distributions of traits between men and women may in part explain why we don't have 50% representation of women in tech and leadership." Among those traits are assertiveness, a drive for status, an orientation toward things rather than people, and a tolerance for stress. He acknowledged that many of the differences in distribution are small and overlap significantly between the sexes, so that one cannot assume on the basis of sex where any given individual falls on the psychological spectrum. Considerable research supports Damore's claims regarding male and female career preferences and personality traits.

Damore affirmed his commitment to diversity and suggested ways to make software engineering more people-oriented. But he pointed out that several of Google's practices for engineering diversity discriminated in favor of women and minorities. And he called for greater openness to ideas that challenge progressive dogma, especially the "science of human nature," which shows that not all differences are "socially constructed or due to discrimination."

Google CEO Sundar Pichai employed the academy's bathetic language of injury in his response to Damore. "The memo has clearly impacted our co-workers, some of whom are hurting and feel judged based on their gender," he asserted in a memo of his own.[25] Yonatan Zunger, a recently departed Google senior engineer, claimed in an online essay that the speculations of Damore, a junior employee, have "caused significant harm to people across this company, and to the company's entire ability to function." He added that "not all conversations about ideas even have basic *legitimacy*" [emphasis in original].[26]

The discrimination lawsuit Damore filed after his termination reveals a workplace culture at the Silicon Valley giant infused with academic victimology that extends beyond his own experience. Google employees denounce the advocacy of gender- and race-blind policies as a "microaggression" and the product of "racism" and "misogyny." Managers apologize for promoting men, even when women are being promoted at a higher rate. All-male research teams are mocked; employees self-righteously offer to protect Google's oppressed women and members of underrepresented minorities from "blinkered, pig-ignorant" conservative opinion. A manager reprimands someone for pointing out that white men are actually underrepresented at Google compared with the general population. The manager informs the errant employee that caring about facts may seem to be a trait of engineers, but "being absolutely correct is inappropriate" when it comes to "discussions of race and justice." Facts are especially inappropriate "in the context of the threat" faced by women and minority members at Google. Needless to say, no woman or underrepresented minority member faces a threat at Google.

The idea that women and members of underrepresented minorities are being discriminated against in STEM is demonstrably false. An Italian physicist, Alessandro Strumia, was fired from Europe's particle physics consortium CERN for pointing out that female physicists, far from being discriminated against, are hired with a thinner research record than males. A physician-scientist at a top medical school describes the environment in which he works as follows:

> The sheer effort that is expended in complete good faith at the graduate, post-graduate, and faculty level chasing after a declining population of minority applicants is astonishing. URMs are encouraged to apply, indeed begged to apply, to medical school and post-graduate medical training programs. Everyone at this level is trying incredibly hard to be fair, generous, forgiving, thoughtful, kind, and encouraging to these applicants. But if the pool of candidates is actually declining, no amount of effort, exhortation, or threat will achieve diversity. It's one thing to do poorly on the MCAT; it's another not even to bother taking it. The latter is now the bigger problem because the academy has already relaxed its standards and come up with all kinds of ways to explain away the need to do well on these tests.[27]

Do we want the best molecular biologists and pharmacologists working on COVID-19 and other pressing medical needs, or do we want the best female, black, and Hispanic molecular biologists and pharmacologists? Sometimes the same person will occupy both categories. But where those categories do not overlap, it is reckless to treat sex and race as superior qualifications.

The extraordinary accomplishments of Western science were achieved without regard to the complexions of its creators. Now, we are to believe that scientific progress will stall unless we pay close attention to identity and try to engineer proportional representation in schools and laboratories. The truth is exactly the opposite: lowering standards and diverting scientists' energy into combating phantom sexism and racism is reckless in a highly competitive, ruthless, and unforgiving global marketplace. Driven by unapologetic meritocracy, China is catching up fast to the United States in science and technology. Identity politics in American science is a political self-indulgence that we cannot afford.

The Sausage Factory

Gail Heriot & Carissa Mulder

The way colleges and universities set admissions policy isn't pretty—
or proper—and nothing in the law or the Constitution requires the
courts to pretend it is.

When the Supreme Court announced its decisions in the twin
cases of *Grutter v. Bollinger* (2003)[1] and *Gratz v. Bollinger*
(2003),[2] a casual reader could have been forgiven for believing
that the battle over affirmative action had resulted in a draw. In
Grutter, the Court upheld the University of Michigan Law School's
race-preferential admissions policy, while in *Gratz* it condemned
the same university's undergraduate policy as unconstitutional.

Appearances, however, can be deceiving. *Grutter* was an enormous loss for those who advocate nondiscrimination. The win
in *Gratz*, on the other hand, was trivial and easily circumvented.

The difference between the two cases was essentially cosmetic.
Prior to the Court's decision, the University of Michigan's College of Literature, Science, and the Arts was adding twenty extra
points, based entirely on race, to students' admissions scores.
Those twenty points were equivalent to an entire letter grade:
An African American student with an unspectacular 2.99 high
school GPA would thus be admitted over an Asian American or
white student with a near-perfect 3.98 GPA, all other things being
equal. Or, to look at those twenty points another way, the most

an applicant could get for achieving a perfect score on the SAT was twelve points.[3] Being African American was thus enough to overcome even the most disappointing scores on the SAT.

By contrast, the law school—which won its case—didn't use a point system. Its admissions officers would simply eyeball the applications and make a decision. But that didn't mean the law school wasn't discriminating based on race. It definitely was. Nor did it mean that the magnitude of discrimination was smaller than at the college. To the contrary, it was greater. The difference was simply the law school did not employ an explicit formula.

In essence, the Court told the college that it needed to hide what it was doing better. But as long as it avoided mathematical formulae, it could go on discriminating. After the *Gratz* decision, the college modified its procedures to look more like those approved in *Grutter*, but the credentials gap between underrepresented minority students and white or Asian American students only grew.[4]

The Supreme Court has since weighed in twice more on the subject of race-preferential admissions—in *Fisher v. University of Texas* (2013)[5] and its sequel, *Fisher v. University of Texas* (2016).[6] They added only a little: While *Fisher I* suggested that the Court might be willing to start putting pressure on colleges and universities that practice *Grutter*-style race discrimination, *Fisher II* proved it wasn't—not yet anyway. The University of Texas was let off the hook entirely.

Grutter thus remains the key case. Unless the Court modifies—or at least clarifies—its stance in *Grutter*, race-preferential admissions policies and the poisonous identity politics they fuel will remain with us for decades to come.

One of the striking aspects of the decision was its idealized view of higher education. The majority opinion—by Justice Sandra Day O'Connor—treated state colleges and universities as more worthy of esteem and deference than elected legislatures and government agencies. The majority was willing to tolerate race discrimination coming out of academia, because…well…academia should be respected. Alas, this rosy image of academics as guardians of wisdom and learning was naïve in 2003 and, in retrospect, seems almost comically so.

The reasons to doubt academia's wisdom are especially strong when it comes to race-based admissions policies. If the Court was under the impression that colleges and universities are guided by a careful consideration of "education science" in setting such policies, that impression can be safely dismissed. In 2015, hoping to get a sense of each university's deliberative process, the two of us worked with the Center for Equal Opportunity to send public-records requests to twenty-two public universities. We asked for any document even mentioning the problem of "mismatch" or the leading empirical studies on that topic (as discussed elsewhere in this volume). We believed—and continue to believe—that no responsible university would develop its admissions policy without at least considering the evidence that preferential treatment decreases, rather than increases, the likelihood of career success for minority students. We got back nothing. The universities evidently hadn't given it a thought.

In the real world, race-based admissions policies are, instead, the product of political winds from both inside and outside each institution—blustery gusts that have more to do with what feels good than what is good. For decades, those winds have originated from many quarters but have always pointed in the same direction—toward greater emphasis on race. In dealing with them, public university administrators—a species not too different from politicians—practice the art of practical politics. Considerations of pedagogy rarely enter into the calculation.

Some of what drives all this is, of course, the reigning ideology in academia. But don't discount the practical side: Money matters in higher education. Pleasing state legislators, foundations, and donors therefore matters. Most educational institutions are quite willing to bend themselves into whatever shape is needed to qualify for more outside funds—even if that means adopting aggressively discriminatory policies that they might not otherwise prefer. Keeping the peace matters, so placating student protestors is also a necessity. Students have caught on to this, so their demands, particularly on matters of race, have escalated in recent years. Alumni must also be kept happy, because, among other things, they provide jobs for recent graduates. Increasingly, they find it satisfying to signal their virtue by calling for more diversity, and college and university officials are happy to accommodate them.

You may be thinking, "Thank goodness we have accreditors, who can make sure that colleges and universities stick to their educational mission and don't allow non-academic considerations to dictate academic policy." But, as this essay will show, accreditors have been part of the problem, not its solution.

The American poet John Godfrey Saxe wrote in 1869, "Laws, like sausages, cease to inspire respect in proportion as we know how they are made." He could have been speaking of modern admissions policies.

STRICT SCRUTINY AND DEFERENCE: A CONTRADICTION IN TERMS

Grutter was one of those 5–4 decisions that the modern Court has become famous for. The one thing that all nine members agreed on was that the law school's policy was racially discriminatory and therefore had to be subjected to "strict scrutiny." Strict scrutiny is the law of equal protection's most demanding standard: A racially discriminatory law or policy can be upheld only if the Court finds the justification for it "compelling" and further finds that the law or policy at issue is "narrowly tailored" to achieve that compelling justification. Prior to *Grutter*, it was rare for anything subjected to strict scrutiny to survive it. Indeed, in 1972, leading constitutional scholar Gerald Gunther referred to the standard as "'strict' in theory and fatal in fact."[7]

But, in *Grutter*, the Court's majority immediately eviscerated the high standard it had set. It held that it should "defer" to the law school's "educational judgment" in determining whether its stated purpose—the desire to capture the educational benefits of diversity for all its students—was compelling.[8]

By purporting to "defer," the Court turned strict scrutiny on its head. Deference is the opposite of strict scrutiny. One cannot strictly scrutinize a government's actions and defer to its judgment at the same time. To do so is to contradict oneself.

The Court sought to justify itself by referring to "academic freedom." But there is no chance whatsoever that academic freedom would have been sufficient to justify any other form of race discrimination. Imagine if the Supreme Court had deferred in the landmark Civil Rights Era cases dealing with education— *Sweatt v. Painter* (1950),[9] *McLaurin v. Oklahoma State Regents* (1950),[10] and *Brown v. Board of Education* (1954).[11] At the time, there was no shortage of education experts that the defendants could produce as expert witnesses who believed—perhaps sincerely—that students learn better in racially segregated schools.[12] The nation should be thankful the Court had the courage to exercise its own judgment.

Why then should higher education be given deference now? The Court never fully explained why, alone among government instrumentalities, public colleges and universities should be exempt from the strong presumption against racially discriminatory laws and policies (or why, alone among industries, private colleges and universities should be exempt). The answer cannot be expertise, since it is always the case that the defendant in an equal protection case will have greater expertise than the Court has concerning its own business. With four law professors and nine lawyers on the Court, there was much less reason to defer in *Grutter* about matters of legal education than there would have been in a case about mail delivery or nuclear power. It also cannot be because colleges and universities have a particularly commendable history of racial equity. Quite the opposite is the case. Discrimination against African Americans at both public and private institutions of higher learning, including many north of the Mason-Dixon line, is a story that should require no elaboration here. Jewish quotas are another blot on higher education's history, particularly at Ivy League and other selective schools. It's not a good record.

What is the explanation for higher education's failures on matters of race? That is a subject that deserves its own multi-volume treatment. But one part of the answer may simply be that the quality of a college education is a difficult thing to judge, especially in the short run. More so than most other products and services, education is thus prone to fads. Over the course of history, fashionable ideas justifying race discrimination have been especially pernicious, but they are hardly the only ill-considered ideas that colleges and universities have unleashed upon the world.[13]

The *Grutter* Court then conferred a second favor on higher education. Not only was it willing to assume that obtaining the educational benefits of diversity was a compelling purpose, it was also willing to assume that, *in fact*, the law school's motivation in adopting race-based admissions was to obtain those benefits. As Justice O'Connor put it, "good faith...*is presumed* absent a showing to the contrary."[14]

All this special treatment was particularly odd, given that there is plenty of reason to believe that obtaining the educational benefits of diversity is unlikely to be the main motivation of colleges and universities that engage in race-preferential admissions.

IDEOLOGICAL MOTIVATIONS

Many academics have been candid that "social justice" or "compensation for past discrimination," rather than the educational benefits of diversity, is what motivates them to support race-based admissions. Columbia University law professor Kent Greenawalt, a skeptic of these policies, once declared, "I have yet to find a professional academic who believes the primary motivation for preferential admission has been to promote diversity in the student body for the better education of all the students."[15]

The same thought has been expressed by many others,[16] including Harvard law professor Alan Dershowitz, who has written:

> The raison d'être for race-specific affirmative action programs has simply never been diversity for the sake of education. The checkered history of "diversity" demonstrates that it was designed largely as a cover to achieve other legally, morally, and politically controversial goals.[17]

Harvard law professor Randall Kennedy, an affirmative-action proponent, put it even more pointedly:

> Let's be honest: Many who defend affirmative action for the sake of "diversity" are actually motivated by a concern that is considerably more compelling. They are not so much animated by a commitment to what is, after all, only a contingent, pedagogical hypothesis. Rather, they are animated by a commitment to social justice. They would rightly defend affirmative action even if social science demonstrated uncontrovertibly that diversity (or its absence) has no effect (or even a negative effect) on the learning environment.[18]

In recent years, the dominant rhetoric in our "woke" culture focuses on combating "structural racism" or "systemic racism," which is suggestive of righting past and present wrongs. The literature on race has concentrated even more on "social justice" themes, including reparations for slavery. While the term "diversity" still gets bandied about, the educational benefits of diversity don't get a lot of mention.[19]

So why did the University of Michigan claim to be motivated by a desire to secure the educational benefits of diversity for its students in *Grutter* and *Gratz*? Why did the University of Texas make the same claim before the Supreme Court in the *Fisher* cases in 2013 and 2016? Why not point to "social justice" instead?

The answer is pretty obvious: In 1978, every university counsel in the country began advising university officials that only one motivation for race-preferential admissions policies has ever received anything approaching Supreme Court approval. That is diversity. Claiming other motivations would be risking a lawsuit.

But, in 1978, the diversity rationale received approval from only one member of the Court—Justice Lewis Powell, in his famously one-justice opinion in *University of California Board of Regents v. Bakke* (1978).[20] The other eight—who were evenly split on what the result should be—did not even consider the argument.

Interestingly, judging from his opinion, Powell did not seem all that keen on race-preferential admissions himself. He sided with plaintiff Allan Bakke in concluding that the policy of the medical school at the University of California at Davis was unconstitutional. In doing so, he formed a majority with the four justices who considered the policy to be an obvious violation of Title VI of the Civil Rights Act of 1964 without even having to consider whether it also violated the Constitution. And he differentiated himself from the four dissenting justices, who viewed the power of the state to discriminate in favor of racial minorities to be quite broad.

But Powell's conciliatory nature caused him to speculate

whether there might be circumstances under which the Constitution would permit race discrimination in admissions. One by one, he rejected the arguments advanced by the medical school. Most importantly, he rejected what he called "past societal discrimination" (and what today might be called "social justice"). As he put it, "the purpose of helping certain groups whom the faculty of the Davis Medical School perceived as victims of 'societal discrimination' does not justify a classification that imposes disadvantages upon persons...who bear no responsibility for whatever harm the beneficiaries of the special admissions program are thought to have suffered." The only argument he saw as potentially legitimate—the educational benefits of diversity—made sense to him because, in theory at least, it directly benefits *all* students.

Suppose the Court were to find, in a future case, that a particular university adopted its race-preferential admissions policy to right past and present wrongs. It is difficult to see how the Court could "defer" on whether this view of social justice constituted a compelling purpose. The higher education industry has no special expertise at evaluating what is or is not required by social justice. If anything, the Court is the better institution to judge such arguments. And as high-minded as this motivation might seem to its proponents, it has been explicitly rejected as unconstitutional by Justice Powell. Later decisions of the Court reinforced this, especially *Wygant v. Jackson Board of Education* (1986),[21] in which a plurality of the Court explicitly rejected "societal discrimination" as a justification for race discrimination by a school district. As Justice Scalia stated in concurrence in *Adarand Constructors, Inc. v. Peña* (1995):[22]

> [U]nder our Constitution there can be no such thing as either a creditor or a debtor race. That concept is alien to the Constitution's focus upon the individual....To pursue the concept of racial entitlement—even for the most admirable and benign of

purposes—is to reinforce and preserve for future mischief the way of thinking that produced race slavery, race privilege and race hatred. In the eyes of government, we are just one race here. It is American.[23]

Under the circumstances, the university's likelihood of prevailing in that future case would not be good.

PRACTICAL MOTIVATIONS

Of course, not everything that colleges and universities do is motivated by a sense of "social justice." Responding to pressure from outside forces plays a significant role in setting policy too. Even at colleges and universities that would have leaned toward race-preferential admissions anyway (which is nearly all of them), outside pressure strengthens the hands of those on campus who favor the most aggressive policies and discourages their more cautious colleagues.

In a poll taken by political scientists Susan Welch and John Gruhl in the late 1990s, more than 23 percent of medical school and 15 percent of law school admissions officers reported that they had felt "significant" or "some" pressure from state or local governments to engage in "affirmative action."[24] As far as we are aware, no recent poll has asked that same question. But given the astonishing growth of identity politics over the last twenty years, any suggestion that the pressure has decreased rather than increased seems far-fetched.

State legislatures control state university budgets, and no public university president ever forgets that. In 1995, Ward Connerly, a member of the University of California Board of Regents, authored a policy ending race-preferential admissions at the University of California and persuaded the board of regents to adopt it. California governor Pete Wilson was sympathetic to Connerly's view, but the legislature's majority definitely was not. Connerly described UC president Jack Peltason's reaction this way:

> Jack said, "look, we got a legislature to deal with...that really has yes or no over our budget." The code for everything that he was saying is that it's a Democratically controlled legislature, Willie Brown was the speaker, and John Vasconcellos was chairing the Budget Committee, and John took a real interest in the University. So Jack's concerns... were that, "God, we're going to run into a buzz saw here," and looking out for the best interests of the University, don't rock the boat.[25]

Usually one would expect legislative pressure to be applied behind closed doors. But sometimes it is very public—as in the case of the University of Delaware in 2015. The *Delaware News Journal* reported:

> Delaware's flagship university is facing new questions about a lack of diversity on campus, with students, state lawmakers and civil rights leaders calling on the University of Delaware to do more to recruit and retain black students....
>
> Sen. Harris McDowell, a Wilmington Democrat and co-chair of the budget committee, said the university's record on diversity is "disappointing."
>
> "The data is very discouraging," McDowell said.
>
> Budget Committee member Rep. James "J.J." Johnson, a New Castle Democrat, said the university must work harder to close the racial gap.[26]

Leaders at the University of Delaware almost certainly understood what to do in order to return to the legislature's good graces: Up the ante on race-preferential admissions.

Sometimes it's unclear whether it's state legislators or someone else who is exerting pressure. Consider the case of the College of Charleston, a state university that depends on the South Carolina legislature for its budget. On Sunday, July 29, 2018, the *Charleston Post and Courier* published an article entitled "Affirmative Action Comes to a Quiet End at College of Charleston":[27]

> The College of Charleston stopped considering race as a factor in student admissions in the summer of 2016, quietly eliminating a tool for increasing diversity as black enrollment stagnated at the public college....
>
> The end of affirmative action came so quietly that even longtime advocates for minority students did not hear about it.

Only two days later, the *Post and Courier*, in "College of Charleston Resumes Affirmative Action After 2-Year Hiatus," reported the college had changed its mind:[28]

> The College of Charleston has begun practicing race-conscious affirmative action in its admissions office again, about two years after quietly discontinuing the practice.
>
> In a statement published on C of C's website Tuesday afternoon, Interim President Stephen Osborne said the college would begin conducting an additional review of students of color who are not initially recommended for admission.

So what happened? Somebody got to the College of Charleston. But it's not clear who. All that's clear is that he, she, or they must have done so quietly. No public protests occurred, and a Freedom of Information Act request revealed no flurry of emails from irate students and faculty. But in a mere two days, who would have that much clout? Was it state legislators who threatened to oppose the college's budget? A major donor? Or did the college president have his own sudden epiphany? We may never know.

One thing is for certain: The change in policy couldn't have been the product of careful research on the educational effects of race-based admissions, not with a two-day turnaround.[29]

Another significant influence on admissions policy is the federal government. Some admissions officials reported to Welch and Gruhl threats of legal action and threats to withhold funds; others reported that the need to fill out federal paperwork effectively pressures them to engage in affirmative action.[30] But, as is often the case with the federal government, it is the carrots rather than the sticks that have the most profound effects. Former UC Santa Cruz dean John M. Ellis, now an opponent of race-preferential admissions, candidly admits in his essay in this volume that, as graduate school dean during the 1970s, he started his school down the wrong road in order to qualify for federal monies:

> At the beginning of my term as graduate dean at UCSC, we had no affirmative-action program for graduate student admissions. And so when my office chief of staff got wind of a soon-to-be announced federal program of grants to campuses to provide fellowships for minority and female graduate students, we both had the same thought: of course we'd like more money to support our graduate students—but mostly we want more money, whatever it may be earmarked for.[31]

Ellis described how he came to regret his decision to pursue these federal funds:

> [W]hen it began, affirmative action seemed so modest and circumscribed, so limited in scope and so well-intended, that it was impossible to imagine the damage it would do.[32]

Private foundations and alumni donors have a similar effect. By offering carrots to institutions to increase race preferences, one can surely assume they get results.[33] Millions of dollars have been dispensed to colleges and universities from foundations like Irvine and Rockefeller for the purpose of increasing campus racial diversity.[34] Millions more have been dispensed for other purposes—but only to colleges and universities that are judged sufficiently "diverse."

It is unlikely that the Court in *Grutter* would have approved the University of Michigan's race-preferential admissions policy if the university's explanation for it had been "This is what our state legislature wants, and it is our judgment that without the legislature's support, our educational mission will suffer" or "The Ford Foundation is very enthusiastic about race-preferential admissions, and that's where the money is." Yet explanations like these are more consistent with aggressive efforts to enroll minority students despite large gaps in academic credentials than is any effort to capture diversity's educational benefits for all students. It is beyond comprehension that a college or university would neglect to consider the pedagogical problems created by the inevitable gaps in academic credentials if the educational benefits of diversity were, in fact, its primary concern.

Of course, it is not all about the money. Appeasing students' demands is part of the story too. In 2011, for example, at the University of Wisconsin, a student mob, egged on by the university's "Vice Provost for Diversity and Climate," overpowered hotel staff, knocking some to the floor, to interrupt a press conference at which the speaker was critical of race-based admissions policies.[35] No doubt this was bad publicity for the University of Wisconsin and its president. The easiest way to calm protesters down is to try to give them at least part of what they want.

The Wisconsin protest was more unsettling than most, but there is an abundance of other examples. At Colgate University in 2014, more than 350 students occupied the admissions hall in order to demand greater diversity.[36] That same year, UCLA law students staged a protest of what they saw as a lack of diversity, despite the school's claim that 35 percent of its students were people of color.[37]

The year 2015 was a particularly big one for diversity demands. One article appearing online found twenty-one schools where students had issued formal demands for increased student diversity.[38] But the demands have continued into the present as well. In 2018, New Mexico State University students marched across campus and into the provost's office with a list of six demands aimed at diversifying the campus.[39] In 2019, it was the turn of students at California Polytechnic State University at San Luis Obispo and the University of Alabama to protest.[40]

The University of Alabama protest involved over two hundred students carrying signs, chanting, and marching to the president's office to demand, among other things, greater diversity. Upon their arrival at the administration building, they were greeted by President Stuart Bell, who agreeably told them that he, too, wanted a safe, inclusive, and diverse university for students. "I appreciate you taking the time out of your schedule," he told them. "You have my pledge that we will take this and we will look at providing action items as we move forward." At that point, one of the protestors told him to shut up.[41]

For a while, the COVID-19 crisis seemed to slow things down, but the quiet didn't last. Students at the University of South Carolina and students and alumni at Michigan State University held diversity-inspired marches in June 2020.[42]

Just as with state legislators and foundation donors, it is unthinkable that the Supreme Court would have upheld the University of Michigan's policy if it had argued, "Some of our students really want more racial diversity in their classes, and we like to please our customers," or even "Some of our students are so exercised over this issue that we think that it is in the best interests of their education—and everyone's education—to give them what they demand." Even under Justice O'Connor's

Constitution, race discrimination cannot be justified by a desire to satisfy the demands of loud student protesters.

FISHER: A DISAPPOINTING INTERLUDE

In 2008, a lawsuit against the University of Texas was filed by Abigail Fisher, a young white Texas woman who had been rejected for admission under circumstances that appeared to involve her race.

After the *Grutter* debacle, advocates of race-neutral admissions needed a very strong case to advance their cause. And it looked like they had it in *Fisher v. University of Texas*. In 1996, well before *Grutter*, the U.S. Court of Appeals for the Fifth Circuit, in a case called *Hopwood v. Texas*,[43] had held that UT's race-preferential admissions policy was unconstitutional and issued an injunction against it. The Fifth Circuit anticipated—incorrectly—that the Supreme Court would ultimately hold race-preferential admissions to be unconstitutional.

The following year—in part, as a response to *Hopwood*—the Texas legislature passed a statute requiring UT to accept any and all graduates of Texas high schools whose high school GPA put them in the top 10 percent of their class.[44] This "Top 10% Plan" made UT more racially diverse than it would otherwise have been and at least had the virtue of not directly considering race. By 2003, UT was admitting higher numbers of African American, Latino, and Asian American students than ever, causing the university to declare that it had *"effectively compensated for the loss of affirmative action."*[45]

When *Grutter* overruled *Hopwood* by implication, colleges and universities in Fifth Circuit states (Texas, Louisiana, and Mississippi) were able to reinstitute race-preferential admissions. But this put UT in an awkward position. It had, after all, publicly declared that it didn't have a diversity problem. With its statutorily mandated Top 10% Plan, its 2004 entering class was already 21.4 percent African American or Latino (as well as 17.9 percent Asian American). Did it really need to go back to considering race to get the diversity it claimed to need? If UT was already diverse without using race preferences, how could it argue that it had a compelling need for more discrimination?

Already diverse or not, UT reinstituted preferential treatment based on race, beginning with the entering class of 2005. It argued that it needed to do so in order to ensure that every classroom, and not just the class as a whole, was diverse. In particular, it claimed to have a diversity problem in its science and engineering classes.

Interestingly, the discriminatory plan affected only a tiny number of seats in UT's class; most of UT's class came in through the Top 10% Plan. Why did the university bother to risk a lawsuit for only a slight gain in racial diversity? We'll never know for sure. Perhaps its leaders wanted to show that they shared the social-justice vision so popular on other campuses. Or perhaps they wanted to avoid giving the impression that, if other schools emulated UT's Top 10% Plan, it would be clear that race preferences were unnecessary.

Even if the Court were to assume that UT was genuinely motivated by the educational benefits of diversity, there were problems for UT. In theory, at least, the diversity rationale does not confer on colleges and universities the authority to discriminate to the point that every racial group is represented according to its proportion in the relevant population. Rather, it allows only for admitting a "critical mass" such that their perspectives will be part of the academic conversation. The question is "What constitutes critical mass?" Supporters of race-neutral admissions hoped that *Fisher v. University of Texas* (2013) would overrule *Grutter* or, failing that, would set a limit on the vague concept of "critical mass."

The Court fulfilled neither hope. The 7-2 decision made no effort to disturb *Grutter*'s deference to the university on the first part of the strict scrutiny test (whether the university had a compelling need for racial diversity in its class). It also declined to articulate a "one size fits all" upper limit for "critical mass." It did, however, hold that it would not defer on the second part of the strict scrutiny test (whether the university's actual policy is narrowly tailored to serve that need) and remanded the case for the lower courts to apply the traditional stringent standard for that part of the test.

That still could have been a lot. A robust application of the narrow tailoring requirement would almost certainly have resulted in a loss for UT. There were too many inconsistencies between UT's claimed pedagogical purpose and its actual policy.

In the end, however, the *Fisher* case came to nothing. The 5-4 opinion for the majority in *Fisher II*, written by Justice Anthony Kennedy, held that UT's race-preferential program was narrowly tailored to serve the compelling interest of diversity. The opinion was inexplicably open-ended, with little serious examination of UT's policy. Anything goes.

In a much quoted passage from *Grutter*, Justice O'Connor had stated, "We expect that 25 years from now, the use of racial preferences will no longer be necessary to further the interest approved today." *Fisher II* came more than halfway into that period, yet preferences had become more entrenched.

Of course, even if *Fisher II* had gone the other way, it is doubtful that much more progress would have been made toward fulfilling Justice O'Connor's expectation. Determining whether a particular college or university's admissions policy is narrowly tailored to serve the interest of reaping the educational benefits of diversity is necessarily a case-by-case analysis. That means that it would take many lawsuits (and many decades) to make a dent in the campus culture of race preferences.

If Justice O'Connor's expectation is to be fulfilled by 2028 (or indeed if it ever is to be fulfilled), the Court will need to reverse course on *Grutter*. And it will need to do so sooner rather than later.

OVERRULING *GRUTTER*: THE CASE FOR DEFERRING IN THE OPPOSITE DIRECTION

If the Court does move away from *Grutter* in the future, we suggest that it move all the way. There is a very different kind of deference that the Court should consider. It just runs in the opposite direction from *Grutter* deference. Higher education deserves no special deference. On the other hand, a court should think once, twice, and three times again before it declares a justification to be compelling if a majority of Americans (or even a large minority) not only disagree that it is compelling, but find it unpersuasive altogether.[46]

Make no mistake: Under no circumstances should a court defer to the judgment of those arguing in *favor* of race discrimination—no matter how wise or wonderful it perceives them to be. It must always satisfy itself that the argument is indeed compelling. But the judgment of those who oppose race discrimination is an entirely different matter. If a large number of Americans—even majorities—believe that a law or policy that racially discriminates is unjustified, it's hard to imagine many circumstances under which the Supreme Court should go ahead and allow the state to engage in such discrimination.

By deferring to higher education in *Grutter*, the Court put a heavy thumb on the scale in favor of race discrimination. But the thumb is supposed to go the other way. The Court is supposed to do everything it can to *avoid* approving race discrimination and instead to favor race neutrality.

It's not just that most Americans find that the justification for race-preferential admissions fails to rise to the level of "compelling." They don't find it convincing at all. They're against such policies. And they have consistently opposed them for decades. For example, Gallup polls asked the following question of Americans in 2003, 2007, and 2013:

> Which comes closer to your view about evaluating students for admission into a college or university—applicants should be admitted solely on the basis of merit, even if that results in few minority students being admitted (or) an applicant's racial and ethnic background should be considered to help promote diversity on college campuses, even if that means admitting some minority students who otherwise would not be admitted?

Every time, the response has been at least 2 to 1 in favor of merit only.[47] Similarly, Pew Research asked the following question in 2019:

> When it comes to decisions about hiring and promotions, do you think companies and organizations should take a person's race and ethnicity into account, in addition to their qualifications, in order to increase diversity in the workplace (or) should only take a person's qualifications into account, even if it results in less diversity in the workplace?

The latter alternative was chosen by 74 percent of the respondents.[48]

This is consistent with the polling results throughout the 1980s and 1990s. During that period, too, polls offered consistent results opposing race-preferential admissions, causing public-opinion experts Paul Sniderman and Thomas Piazza to write that the race-preferential policy agenda "is controversial precisely because most Americans do *not* disagree about it."[49] There is even evidence that a majority of college and university faculty members oppose race-based admissions policies.[50]

Similarly, voters in California (in 1996),[51] Washington State (in 1998),[52] Michigan (in 2006),[53] Nebraska (in 2008),[54] and Arizona (in 2010)[55] have taken advantage of the ballot-initiative process in those states to pass (by decisive and sometimes overwhelming margins) initiatives that, among other things, prohibit race-preferential admissions in state universities. Only in one state—Colorado (2008)—has such an initiative been defeated, and then only by a razor-slim margin.[56] In Washington State, an effort by the legislature to repeal its 1998 initiative was defeated at the ballot box in 2019, albeit by a slim margin.[57] In California, a similar effort known as Proposition 16 was decisively defeated in 2020, despite its supporters outspending its opponents almost 16 to 1.

Indeed, those states that have prohibited race-preferential admissions have been an interesting laboratory for studying the diversity rationale. If college and university officials who claim the educational justification for discriminating is compelling were right, one would expect the quality of the institutions in those states to fall considerably. But that does not appear to have happened. Those states have managed to continue the work of their state universities without any loss of status. Before the University of California's flagship Berkeley campus was required to have race-neutral admissions policies, in 1996–97, it was ranked 23rd by *U.S. News.* By 2010, its rank was 21st, and in 2020 it was 22nd.[58] In fact, in 2006, *U.S. News* ranked Berkeley as the best public university in the nation.[59] Arizona State University rose from number 121 in 2010[60] to number 117 in 2020. The University of Michigan–Ann Arbor was ranked 29th in the country in 2010 and 25th in the country in 2020.[61]

Constitutional law should be something more than the likes and dislikes of five of the nine lawyers who happen at any one time to be on the Supreme Court. It should have an objective component. A compelling interest should be one that all, or nearly all, Americans can agree is necessary. It should be rare. Of course, on those (we hope rare) occasions when Americans do view the justification for discrimination on the basis of race to be compelling, the Court should still independently satisfy itself of the need.

The Supreme Court is supposed to be the institution that pulls us back from the brink when we are tempted by the path of race discrimination—a path that Americans have always come to regret. But the court didn't do its job in *Grutter*. Instead, by deferring to the University of Michigan Law School, it dragged us kicking and screaming over the edge.

ACCREDITING AGENCIES

Accrediting agencies are a special case, and a special approach may be possible with them—perhaps even one that involves legislation. Because they can decide whether particular colleges or universities will be eligible for federal funding, including funding for student loans, they have the power of life or death over these institutions. When accreditors speak, colleges and universities must listen.

Every seven years or so, accrediting agencies inspect each school and determine whether its accreditation should be renewed. Schools prepare for these visits many months in advance. The inspection teams typically include a number of faculty members from other, sometimes competing, schools. In addition, law school inspection teams usually include lawyers and judges, and medical school inspection teams usually include physicians.

Accreditors are frequently the most eager enforcers of diversity demands. They make it very difficult for an institution to be a dissenter. In a sense, the accreditor functions as the enforcer of a cartel. Many faculty members who favor race-based admissions at their own institutions would, for ideological reasons, like to see other institutions follow suit. But sometimes their reasons may have more to do with controlling the competition. If one law school engages in aggressive race preferences (or any kind of preference), it risks bringing down its bar passage rate and ultimately its all-important ranking in *U.S. News*. But if all law schools are required to do the same, its ranking will be unaffected. Similarly, a college that is big on race-preferential admissions may end up hurting the academic profile of its student body, which also forms part of the basis for its ranking. If that college can force other colleges to follow its example, it can protect itself.

Anyone who wonders why colleges and universities seem to march in lockstep on race-preferential admissions needs to keep this in mind. Accreditors make it nearly impossible to do anything else. But that poses a legal problem: If accreditors rather than individual schools are pulling the strings, then the resulting admissions policies would likely be considered inconsistent with *Grutter*. However misguided that opinion may have been in the context of state-sponsored race discrimination, its aim was to allow colleges and universities some measure of autonomy, not to foster academic conformity. It is hard to imagine the *Grutter* decision garnering five votes if it had been apparent that it would create for accreditors—backed by the life-or-death power of federal funding—the opportunity to insist on an orthodoxy of race preferences.

The earliest such case to come to public attention was that of Baruch College, a constituent college of the City University of New York. Since the accreditation process is confidential, and schools don't boast about their difficulties in getting reaccredited, we cannot know how many cases came before or after. But in 1990, Baruch was threatened with the loss of accreditation, not for a poor student-faculty ratio or a poorly stocked library—both those things were fine at Baruch. Its science laboratories were well equipped, its finances were in order, and its faculty was excellent, including as it did a Nobel laureate in economics. Instead, it was faulted for its failure to hire a sufficient number of minority faculty members and its failure to retain a sufficient number of black and Latino students. The Middle States Association of Colleges and Schools thus deferred Baruch's reaccreditation—which, after it was reported in the *New York Times*, caused huge embarrassment to the college.[62]

Eventually, Secretary of Education Lamar Alexander came to Baruch's rescue by administering Middle States some of its own medicine—deferring the renewal of its status as a federally recognized accrediting agency. Middle States backed off, but the push toward accreditors' forcing race-preferential hiring and admissions policies on colleges and universities was just getting started.[63]

In 1988, the Western Association of Schools and Colleges (WASC) had quietly adopted diversity standards for the colleges and universities it accredited. The most significant provision required institutions to make "positive efforts to foster...diversity." These efforts and the results were to be "monitored and periodically reviewed." Few took note, until WASC began to pressure the Rand Graduate School of Policy Studies in late 1990. Rand was informed that it had met the other requirements for reaccreditation but that it was "missing an opportunity to take leadership and responsibility" in the areas of race, sex, and ethnicity. Rand was required to report back to WASC: "Specifically, the Commission requests that the School more clearly delineate its goals with respect to increasing the representation of minorities and women in its faculty and student body and the inclusion of the study and analysis of issues related to diversity in its curriculum and the progress made in reaching those goals."[64]

Next came tiny Thomas Aquinas College in Santa Paula,

California. Unlike Rand, Thomas Aquinas fought back, making it clear its policy was of nondiscrimination and that it had no interest in changing that. When WASC tried to apply pressure, other colleges and universities began to notice the threat to their autonomy that WASC's diversity standard posed.

By 1994, fourteen schools—including Caltech, Stanford, and USC—were objecting to WASC's decision to promulgate an official "diversity statement" to guide the institutions it accredited. Stanford University president Gerhard Casper made the point as gingerly as possible but nevertheless effectively: "I obviously have no objection to diversity as a general goal," he said. "My objection is to diversity as a standard that is enforceable through the accreditation process." Stanford's faculty senate unanimously backed him up. Caltech president Thomas E. Everhart was less diplomatic. He told WASC flatly that its statement was politically motivated and that WASC leaders should "stick to their knitting."[65]

Martin Trow, a distinguished UC Berkeley sociology professor and former chair of the National Advisory Committee on Accreditation, described the situation this way: "This is a fiercely evangelical movement," he said. WASC's diversity statement "is nothing else than a political position which claims moral superiority to alternatives."[66] The UC Academic Council evidently agreed. Without a dissenting vote, it passed a resolution expressing concern over the "substantial threat to institutional autonomy" WASC's diversity policy represented.

None of this stopped WASC. On February 23, 1994, its fifteen-member commission reaffirmed its policy. Most of the schools that it accredited supported it—though some may have done so only on a very limited basis. UC Berkeley chancellor Chang-Lin Tien, in a break with his academic council, supported the policy based on his understanding that the policy would never be used as a club. In a letter, he wrote: "My decision was based, in part, on assurances from the Accrediting Commission that accreditation will not be withheld on the grounds of diversity, thereby preserving institutional autonomy."

Given the confidentiality of the accreditation process, it is hard to come by information on it. But by the late 1990s, fully 31 percent of law schools and 24 percent of medical schools polled by Welch and Gruhl reported that they "felt pressure" "to take race into account in making admissions decisions" from "accreditation agencies." What is interesting is that Welch and Gruhl didn't ask directly about accreditation agencies. As discussed above, they asked respondents to the poll about pressure from the federal, state, or local government. Only after that did they ask, in a catch-all question, whether respondents had felt pressure from other sources. If they answered "yes," they were asked to specify which groups.[67] The information about accreditors was thus volunteered and likely to be understated.

The two accreditation agencies that the law and medical school respondents would have been referring to are the Council of the American Bar Association's Section on Legal Education and Admissions to the Bar ("ABA") and the Liaison Committee on Medical Education ("LCME"). Neither the ABA nor LCME is an academic institution itself. LCME, for example, describes itself as consisting of "medical educators and administrators, practicing physicians, public members and medical students."[68] The ABA is similar in that practicing lawyers and others are represented.

There is evidence that the pressure from accreditors to increase diversity grew after the 1990s (and we are aware of no evidence to the contrary). Just a few years ago, one of us (Heriot) cooperated with the National Association of Scholars in conducting a round of state public-records requests of state medical schools. Out of the sixteen schools that have responded or partially responded, half had been cited by LCME for problems with diversity. At the University of Nevada, Reno School of Medicine, for example, the 2009 Survey Team found that "the numbers of students and faculty of diverse backgrounds have been consistently low," and the 2012 Survey Team found the school to be "noncompliant" with diversity accreditation standards.[69] Similarly, the 2009 Survey Team for Wright State University's Boonshoft School of Medicine reported:

> Diversity of the student body has been somewhat problematic. There has been a steady decline in the number of African-American student applicants and students from 309 applicants in 2001 to 241 in 2007, and from 50 total African-American students in 2001 to 32 in 2007. At the same time there are no Hispanic students. The number of Asian students has increased.[70]

As a result, the accreditor classified Wright State's diversity as an area "of transition, whose outcome could affect the school's ongoing compliance with accreditation standards."

At the University of South Alabama College of Medicine, the accreditor named diversity as an area of "partial or substantial noncompliance," finding that "[d]iversity among faculty and students has not increased notably in the past seven years."[71]

When complaints like these are made by the Survey Team, the medical school is expected to fix them or face the consequences.

Like LCME, the ABA requires law schools to demonstrate their commitment to diversity. Not long after *Grutter*, the ABA ramped up its requirements for diversity, apparently in the mistaken belief that *Grutter* empowered it rather than actual law schools.[72] In essence, the ABA was insulating schools that give large preferences from competition on issues like bar passage rate with schools that would rather give smaller preferences or none at all.

The ABA is fully aware that the only way to comply with its standards is to give preferential treatment to students from designated minorities. In its amicus brief in *Grutter*, it told the

Court that "race-conscious admissions are essential to increasing minority representation in the legal system." "[I]t is unquestionable," the ABA wrote, "that the improvement in minority participation...has been achieved largely by the use of race-conscious admissions policies such as those under attack here."[73] Nine years later, it took the same position in its amicus curiae brief in *Fisher I*.[74]

The ABA has not hesitated to overrule the educational judgment of the law schools it regulates. In 2006, for example, the Charleston School of Law unexpectedly failed to win accreditation from the ABA after a favorable recommendation from its accreditation committee. According to news reports, the ABA's concerns focused in part on race.[75] Final accreditation was not awarded until the dean had declared that "[w]hatever we have to do [to win accreditation], we'll do it" and a new director of diversity was publicly announced.[76]

The case of George Mason University School of Law is particularly troubling. Its story began with the ABA's site-evaluation team visit in 2000. The site-evaluation team was unhappy that only 6.5 percent of entering day students and 9.5 percent of entering evening students were minority members.[77]

Nobody could argue that GMU's problem was lack of outreach. Even the site-evaluation team conceded that GMU had a "very active effort to recruit minorities." Indeed, it described those efforts at length. It noted, however, that GMU had been "unwilling to engage in any significant preferential affirmative action admissions program." Since most law schools were willing to admit minority students with dramatically lower academic credentials, GMU was at a recruitment disadvantage.[78]

GMU's faculty members did not all have the same views on affirmative action. Some members considered even small admissions preferences to be morally repugnant; others believed admissions preferences would hurt, rather than help, their intended beneficiaries. But some were willing to put a slight thumb on the scale in favor of African Americans and Hispanics. What set GMU apart from many law schools was that a strong majority opposed the overwhelming preferential treatment commonly practiced elsewhere. The site-evaluation team noted its "serious concerns" with GMU's policy.

Over the next few years, the ABA repeatedly refused to renew GMU's accreditation, citing its lack of a "significant preferential affirmative action program" and supposed lack of diversity. Back and forth the negotiations went. Although GMU could and did step up its already-extensive recruitment efforts, it was forced to back away from its opposition to significant preferential treatment. It was thus able to raise the proportion of minority members in its entering class to 10.98 percent in 2001 and 16.16 percent in 2002.[79]

None of this was enough. The ABA didn't want slow, deliberate movement in its direction; it wanted utter capitulation. Shortly after the Court's decision in *Grutter*, an emboldened ABA summoned the GMU president and the law school dean to appear before it personally and threatened the institution with revocation of its accreditation on account of its alleged diversity problem. This would not just make GMU ineligible for federal funds, including student loans; it would also cut its students off from sitting for the bar examination, since nearly all states require a degree from an ABA-approved law school for that. GMU responded by further lowering minority admissions standards and expanding resources devoted to diversity, all in hopes of soothing the ABA's wrath. As a result, 17.3 percent of its entering students in 2003 and 19 percent in 2004 were minority members.[80]

Still the ABA was not satisfied. This time its focus was on African American students specifically. "Of the 99 minority students in 2003, only 23 were African-American; of 111 minority students in 2004, the number of African Americans held at 23," the ABA complained. It didn't seem to matter that sixty-three

African Americans had been offered admission or that the only way to admit more was to lower admissions standards to alarming levels. It didn't even matter that many students admitted under those circumstances would incur heavy debt but never graduate and pass the bar. GMU's skepticism about race preferences was heresy, and the ABA was determined to stamp it out.[81]

GMU finally got its reaccreditation after six long years of abuse—just in time for the next round in the seven-year re-accreditation process.[82] Sure enough, the ABA's 2007 site-evaluation team report again raised concerns that GMU was not in compliance with ABA diversity standards.

Meanwhile, an important question was not being asked: What happened to the minority students who were admitted in the first round, against the GMU faculty's better judgment? The ABA was apparently not so interested in that. The ABA was not making an educational judgment about pedagogy; it was preening itself in an effort to show its highly superficial concern for social justice (as well as making sure an up-and-coming law school would not be able to improve its bar passage rate and hence its ranking).

But GMU's dean, Daniel D. Polsby, was very interested in the fate of his students. In a letter dated January 3, 2008, to the ABA's Hulett H. Askew, responding to the ABA's 2007 site-evaluation report, Polsby patiently explained the damage inflicted by the ABA's enforcement of diversity standards.[83]

As the ABA failed to recognize, when students attend a school at which their entering academic credentials are well below those of their peers, they will usually earn grades to match. During the period from 2003 to 2005, while GMU was under pressure to increase its racial diversity, African American students experienced dramatically higher rates of academic failure (defined in GMU's academic rules as a GPA below 2.15). Fully 45 percent of African American law students at GMU experienced academic failure, as opposed to only 4 percent of students of other races.[84]

Polsby put the problem plainly: "We have an obligation to refrain from victimizing applicants, regardless of race or color, by admitting them to an educational program in which they appear likely to fail."[85]

Part of the tragedy, of course, is that the empirical evidence indicates that many of these students would have stood a greater chance at success in their goal of becoming lawyers if they had attended a law school at which their entering academic credentials had been more like the median student's. But the ABA prevented that.

If institutional autonomy is to be protected, the solution is obvious. Accreditors should be prevented from intervening in ideologically charged issues like diversity. It is highly unlikely that the Supreme Court would have defended the University of Michigan Law School if the university had argued, "We discriminate because otherwise our ideologically skewed accrediting agency would cut us off from federal aid and cut our students off from taking the bar exam." The U.S. Department of Education should not recognize an accreditor that attempts to bully institutions in this way. If it persists in recognizing such accreditors, Congress should act. Unlike other efforts to discourage race-preferential admissions, this one could be reasonably popular among higher education officials. At least in other contexts, colleges and universities are seldom enthusiastic about being bullied.

CONCLUSION

In *Grutter*, the Supreme Court abandoned its practice of placing a strong thumb on the scale in favor of nondiscrimination. Instead, it deferred to a discriminator. Given what we know about colleges and universities, their motivations, their own ideological leanings, and the pressures put on them to engage in race-preferential admissions, there was nothing to justify this.

Race Preferences and Discrimination against Asian Americans in Higher Education

Lance Izumi & Rowena Itchon

" **I**n my mind," an anonymous Asian American high school student wrote in 2020, "introduction of race into the dialogue is dangerous in and of itself," because it "perpetuates stereotypes, both among the population and in students themselves."[1] While written to oppose the repeal of California's Proposition 209, which banned government discrimination based on race and other factors, this student's appeal should also be a reminder of the painful history of injecting race into American laws, which adversely affected various groups, especially Asian Americans.

The list of government actions explicitly directed against Asians has ranged from the Chinese Exclusion Act, which stopped immigration of Chinese laborers into the United States; to the Gentlemen's Agreement of 1907, which restricted Japanese immigration; to California laws restricting land ownership by the Japanese; to the Tydings-McDuffie Act, which limited Filipino immigration; to Franklin Roosevelt's Executive Order 9066, which resulted in the relocation of Japanese Americans to internment camps for the duration of World War II.[2]

Yet, while laws explicitly directed against Asian Americans have been repealed or overturned, other less explicit laws and practices continue to work against Asian Americans. Nowhere has this anti-Asian bias been stronger and more insidious than in higher education admissions.

In California, for example, prior to 1995, the selection process for admission to the prestigious University of California system included race as one significant factor, among others. This was then used to advantage students of certain racial backgrounds and disadvantage students from other backgrounds, including Asian Americans.

Further, UC's use of race extended beyond admissions to a wide variety of other programs. In fact, the use of race was so widespread and such a hodgepodge throughout the then nine-campus system that, according to John Aubrey Douglass, a senior research fellow at the Center for Studies in Higher Education at UC Berkeley's Goldman School of Public Policy, "The cumulative process of incorporating racial preferences into university admissions practices and faculty hiring did not create a coherent policy regime."[3]

"Campuses within the system had seemingly created their own array of affirmative action programs and their own set of admissions practices," noted Douglass. "Arguably, no single person in the University of California had a solid understanding of affirmative action programs that had sprung up over the years or the discretionary use of racial preferences in campus decision-making."[4]

While no one may have been able to explain the true breadth, reach, and impact of race preferences throughout the UC system, one thing was beyond doubt—Asian Americans were hurt by the system's race-preference regime.

Examples of the victimization of Asian Americans were often stark and shocking. For instance, a 1995 study by the Pacific Research Institute (PRI), a California-based public policy think tank, used UC's own data to analyze admissions results at UC schools of medicine.

The PRI study found that, in 1993, the UC Davis School of Medicine accepted African Americans at thirteen times the rate of Japanese Americans, with 23 out of 243 African American applicants accepted versus only 1 out of 90 Japanese American applicants.[5] Mexican Americans were accepted at nearly fourteen times the rate of Korean Americans, with 40 out of 235 Mexican American applicants accepted, compared to only 3 out of 241 Korean American applicants.[6]

UC Davis argued at the time that it gave no special preference based on race or ethnicity, but the PRI study calculated the probability of such discrepancies in acceptance rates occurring by chance as one in a million.[7]

Indeed, applicants from underrepresented minority groups, including African Americans, Hispanics, and Native Americans, were awarded 20 to 30 percent of admissions, even though they were only about 10 percent of the applicant pool.[8]

Particularly interesting was the fact that, even holding students' undergraduate institution constant, UC's race-preference system disadvantaged Asian American students.

The PRI study looked at UC medical school applicants who had received their undergraduate degrees at UC Irvine in 1993. Among UCI graduates, applicants from underrepresented minority groups were nearly three times as likely to be accepted to a UC medical school as were Vietnamese American applicants, who had a group GPA of 3.8, the highest of any group. Indeed, two-thirds of Vietnamese American applicants who were denied admission had a mean GPA that was higher than the mean GPA of the underrepresented minority applicants who were admitted.[9]

Such obvious discrimination against Asian Americans was a key reason why, in 1995, the UC Board of Regents adopted SP-1, a policy that eliminated the use of race, ethnicity, and gender as factors in admissions and required that between 50 and 75 percent of admissions be based solely on academic achievement.[10]

California state assemblyman Nao Takasugi, a Japanese American who for many years was the only Asian American member of the state legislature, testified to the UC regents in favor of eliminating race preferences in admissions and recalled his experience being interned at a camp during World War II:

> During the internment, I saw families torn apart, ruined and deprived of their rights as Americans. Let us be clear, what we are discussing today with UC's special preferential admissions policy is nothing more or nothing less than state-mandated discrimination based on race, the same discrimination that locked me and my family away in the prison of injustice in [the internment camp at] Gila River, Arizona.[11]

As the statistical evidence showed, Asian Americans were being affected very personally by UC's race-preference system. Ward Connerly, the fearless African American UC regent who proposed SP-1, observed that underrepresented minority applicants "who score very low in academic achievement but who are from relatively affluent families get boosted towards the front of the line on race alone," while "Asians and whites who score in the top levels on academics and who are from relatively poor families are dropped way down the admissions line based solely on race."[12]

UC's race-preference policies and programs, therefore, acted as the very definition of government-sanctioned systemic racism against Asian Americans.

Following the UC regents' vote, in 1996 Californians approved Proposition 209, a ballot initiative that eliminated race-based preferences throughout California government. Modeled on the federal Civil Rights Act of 1964, the initiative language stated: "The state shall not discriminate against, or grant preferential treatment to, any individual or group on the basis of race, sex, color, ethnicity, or national origin in the operation of public employment, public education, or public contracting."[13]

Proposition 209's impact has been huge—not only in California, but across the nation. In the years following the passage of California's landmark initiative, Washington, Arizona, Michigan, Idaho, Nebraska, Oklahoma, New Hampshire, and Florida have enacted prohibitions against the use of race preferences in admissions to institutions of higher education.[14]

Yet, despite the positive influence of Proposition 209, race preferences continue to be used in higher education in many places, to the detriment of Asian Americans. And even in states that have outlawed race preferences, preference supporters continue to launch efforts to repeal these bans.

CALIFORNIA: THE FIRST ATTEMPT TO OVERTHROW PROPOSITION 209: SENATE CONSTITUTIONAL AMENDMENT 5

The first statewide attempt to repeal Proposition 209 was in 2012, when California state senator Edward Hernandez (D-West Covina) introduced Senate Constitutional Amendment 5,[15] a ballot measure that asked voters to eliminate Proposition 209's ban on the use of race preferences in admissions at California's public universities and colleges.

Hernandez had begun his effort the prior year through conventional means, by introducing a senate bill that, he hoped, would pass the legislature and be signed into law by the governor. Senate Bill 185 authorized the University of California and required the California State University systems to "consider" race "so long as no preference is given" in their admission policies.[16] The bill didn't bother to explain how these universities were supposed to "consider" race without giving a preference on the basis of race. While it passed the assembly and senate, the bill was ultimately vetoed by Governor Jerry Brown. In his veto message, Brown wrote that he agreed with the spirit of the bill but that "Signing this bill is unlikely to impact how Proposition 209 is ultimately interpreted by the courts; it will just encourage the 209 advocates to file more costly and confusing lawsuits."[17] On this issue, Brown applied his self-described "canoe" style of governance: paddle a little to the left, then a little to the right, taking you right down the middle.

Not ready to give up, Hernandez turned SB 185 into a ballot initiative. He had reason to be optimistic. California's political and demographic makeup was on his side. For a proposed constitutional amendment to make it onto the state ballot, it must first pass the state assembly and senate. Democratic supermajorities in both houses assured smooth sailing. Moreover, by 2012, California had become a solidly blue state, with nearly 44 percent[18] of the population registering Democrat and a 56 percent majority minority population.[19] If SCA 5 made it onto the ballot, its chances of passage seemed very good.

In making his case, Hernandez argued that because of Proposition 209, "there has been a precipitous drop in the percentage of Latino, African American, and Native American students at California public universities, despite the fact that those same groups have seen steady increases in their percentages of college-eligible high school graduates."[20]

However, Hernandez's charges that certain racial groups were disadvantaged by Proposition 209 could not be substantiated. In publicly accessible data, in both absolute numbers and percentages, more minority students were attending the University of California.[21] Comparing data from 1996 (the year Proposition 209 was passed) to data from 2013, the African American student population increased slightly, from 4 percent to 4.3 percent (by comparison, 6.6 percent of California's population is African American). The percentage of Hispanic students rose from 14.3

percent to 27.8 percent (38.2 percent of California's population is Hispanic). Asian American students increased from 32 percent to 35.9 percent (13.9 percent of California's population is Asian American). The only racial group with decreased student population was whites, whose share fell from 41 percent to 27.9 percent (39.4 percent of the state's population is white).

Further, the UC system already led the nation in its admission of economically disadvantaged students. In 2011–12, 41 percent of the enrolled students at UC and CSU were Pell Grant recipients.[22]

In addition to the majority of legislators, SCA 5 also enjoyed the support of Sacramento's most powerful unions, including the American Federation of State, County, and Municipal Employees (AFSCME), the California Teachers Association, the California Nurses Association, and the California Hospital Association.[23]

They were also joined by California's higher education establishment. Long opposed to Proposition 209, California's progressive academics saw SCA 5 as an opportunity to bring back race-preferential admissions policies to state colleges and universities. UCLA chancellor Gene D. Block wrote an open letter to students and faculty opposing Proposition 209: "Nearly two decades have passed since Californians voted to end affirmative action in admission to public colleges and universities. Today it is clear that we have suffered for it."[24] Ironically, he acknowledged in his letter that an offensive flyer sent to UCLA's Asian American Studies Center at the time was "another horrifying reminder" of racism and bigotry. "What matters is how we respond," he wrote. "We must support each other. We must listen to one another."[25] Nevertheless, he seemed to turn a deaf ear to the voices of Asian Americans, who he surely knew would be negatively impacted by the repeal of Proposition 209.

SCA 5 won easy passage in the state senate in January 2014. Its principal coauthor was African American assemblyman Steven Bradford (D-Gardena), and its coauthors were some of the

Democratic Party's heaviest hitters, including Darrell Steinberg (D-Sacramento), Kevin De Leon (D-Los Angeles), and
Ricardo Lara (D-Long Beach). Senators of Asian descent Ted
Lieu (D-Riverside), Carol Liu (D-La Cañada-Flintridge), and
Leland Yee (D-San Francisco, who in the following year pleaded
guilty to felony racketeering charges), were among those who
voted for SCA 5.

Not long after SCA 5's passage in the state senate, Chinese-
language media outlets began covering the legislation. Asian
American parents were angered by the bill, fearing that their
children would be denied admission to universities in favor of
applicants from other racial groups. Their fear was justified. The
most comprehensive study at the time, by researchers Thomas
Espenshade and Alexandria Radford in their 2009 book *No Longer
Separate, Not Yet Equal*, found that, in admissions practices at the
most highly selective private universities, "Asian applicants have
67 percent lower odds of admission than white applicants with
comparable test scores."[26]

While Asians are vastly diverse—with different religions,
ethnicities, languages, and cultures—the one thing nearly all
have in common is a deep, almost sacred, reverence for education. In South Korea, for example, one of the allegations that
led to the impeachment of President Park Geun-hye involved
a close advisor who used her connections to get her daughter
into a prestigious university in Seoul. South Koreans found this
especially irksome, reported *Los Angeles Times* journalist Steven
Boroweic.[27] He explained that in South Korea "education is a
national passion and competition for spots at top schools is cutthroat."[28] The president of the college was eventually forced to
resign over the scandal.

In California, SCA 5 touched a nerve among Asian Americans. While registered mostly as Democrats, they have historically stayed away from state politics. "Chinese people care about

education, but do not do politics," said Cathy and Alan Zhang, who hosted a San Francisco Bay Area radio show for Chinese Americans.[29] It was Asian-language media outlets like those of the Zhangs, along with social media, that brought SCA 5 under intense scrutiny.

The ballot measure became a hot issue on Facebook. Bulletin board systems (BBS) like Chinese-language forum mitbbs. com held lengthy discussions. WeChat, a phone-based messaging platform, and Weibo, a Chinese-language social network, were critical in organizing the Chinese American community.[30] A Change.org petition started by Chunhua Liao, a scientist and father of two young boys, drew more than 114,000 signatures.[31]

Asian American communities also began organizing rallies and town-hall meetings in the San Gabriel Valley in Southern California and Silicon Valley in Northern California, both areas with large Asian American populations. "No! No! No!" a crowd chanted in response to "SCA 5" shouted over a megaphone outside a hall in Cupertino,[32] an affluent community and headquarters of tech powerhouse Apple and other prominent technology firms. As the *Los Angeles Times* reported, "the coalition that shot down SCA-5 was not a traditional political movement.... Some were simply mothers with children preparing for college."[33]

While the most active opposition came from Chinese American groups—such as the Joint Chinese University Alumni Association, Chinese Alliance for Equality, and the Silicon Valley Chinese Association—other Asian American groups joined forces, including the Vietnamese Cambodia and Laos Association of America and the Indian American Forum for Political Education.[34] There were also pan-Asian groups, such as the 80-20 National Asian American PAC, and the American Civil Rights Institute, founded by Ward Connerly, whose leadership had been instrumental in the passage of Proposition 209.

Although SCA 5 was couched in terms of "diversity," many

Asian Americans were taken aback by Sacramento's progressive politicians who brushed over the fact that the measure discriminated against their children.

"I am so appalled to see this bill was proposed," said the father of a tenth-grader.[35] "My wife and I spend the majority of our salaries on our daughter's education so that she can take piano lessons and learn all the skills that will get her to better universities one day.... College admission should be solely based on merit. SCA-5 reverses the history and that's not American."[36]

Protestors were often seen carrying signs quoting civil rights leader Martin Luther King's "I Have a Dream" speech: "a dream that my four little children will not be judged by the color of their skin but the content of their character." SCA 5 soon became known as the Skin Color Act.[37]

It was Asian American politicians who drew the most fire. State senators Ted Lieu, Leland Yee, and Carol Liu were bombarded with thousands of phone calls and emails from constituents who believed that race preferences would ultimately hurt Asian Americans. The backlash forced the three to backpedal their support. In a joint letter to Hernandez and Assembly Speaker John Pérez, they asked that SCA 5 be prevented from advancing further. "As lifelong advocates for the Asian American and other communities, we would never support a policy that we believed would negatively impact our children," the letter stated.[38]

Meanwhile, in the assembly, some Democrats began to waffle. According to an analysis by the *San Jose Mercury News* at the time, if two or more of the eight assembly Democrats belonging to the Asian and Pacific Islander Legislative Caucus voted "no," the bill would fail.[39] Caucus chairman Paul Fong (D-San Jose) began to have concerns about the proposal: "I believe every student should have equal access and opportunity to a quality and affordable education," said Fong, a former teacher.[40]

Ed Chau (D-Monterey Park) was confronted by protestors

outside his district office.[41] He pledged not to support SCA 5 in its current form. Phil Ting (D-San Francisco) announced that he wasn't ready to vote for it,[42] as did assembly member Sharon Quirk-Silva (D-Fullerton). Quirk-Silva was in a competitive race with Korean American Republican Young Kim, who came out against SCA 5.[43] Congresswoman Judy Chu, a progressive Asian American politician who represented Pasadena and the San Gabriel Valley, also opposed it.

By March 17, 2014, just six weeks after its passage in the state senate, Speaker Pérez announced that he was withdrawing SCA 5 from consideration because he did not have the votes to pass it. He sent the bill back to the senate, essentially killing the bill for the rest of the legislative session.

Darrell Steinberg, president pro tempore of the state senate, said in a statement that he was "deeply concerned anytime one ethnic group turns on another," essentially blaming Asian Americans.[44] He didn't see the irony of his statement, in that it was actually Sacramento's progressive politicians who had turned on—or at least forgotten—their own constituents.

As is the standard political practice on thorny policy issues, Pérez and Steinberg created a "task force" to attempt to mollify all sides. The task was to look for ways to "expand access" to the public university system and "engage in a very broad conversation with all interested stakeholders, with academics and with leaders of our institutions of higher education to understand where we are and where we'd like to get as a state to have the broadest access to our public university system as possible."[45]

Six years later, the pursuit of race preferences would return in California.

WASHINGTON STATE: THE ATTEMPT TO OVERTHROW INITIATIVE 200: INITIATIVE 1000 AND REFERENDUM 88

After California passed Proposition 209 in 1996, Washington State followed suit in 1998 with a similar ban. Initiative 200 (I-200) prohibited discrimination or giving preferential treatment based on race, sex, color, ethnicity, or national origin in public education and government employment and contracting.[46]

But two decades later, emboldened by the "equity" movement, whose ranks included progressive educators and union members, the Washington legislature attempted to roll back I-200 by defining the terms of the original law idiosyncratically.

Under the proposed Initiative 1000,[47] *preferential treatment* was prohibited. But the initiative defined "preferential treatment" as using race, ethnicity, national origin, sex, color, or age as the *sole factor* for selecting a less-qualified candidate over someone more qualified. *Affirmative action*, however, would be allowed. I-1000 defined "affirmative action" as using the same characteristics as *factors* when considering a person for educational or employment opportunities. This bit of wordsmithing would have allowed the state to implement affirmative-action laws and policies while continuing to "ban" preferential treatment and discrimination. As crafted, both laws would be compatible.

I-1000 also established the Governor's Commission on Diversity, Equity, and Inclusion that would be responsible for ensuring compliance and producing an annual report on the progress of state agencies for achieving the goals of the initiative. The governor would be responsible for appointing most members of the commission, which would have the power to set and enforce college admissions and hiring goals.

Like the progressive legislators in Sacramento, Olympia's political elites were confident that I-1000 would sail through. The rumblings from Washington's Asian American community were a mere distraction. Indeed, concerned citizens who made the trip to Olympia felt dismissed by Democrat legislators. One Asian American recounted the trip in a post on the *WA Asians for Equality* blog:

We were treated very badly by many legislators in Olympia (all were Democrats). We could not get appointments with them. Out of our [repeated] requests, [Senate] Majority Leader, Andy Billig, met us. Yet, he spoke to us in a condescending manner throughout the meeting. He even said that he did us a favor meeting us, because we were not from his district!—Really? Senator Billig, as a Senate Majority Leader, we are very sure you meet people out of your districts A LOT! [emphasis in original][48]

During the legislative session for I-1000, more than three hundred Asian Americans showed up in Olympia at five in the morning to attend the committee hearing and voice their opposition.[49] In contrast, one observer wrote that only "a handful of executives from special interest organizations testified in support of I-1000. And on April 22, 2019, more than 160 concerned Asians lobbied against I-1000 in Olympia, in contrast to fewer than 25 who showed up in support of I-1000. I-1000 supporters had to cancel their planned event in Olympia due to lack of community support."[50]

Nevertheless, I-1000 passed along party lines, 56-42 in the state house and 26-22 in the state senate, with all Democrats voting in favor with the exception of Representative Brian Blake and Senators Tim Sheldon and Mark Mullet, who voted with Republicans.[51]

Mullet would pay for his independence. *WA Asians for Equality* wrote that Mullet was being

attacked when he "regularly bucked the Democrat caucus, often being the only member to cast certain votes." His NO vote on I-1000 is listed as a proof of his disobedience of the Democratic Party. Yet, Senator Mullet's vote clearly represented the will of his constituents.... He stood against pressure from his own party and voted NO on I-1000. At the [Senate] Floor, Senator Mullet said that he made a verbal promise to these groups (i.e. us) before the session started and was going to hold that verbal promise and would be voting NO.[52]

The writer went on to urge both Democrats and Republicans in Mullet's district to cast their vote for him.

I-1000 was set to become law in July. Democratic state senator Bob Hasegawa, who voted for the initiative but was conscious of the opposition's deep disappointment, suggested they collect "200,000" signatures to run a ballot measure to repeal the law.[53]

That's exactly what they did.

In Washington State, a bill can be prevented from becoming law through a veto referendum. To qualify such a referendum for the ballot, supporters need to gather and submit nearly 130,000 signatures ninety days following the adjournment of the legislative session during which the bill was passed.[54]

Within months, Washington Asians for Equality volunteers, most with little political experience, collected 213,268 signatures, astonishing Olympia's political elite. On August 7, 2019, Washington's secretary of state certified Referendum Measure 88 (R-88) for the November general election. "We set a record for the number of signatures backing a referendum measure," said Linda Yang, a leader of Washington Asians for Equality. "And this is the first time in Washington State's history and in this country's history that Asian Americans led the pack and sent a referendum measure to the ballot."[55]

Opponents of I-1000 faced a Who's Who of progressive groups, including the ACLU of Washington, the Washington State Democratic Central Committee, the Washington Education Association, Democrats for Diversity and Inclusion, El Centro La Raza, the NAACP, and even Microsoft. All were united in the goal of reversing the "inequitable trends" resulting from I-200.[56]

The Washington Fairness campaign argued that I-1000 would

allow the state to "take tangible, collective action to level the playing field for working families with the most urgent unmet needs, and we should strive to make Washington a place where someone's race, ethnicity, gender, or other status isn't a generational determinant of their ability to thrive or share equitably in the prosperity afforded to our region."[57]

"The fight over I-1000," wrote John Carlson, a Seattle radio host who, with the help of Ward Connerly, led the I-200 campaign two decades earlier, is "a classic clash between equality and equity. Equality means everyone plays by the same rules. Equity requires the rules to be different because people are different." But he noted that while the fight was familiar, the players weren't.[58]

During I-200, Carlson said he "tried but failed to engage the Asian-American community in that campaign. The tech community in those days was also largely uninterested. Almost every corner of the state's cultural and political establishment was against us."[59] This time, however, it was different. After two decades of largely staying away from the political fray, Washington's Asian Americans were all in.

"In this state, there is a dark history with Chinese Americans," said Kan Qiu, co-chair of Let People Vote and a small-business owner from Bellevue.[60] "Back in the 1880s, right after Chinese labor was used to finish the transcontinental railroad, back then, Chinese immigrants were the second largest ethnic group, behind white, in the State of Washington."[61] Qiu noted that discrimination was common during those times, spreading fears of Chinese immigrants stealing jobs. Eventually, exclusionary laws were passed, many of which disallowed land ownership for Asian immigrants. It's this sensitivity to the region's racist past that informed Qiu's opposition to affirmative action.[62]

To Asian Americans, I-1000 was "a 21st-century Chinese Exclusion Act" that would "bring back different rules for different races.... They have co-opted the rhetoric of identity politics and used it to attack progressives," wrote Christopher Rufo, a Seattle-based writer and filmmaker.[63] Progressives "claim to fight for diversity but they oppose the interests of 'inconvenient minorities' like Asian Americans, who contradict their belief that all minorities are victims of oppression."[64]

It was Washington's Asian Americans who called out I-1000's authors' sleight of hand in redefining Initiative 200. "I-1000's ballot title also claims that it doesn't allow 'preferential treatment', but only because the measure changes the definition of preferential treatment," argued Washington Asians for Equality.[65] "In short, it exists only when one applicant is chosen over another solely because of race. That means discrimination can take place if race is used in addition to one other quality. This is the very definition of discrimination. I-1000's ballot title claims that it does not allow 'quotas'. The truth is that racial quotas would be implemented... with a 'disparity' study to count by race, goals to enroll and hire by race, and timetables enforced by bureaucrats."[66]

More than $1 million was raised for the campaign, primarily from Chinese American business owners and tech employees from the Seattle suburbs. Washington Asians for Equality also collected more than 650 donations from Microsoft employees, even as the company, headquartered in Redmond, officially endorsed I-1000. As of mid-October 2019, not a single Microsoft worker had made a donation to support I-1000.[67]

The campaign also collected more than 270 donations from Amazon employees by May. Employees at Google, Facebook, and eBay also donated, suggesting that while senior management might have subscribed to the "diversity" party line, armies of tech workers weren't impressed by identity politics.[68]

"Close to 2,000 people donated to this Referendum," said Yang. "This is a true grassroots campaign.... The other side is dishonest. They owed signature collectors $1.3 million... and launched a new PAC to avoid paying down the debt."[69] Yang was referring to the pro-I-1000 One Washington Equality campaign, which ran out of money and started a new PAC in order to avoid paying its signature-gatherers.

"The message from Washington Asians for Equality is simple," wrote Rufo, "race-based discrimination is wrong. Progressive activists claim that they oppose racism, but I-1000's affirmative-action program would add another layer of bureaucracy, with the sole purpose of discriminating based on race—the definition of 'institutionalized racism.'"[70]

Referendum 88 was ultimately defeated narrowly by 50.4 percent of the vote with a margin of just 14,000 votes, meaning that I-1000 would not go into effect. Yang, an émigré who had come to the United States with just $200 in her pocket, summed it up: "The other side has tried to portray this extraordinarily successful campaign as a group of Asian Americans worried about losing spots at [the University of Washington]. This is clearly about a much larger issue. This is about a basic fundamental American value: Individual rights for every person! Race has no place in American life or law."[71]

HARVARD UNIVERSITY: RACE-PREFERENTIAL ADMISSIONS

It turned out that 2014 was an important year in Asian Americans' fight against race discrimination. Not only did Asian Americans defeat the attempt to overturn Proposition 209 in California, but also a lawsuit was brought in federal court against Harvard University, alleging that the university "is engaging in a campaign of invidious discrimination by strictly limiting the number of Asian Americans it will admit each year and by engaging in racial balancing year after year."[72]

The lawsuit was brought by the organization Students for Fair Admissions (SFFA), which charged that "Asian Americans must have far higher qualifications than other students to be admitted to Harvard" and that "Asian Americans face an uphill battle, as Harvard will cap their admission in the belief that too many Asian Americans will destroy the character of the student body."[73]

SFFA's complaint alleged that Harvard violated Title VI of the U.S. Civil Rights Act of 1964, which prohibits discrimination based on race and ethnicity. The complaint said that there were four ways that Harvard was violating Title VI.[74]

First, the complaint alleged that Harvard used a so-called "holistic" admissions system "to disguise the fact that it holds Asian Americans to a higher standard than other students and essentially forces them to compete against each other."

For example, survey data showed that Asian American students entering Harvard in 2013 had an average SAT score of 2299, while entering African American students' average score was 2107.[75]

Second, Harvard was alleged to engage in racial balancing, which creates a largely set racial composition of the student body. "Over an extended period," said the complaint, "Harvard's admission and enrollment figures for each racial category have shown almost no change." Every year, the same percentages of African Americans, Hispanics, whites, and Asian Americans were admitted, even though application rates and qualifications for each racial group underwent changes over time.[76]

The Asian American admission rate at Harvard always seemed to hover between 18 and 20 percent. This years-long stability in racial composition is, according to SFFA, "the deliberate result of systemwide intentional racial discrimination designed to achieve a predetermined racial balance of its student body."[77]

Third, SFFA charged that Harvard used race not just as a plus factor, but as a "dominant factor," which accounted for "the remarkably low admission rate for high-achieving Asian-American applicants" despite their broad diversity and eclectic abilities and interests.[78]

Finally, the complaint alleged that Harvard used race as a key factor in admissions when race-neutral alternatives, such as socioeconomic status, could promote diversity equally as well.[79]

The U.S. Supreme Court has stated that race can be used as a factor in university admissions if it serves a compelling interest. One compelling interest the Court has been willing to defer to is the promotion of student diversity. Yet, the Court has said that applicants must be evaluated as individuals and race cannot be used as the defining feature of the admissions evaluation.

The trial began in 2018 in front of U.S. District Court Judge Allison Burroughs, an Obama appointee who had gained national notoriety in 2017 for issuing a temporary restraining order against President Donald Trump's ban on travel from top terrorism-promoting countries.

One ominous sign for the plaintiffs came in the run-up to the trial, when Judge Burroughs ruled that Harvard did not have to produce any data on its widely criticized history of anti-Jewish admissions practices.[80]

In order to prove empirically that Harvard discriminated against Asian American applicants, the plaintiffs relied on expert testimony and research by Duke University professor of economics Peter Arcidiacono. In his expert report for the case, Arcidiacono put together an extensive two-decades-long admissions database that allowed him to analyze how various factors, including race and ethnicity, affected admissions decisions at Harvard.[81]

Arcidiacono's findings were shocking. First, he found that Asian American applicants "as a whole are stronger on many objective measures than any other racial/ethnic group including test scores, academic achievement, and extracurricular activities." Specifically, Asian Americans' average SAT score was 25 points higher than that of white applicants, 154 points higher than that of Hispanic applicants, and 218 points higher than that of African American applicants. Further, Asian Americans had the highest academic index, which is the combined score for standardized testing and high school performance.[82]

Yet, despite this overall excellence, he found:

> Race plays a significant role in admissions decisions. Consider the example of an Asian-American applicant who is male, is not disadvantaged, and has other characteristics that result in a 25% chance of admission. Simply changing the race of this applicant to white—and leaving all his other characteristics the same—would increase his chance of admission to 36%. Changing his race to Hispanic (and leaving all other characteristics the same) would increase his chance of admission to 77%. Changing his race to African-American (again, leaving all other characteristics the same) would increase his chance of admission to 95%.[83]

In fact, "Despite being more academically qualified than the other three major racial/ethnic groups (whites, African Americans, and Hispanics), Asian-American applicants had the lowest admissions rates." Harvard's own data "show that this has been true for every admissions cycle for the classes of 2000 to 2019."[84]

A key way that Harvard penalizes Asian Americans is to give them relatively low personal ratings, which entails judgments on traits such as likability, integrity, helpfulness, courage, and kindness.[85] Arcidiacono found that Asian Americans in the top decile in the academic rating received a significantly lower score in personal rating than "African Americans at the third decile (from the bottom) of the academic index."[86]

Arcidiacono concluded that removing racial and ethnic preferences would have increased Asian American admissions by more than 46 percent over a six-year period.[87]

Harvard, of course, disputed Arcidiacono's findings. The university's expert witnesses said that their own analyses showed no evidence of discrimination against Asian Americans. Interestingly, though, research by Harvard's own Office of Institutional Research (OIR), prepared a year before the lawsuit was filed, found that Asian American applicants, on average, had stronger academic credentials than other applicants and would make up 43 percent of the admitted class based on academic credentials alone.[88] In contrast, remember that, over decades, the Asian American share of Harvard admissions was below 20 percent.

Like Arcidiacono's research, Harvard's own OIR research showed that the use of personal and extracurricular scores had a negative effect on the admissions rate of Asian Americans but not on the applicants of any other race.[89]

The U.S. Department of Justice weighed in on the Harvard case by filing a statement of interest. According to the statement, "Harvard provides no meaningful criteria to cabin its use of race; uses a vague 'personal rating' that harms Asian-American applicants' chances for admission and may be infected with racial bias; engages in unlawful racial balancing; and has never seriously considered race-neutral alternatives in its more than 45 years of using race to make admissions decisions."[90]

In an accompanying statement, U.S. Attorney General Jeff Sessions specifically said:

> While Harvard admits to using race in its admissions process, it has failed to provide any meaningful criteria to explain how it weighs race against other factors in a candidate's application (e.g., test scores and extracurricular activities), and how it limits its use of race to ensure that no illegal discrimination occurs. Supreme Court precedent requires Harvard to provide such an explanation, which it has failed to do in this case.
>
> Further, the evidence shows that Harvard uses a "personal rating" that may be biased against Asian Americans. Based solely on a review of the applicant's file, Harvard scores its applicants

based on "subjective" factors such as "likability" and being a "good person" with "human qualities." Harvard admits that, on average, it scores Asian-American applicants lower on this "personal rating" than applicants of other races.

Substantial evidence also demonstrates that Harvard admissions officers and committees consistently monitor and manipulate the racial makeup of incoming classes, which has resulted in stable racial demographics in Harvard's admitted classes from year to year. The Supreme Court has called such attempts to "racially balance" the makeup of a student body "patently unconstitutional."[91]

Unfortunately, Judge Burroughs not only decided against SFFA and Asian Americans, she sent Harvard a love letter in the form of her opinion.

Burroughs actually called Harvard's discriminatory admissions "a very fine admissions program."[92] Yet she admitted that Harvard's admissions policy was "not perfect" and that Asian Americans would be admitted at a higher rate "if admissions decisions were made based solely on academic and extracurricular ratings," and she acknowledged that Asian Americans received lower personal ratings, where admissions officers may have "provided tips in the personal rating, particularly to African American and Hispanic applicants."[93]

Further, Burroughs acknowledged, "it may be that there is overt discrimination or implicit bias at work to the disadvantage of Asian American applicants."[94] Such doubt should have discredited Harvard's defense of its admissions system.

Yet, these discriminatory practices against Asian Americans are allowable because Burroughs essentially liked what she saw as the end result of this discrimination:

The students who are admitted to Harvard and choose to attend will live and learn surrounded by all sorts of people, with all sorts of experiences, beliefs and talents. They will have the opportunity to know and understand one another beyond race, as whole individuals with unique histories and experiences.[95]

It never seemed to occur to Burroughs that those Asian Americans who would never attend Harvard are individuals with unique individual experiences, beliefs, and talents. As liberals like to say when it suits their narrative, Asian Americans are not monolithic. But when it comes to college admissions, they are monolithic and, thus, cannot contribute the necessary variety of experiences, which makes them expendable.

Amazingly, not only did Burroughs dismiss Professor Arcidiacono's empirical evidence, she also dismissed Harvard's own OIR research that showed the negative impact of Harvard's race preferences on Asian Americans. Instead, as Asian American Coalition for Education (AACE) director of administration Wenyuan Wu observed, Burroughs took all of Harvard's arguments "at face value."[96]

For instance, the plaintiffs' final brief said: "Why does being Asian American systematically lead to a lower rating of an applicant's personal qualities? SFFA's answer is that Harvard engages in racial stereotyping, a form of intentional discrimination, and that the record contains extensive statistical and other circumstantial evidence to substantiate that charge."[97]

Burroughs's response? In her decision, she said that "the self-selected group of Asian Americans that applied to Harvard...did not possess the personal qualities that Harvard is looking for."[98]

"All in all," said Wu, "the Burroughs ruling is crafted on cherry-picking evidence and a stubborn confirmation bias to validate her presumption of Harvard's innocence." Indeed, "[i]t only reflects the judge's rigid view on campus diversity and an unfortunate failure to look beyond her own preconceived notions of political correctness."[99]

SFFA appealed Judge Burroughs's decision to the U.S. Court of Appeals for the First Circuit.[100] Its opening appellate brief argued that even though Judge Burroughs believed Harvard's claims, Harvard's data and actions show that it "imposes a racial penalty on Asian-American applicants":

> The district court's own "preferred" model proves that Harvard's admissions system has a disproportionately negative effect on Asian Americans vis-à-vis similarly situated white applicants—a penalty that cannot be explained on non-discriminatory grounds under strict scrutiny. But not only did the court find this penalty, Harvard did too. Harvard was aware that admissions officers racially stereotyped Asian-American applicants and, by 2013, it knew that those applicants were suffering an admissions penalty. But Harvard took no steps to remedy the problem—at least not until it was sued. It was then that the admissions numbers for Asian Americans began to sharply rise, Harvard revised its procedures to address racial stereotyping and its broader misuse of race in the personal rating, and Harvard suddenly feigned interest in race-neutral alternatives. It turns out, then, that the suspicions of Asian-American alumni, students, and applicants were right all along: Harvard today engages in the same kind of discrimination and stereotyping that it used to justify quotas on Jewish applicants in the 1920s and 1930s.[101]

While the appeal was pending, there was an important research development. Professor Arcidiacono coauthored a new study, released in April 2020, which accounted for Burroughs's criticisms of his statistical model and still found a "substantial penalty against Asian Americans in [Harvard's] admissions."[102] His findings underscore just how political and ideological Burroughs's decision was.

Nevertheless, in another disappointing outcome, the First Circuit upheld Judge Burroughs's decision.

Thankfully, that decision is not the end of the Harvard case.

SFFA will seek review of the Circuit Court ruling in the U.S. Supreme Court.[103] With luck, at the end of this marathon legal battle, Asian Americans will receive the justice that our nation's laws guarantee.

YALE UNIVERSITY: THE U.S. DEPARTMENT OF JUSTICE DETERMINES YALE VIOLATED THE 1964 CIVIL RIGHTS ACT

For those who may have thought that the U.S. District Court decision in the Harvard case had put an end to investigations into race-based preferences in college admissions, the U.S. Department of Justice (DOJ) put an end to that speculation—at least for a brief moment—by declaring in August 2020 that Yale University had violated Title VI of the 1964 Civil Rights Act, which says that any program receiving federal funding cannot discriminate based on race, color, or national origin.[104]

DOJ's action was in response to a complaint filed by AACE in 2016 on behalf of 132 Asian American organizations. AACE alleged that Yale "applied *de facto* racial quotas, racial stereotypes and higher admissions standards to discriminate against Asian American applicants."[105]

According to DOJ, Yale, which receives a great deal of federal funding in one form or another, violated and continues to violate the Civil Rights Act "by discriminating on the basis of race and national origin in its undergraduate admissions." This discrimination "is long-standing and ongoing."[106]

After a more than two-year investigation, in which it reviewed extensive admissions documentation, analyzed admissions data, and interviewed admissions officials, DOJ found that "Yale's race discrimination imposes undue and unlawful penalties on racially-disfavored applicants, including in particular Asian American and white applicants."[107]

Specifically, Yale's own data showed that Asian American

applicants "have a much lower chance of admission than do Yale's preferred racial groups, even when those Asian Americans have much higher academic qualifications and comparable ratings by Yale's admissions officers."[108]

Each year from 2000 to 2017, Asian Americans were admitted into Yale at rates significantly below their proportion of the applicant pool. During that same time period, Yale granted admission to favored racial groups, such as African Americans and Hispanics, at rates higher than their representation in the applicant pool.[109]

DOJ found, "For the great majority of applicants, Asian American and White applicants have only one-tenth to one-fourth of the likelihood of admissions as African-American applicants with comparable academic credentials."[110]

While the U.S. Supreme Court allows race to be used as one factor in university admissions, racial considerations in admissions cannot unduly burden those, such as Asian Americans, who are not members of favored racial groups. Thus, any use of race must be narrowly tailored and cannot be the predominant factor in practice.[111]

Rather than using race as just one factor among many, DOJ asserted, Yale gave outsized consideration to race at every step of its admissions process. Yale's "use of race at multiple steps of its admissions process," it said, "results in a multiplied effect of race on an applicant's likelihood of admission."[112]

Importantly, Yale's own admissions data and information showed that race is not just one factor among many. Rather, racial criteria are used as the "predominant criteria that in practice are determinative in many admissions decisions" and that the determinative impact of race "is multiplied for competitive applicants."[113]

Yale's predominant use of race contrasts with the University of Texas's use of race in its admissions process. The U.S. Supreme Court, in 2016, found that UT used race as "a factor of a factor of a factor" in its admissions calculus and that the admissions officers who made the decision as to whether a particular applicant would be admitted made that decision without knowing the race of the applicant.[114]

Yale, of course, defends its use of race, claiming that its goal of racial diversity satisfies the Supreme Court's requirement of a compelling interest. Yet, the Court has said that in order for diversity considerations to be a compelling interest, they "cannot be elusory or amorphous—they must be sufficiently measurable to permit judicial scrutiny of the policies adopted to reach them."[115] Yale, however, failed to meet this measurability bar.

DOJ's investigation found that "Yale's use of race appears to be standardless, and Yale does virtually nothing to cabin, limit, or define its use of race during the Yale College admissions process."[116] Overall, "Yale's race discrimination dates back more than four decades, to at least the 1970s" and the university's race discrimination "affects hundreds of admissions decisions each year."[117]

DOJ, therefore, said: "Yale must agree not to use race or national origin in its upcoming 2020-21 undergraduate admissions cycle, and, if Yale proposes to consider race or national origin in future admissions cycles, it must first submit to the Department of Justice a plan demonstrating that its proposal is narrowly tailored as required by law."[118] And, given that Yale "admits that it intends to continue its race-based admissions process for the 'foreseeable future,'" any narrowly tailored use of race must have an end date.[119]

If Yale failed to comply, DOJ threatened to file a lawsuit to enforce Yale's obligations under Title VI of the Civil Rights Act.[120]

Yale president Peter Salovey, of course, denied the merits of DOJ's findings, saying, "The department's allegation is baseless."[121] Others, however, felt differently.

Swan Lee, cofounder of AACE, said that DOJ's actions were

"a breath of fresh air for a lot of Asian-American parents." These parents, Lee said, felt that their children were being held to a higher standard than others from favored racial groups.[122]

"All American children should be judged by their merits and the content of their character, not the color of their skin," said AACE president Yukong Zhao, who observed that Asian American children "have been long scapegoated by racial preferences in education."[123]

America's top political observers also took note.

Fox News's Tucker Carlson, host of the highest-rated cable news program in television history, discussed the Yale case during one of his popular opening monologues:

> There's not really any question about the evidence. It's overwhelming. And by the way, everyone knows it's true. Ask any Chinese or Korean-American parent you know. They're highly aware of this. Their kid could have straight A's and an amazing SAT score, but he's not going to Princeton—he'd be lucky to get into Boston College—because he's the wrong color. Is there a single American who doesn't know this? Everybody knows it. Are we OK with that?[124]

The answer is no, Americans are not okay with that. And it does not matter what color your skin is; Americans understand that race preferences are fundamentally unfair.

In the wake of DOJ's findings against Yale, Edward Blum, the president of SFFA and the force behind the lawsuit against Harvard's race-preferential admissions, said: "All of the Ivy League and other competitive universities admit to using racial classifications and preferences in their admissions policies. This investigation reinforces the need for all universities to end race-based admissions policies."[125]

The editors of the *American Mind*, a publication of the Claremont Institute think tank, observed that the federal involvement in the Yale and Harvard cases was "long overdue but extremely significant." According to their statement:

> They are a good start towards revealing—and correcting—the Left's increasingly tyrannical hegemony over American educational institutions. The notion of "disparate impact," or the idea that inequality between identity groups must result from bigoted discrimination, is driving much of our present regime crisis. If this faulty premise is accepted then political revolution, culminating in the destruction of the American regime and the Constitution as we've known it, is justified.[126]

Yale alumnus Aaron Sibarium, an editor at the *Washington Free Beacon*, noted, "Asians have historically suffered all sorts of discrimination—the Chinese Exclusion Act, the internment of Japanese Americans, and, this year, hate crimes associated with COVID-19—of which Yale's policy is yet another example."[127]

"Even if one stipulates," observed Sibarium, "that only historically oppressed groups can be victims of racism, the fact is that Asian-Americans have historically been oppressed."[128]

The reality, Sibarium pointed out, is straightforward:

> Given the finite number of slots, college admissions are necessarily zero-sum: the more students you admit from one group, the fewer students you can admit from another. Any attempt at racial balancing, then, will impose disproportionate penalties on the highest performing racial groups; if disparate impact suffices for discrimination, it means that racial preferences are inherently discriminatory.[129]

And according to DOJ, "Yale's data and other information show that Yale is racially balancing its admitted class."[130]

For those battling for Asian American parents and their children, DOJ's actions were a welcome validation of their fight for equal rights. Said Lee, "It feels great to finally have our existence be recognized by the government."[131]

Alas, it didn't last. One of the Biden administration's first acts was to dismiss the lawsuit without explanation.[132]

CALIFORNIA: THE SECOND ATTEMPT TO OVERTHROW PROPOSITION 209: ACA 5/PROPOSITION 16

When SCA 5 was unexpectedly derailed by an outcry from the Asian American community in 2014, it was thought that the issue of repealing Proposition 209's ban on race preferences had been settled. That belief, however, did not factor in political calculations in the Democrat-dominated California legislature.

In 2020, with COVID-19 lockdowns hampering effective public input to the legislature and with the presidential election believed to ensure a more liberal-voting electorate, Democrats in the state assembly decided to ram through ACA 5, authored by assembly members Shirley Weber (D-San Diego), Mike Gipson (D-Compton), and Miguel Santiago (D-Los Angeles), which would place a proposition on the November 2020 ballot that would repeal Proposition 209.[133]

ACA 5 included a host of "Whereas" clauses that purported to show why Proposition 209 had to be repealed, including accusations such as "The University of California has never recovered the same level of diversity that it had before the loss of affirmative action nearly 20 years ago" and "Since the passage of Proposition 209, diversity within public educational institutions has been stymied."[134]

The public was given only 24 hours' notice that the state assembly had scheduled a hearing on the legislation for May 5, 2020.

It was obvious that the political fix was in, and the Democratic supermajority in the legislature quickly passed ACA 5 and placed it on the November 2020 ballot as Proposition 16.

Yet ACA 5/Proposition 16 was full of faulty premises.

For example, ACA 5's claim that the University of California never recovered the same level of diversity that it had prior to Proposition 209's passage was the basis of the argument used by UC president Janet Napolitano in successfully pushing the UC Board of Regents to support ACA 5. According to Napolitano, since the passage of Proposition 209, "the number of students of underrepresented groups at UC declined and plateaued."[135] UC's own data, however, show otherwise.

Looking back to 1998, two years after the passage of Proposition 209, about 15 percent of new freshmen were from underrepresented minorities, which included Latinos, African Americans, and Native Americans.[136]

A 2020 report by the UC Academic Senate found that in 2017, the most recent year for which information was available, "31 percent of freshmen enrollees to UC were [members of underrepresented minorities]," double the percentage two decades prior.[137]

Race-preference proponents would argue that 61 percent of California's high school graduates in 2017 were from underrepresented minority groups, which is almost double the 31 percent of UC freshmen from those groups.[138] However, the reasons for that disparity do not stem from Proposition 209.

Indeed, poor K-12 public education, not Proposition 209, is the crucial reason for the disparities in UC enrollment of underrepresented minorities.

The UC Academic Senate report said that the gap between the share of underrepresented minorities in grade 12 in California and the pool of those minority students admitted by UC is explained by factors "that precede admissions."

Specifically, K-12 public schools fail to prepare those minority students for college.

For instance, a foundational requirement for admission to the UC system is that students take a set of designated college-preparatory courses called the A-G requirement. The academic senate report found that for underrepresented minorities, the most significant factor preventing UC eligibility was not Proposition 209, but the "failure to complete all required A-G courses with a C or better."

President Napolitano's office acknowledged that "the biggest contributor to underrepresentation at UC is that students do not fulfill A-G subject requirements for admissions."[139]

According to the California Department of Education, in 2017–18, 43 percent of Hispanic and less than 40 percent of African American students met the A-G requirement. In contrast, 55 percent of white and 75 percent of Asian American students met the requirement.[140]

Further, the academic senate report found that "lower high school graduation rates for [underrepresented minorities]" and "lower application rates" were other key reasons for the eligibility gap.[141]

Data from California's Department of Education from 2018–19 show that the high school graduation rate for African Americans was 77 percent, while the rate for Hispanics was 82 percent. In contrast, the graduation rate for whites was 88 percent, and for Asian Americans it was 94 percent.[142]

The low quality of public K-12 education in low-income African American and Hispanic communities is well known within these communities. Knowing that the public K-12 system is the problem, members of these communities realize that race preferences are not the answer.

A 2019 national Pew Research Center poll found that more than six out of ten Hispanics and African Americans opposed considering race in college admissions.[143] Also, a 2017 Public Policy Institute of California poll found that seven out of ten Hispanics and African Americans in California supported tax-funded school vouchers that could pay for tuition at private schools.[144]

As AACE president Yukong Zhao has rightly said, "Politicians, who have instituted failing policies in too many black and Hispanic communities, not hardworking Asian-American children, should be blamed for the persistent racial achievement gaps."[145]

As in the case of SCA 5 in 2014, Asian Americans in California, although they were initially blindsided by the introduction of ACA 5, quickly organized in grassroots efforts to oppose the legislation and the subsequent ballot proposition.

While insider and established liberal advocacy groups, such as the California Asian and Pacific Islander Legislative Caucus and Asian Americans Advancing Justice, pushed for ACA 5, one news report observed, "The [Asian American] opposition has been more homegrown, led by concerned parents and students who worry that California's public universities will shut them out."[146] A grassroots petition quickly gathered more than 100,000 signatures.[147]

Fenglan Liu, a community organizer in Southern California and an opponent of Proposition 16, called the ballot measure "unacceptable, unconstitutional, and unfair to Asians."[148]

Wenyuan Wu, AACE director of administration and executive director of Californians for Equal Rights, said:

> [Proposition 16] fundamentally rejects the principle of equal treatment by trying to legalize preferential treatment. [It] does nothing about addressing root causes behind the disparities and achievement gaps in education. We need equal opportunities, not equal outcomes.[149]

Asian Americans rightly fear that introducing race as a factor in university admissions will naturally lead to racial balancing—

that is, enforcing an artificial composition of students based on race. DOJ, for instance, found that "Yale is racially balancing its admitted class, with major racial groups remaining remarkably stable for approximately the last decade."[150]

Crystal Lu, president of the Silicon Valley Chinese Association Foundation, said she worries when people talk about the overrepresentation of Asian Americans in universities. The implication is that the student body must be proportional to the percentages of various races in the general population. "It shows the intention is to conduct racial balancing," said Lu. "It is a hidden quota system," one which will result in fewer spaces for Asian Americans.[151]

The *San Francisco Chronicle* found that the attempt to reintroduce race preferences into California public university admissions "galvanized a new class of activists in state politics: largely first-generation Chinese Americans." The newspaper found that the issue is very personal for these immigrants. They "emigrated from China to attend college or graduate school in the U.S. and say they overcame a poor upbringing through their education to rise into the middle class."[152]

As Lu said: "We just feel this passionate about racial equality. The true sense of equality, where nobody is above anybody else."[153]

In the end, California voters agreed. Proposition 16 was rejected by a margin of 57.2 to 42.8 percent. The Asian Americans who worked hard to defeat the measure might justifiably feel that David, not Goliath, had prevailed.

CONCLUSION

President Bill Clinton infamously said that, under Proposition 209, some California universities would have "nothing but Asian Americans."[154] Such an appalling statement betrays both stereotyping and, even more important, a willingness to discriminate against Asian Americans. People like President Clinton and Judge Burroughs should listen to people like Sohini Ashoke.

Writing in 2017 on her school's news site, Ashoke, a junior at Henry M. Gunn High School in Palo Alto, California, criticized "the blanket approach of generalizing all Asians during college admissions," which does not account for Cambodian Americans, Laotian Americans, and other Asian American groups that have statistically lower standardized test scores.[155]

Because 44 percent of her fellow students were Asian Americans, Ashoke said, "how colleges handle affirmative action has a direct impact on Gunn students." In a foretelling of Judge Burroughs's decision, she observed, "One of the main reasons why Asian-American applicants are at a disadvantage during college applications is because of the rising policy adopted by colleges to promote diversity on campus."[156] "Their prioritization," she observed, "of non-Asian races during college applications has created the significant and unjustified disadvantage that Asians face during college applications."[157]

Cutting through the utopian wish fulfillment and obfuscating legal jargon, Ashoke wrote: "Creating racial quotas and trying to diversify a campus is most definitely not a step towards equality, and it is not a way to counteract racism. American colleges have now changed their narrative to promote a more diverse environment rather than fight discrimination—evident in their treatment of Asian-American students."[158] Piercing a common Asian American stereotype, she noted that "when it comes to living in an environment that values education, this can not be considered a privilege as it very clearly can vary among all Asian-Americans and is therefore subjective."[159]

In the end, Ashoke urged, "It is crucial to stop allowing race to overshadow personal merit or achievement when it comes to determining who the future college students of this country are."[160]

For those who belittle and minimize the harm that discriminatory race preferences have on Asian Americans, the perspective of Stephen Nakashima is critical. Nakashima, a Japanese American UC regent who voted in 1995 to eliminate race preferences in the UC system, explained his vote by harkening back to his internment during World War II. He pointed out that race preferences are viewed as benign or harmful, depending on whether one is personally being victimized by the practice:

> What it was depended on how you looked at it. From the outside looking into Poston III, where I was, it's an internment camp. But if you're inside behind barbed wire and armed guards looking out, it's a concentration camp. The same goes with respect to affirmative action. It depends on how it affects you personally.[161]

Similarly, decades later, young Sohini Ashoke would write, "modern-day affirmative action works counterintuitively to its original purpose by discriminating against high-achieving minorities and disregarding the injustices they face."[162]

The more things change, sadly, the more they stay the same.

But, as the lawsuits against prestigious universities and the grassroots efforts to protect anti-discrimination laws demonstrate, Asian Americans are breaking the "silent minority" stereotype.

America stands on the cusp of finally throwing preferences based on race onto the ash heap of history. When that happens, Asian Americans will have been one of the catalysts for the demise of that shameful practice.

A Class Act? Social-Class Affirmative Action and Higher Education

Maimon Schwarzschild

How much are people the products of their parents' genes, how much are they the products of their upbringing, and how much do they owe their successes and failures in life to their own efforts? These are notoriously, almost comically, unanswerable questions. But scarcely anyone doubts that nature and nurture—or at a minimum, nature *or* nurture—greatly affect who we are and what happens to us in life. And plainly, people are not morally responsible for their genes or (on the whole) for their upbringing. "Choose your parents wisely" is a wry, but obvious, truth.

One's parents' fate is not necessarily one's own, of course. Education has traditionally been a means to social mobility. "Careers open to talent" were a byword of the Enlightenment struggle against hereditary privilege. Today, more than ever, education opens the way to careers. There is a strong correlation between education, earnings, and social status: the lifetime earnings of college graduates in the United States, on average, are nearly double those of high school graduates.[1] But heredity still matters—in education as in other spheres of life. "Native intelligence," presumably, has some part in educational success. Upbringing surely has as well. Although there are no guarantees of scholastic success for those whose parents are well educated, well connected, and well off, they start with obvious educational advantages. Scores on college admission tests go up, on average, with parental income; and college students, especially at prestigious universities, are disproportionately the children of comfortable families.[2]

Affirmative action on the basis of social class might therefore seem an attractive way to counteract, and at least partially to balance, the unearned caprices of birth. Barack Obama, as his campaign for the presidency got underway in 2007, implied that he might support affirmative action on the basis of class, rather than on the basis of race. Asked whether his own daughters should benefit from affirmative action, Obama said they "should probably be treated by any admissions officer as folks who are pretty advantaged." But as for social class, "I think that we should take into account white kids who have been disadvantaged and have grown up in poverty and have shown themselves to have what it takes to succeed."[3]

Senator Obama (as he then was) put the suggestion in terms that few could disagree with. But systematic affirmative action on the basis of social class would almost certainly mean more than seeking out college applicants from lower-class families or offering more "need-based" scholarships. It would mean more than informally making allowances for a promising applicant where there is genuine reason to think that a test score or other qualification understates the applicant's ability. As with racial affirmative action, such measures would arouse little, if any, controversy. But realistically, class affirmative action almost certainly means systematic admissions preferences based on class, comparable to affirmative action as it now exists on the basis of race: a program for admitting lower-class students with lesser academic qualifications over other applicants with higher qualifications. Prominent authors have advocated such preferential programs, and several universities and colleges, including various divisions of the University of California, have instituted such class affirmative action in their undergraduate and graduate admissions.[4]

Class preferences are often suggested as a better or more acceptable alternative to conventional affirmative action on the basis of race, ethnicity, or sex. After all, if affirmative action is meant to help the underprivileged, surely it is more straightforward to offer preferences to the underprivileged, rather than to groups whose members are not all underprivileged, while many underprivileged people are not members of such groups. Class preferences may be especially attractive to affirmative action–minded colleges and universities in states where—as a result of statewide referenda or otherwise—it is, at least nominally, illegal for public bodies to discriminate, or to prefer, on the basis of race, ethnicity, or sex.[5]

But there are good reasons to think twice about class-based affirmative action. Some of the problems with class preference are common to any educational preferences based on group membership rather than educational qualifications. But some of the most important reasons for caution are specific to preferences based on social class.

Comparing class preferences with race preferences will point up some of the reasons for the allure of class preferences but will also point up some of the problems. A crucial consideration is the question of who is to receive class preference. For example, what about immigrants and their children? In general, social class is difficult to define, and this very difficulty confers great discretion and power on faculties and academic administrators who undertake to bestow class preferences: discretion that is open to abuse for political, ideological, and other ends. Finally, there is the question of whether preferential treatment is necessary to increase educational opportunities for the less privileged, or whether the call for class preferences reflects a mindset inimical to impartial standards and prone to preferences as a first, rather than a last, resort.

CLASS VS. RACE

Race quotas and preferences, especially in higher education, have serious drawbacks, as even their supporters sometimes acknowledge. The case against racial affirmative action is well known. Race preferences enhance race consciousness in a country (and in a world) in which racism has already done incalculable mischief. They systematically mismatch minority students with institutions where their qualifications are significantly below average, hence maximizing these students' self-doubts and the likelihood that they will fail or perform poorly. They stigmatize minority students and graduates as recipients of unearned favor. They promote self-segregation, through the reluctance of minority students to expose themselves to embarrassment by their academically better-prepared fellows. They diminish incentives, or create perverse incentives, by conveying to minority young people that they need not strive too hard to learn and to achieve. They weaken academic standards, because preferences ensure that minority students have lower qualifications on average, and faculties may be loath to maintain high standards at the price of conspicuous minority failure. They may also encourage nihilism about the very idea of high academic standards. And they are widely felt to be unfair, both because educational institutions are generally expected to judge by educational criteria, not by racial ones, and because many of the beneficiaries of race preferences are children of comfortable families, whereas many who are passed over despite their stronger academic achievements are themselves the children of less comfortable homes.[6]

Affirmative action based on social class, if more widely adopted, would at least have the virtue of not being based on race. Racial animosity, which racial affirmative action might be thought to aggravate, holds particular social and political dangers, a fact that is borne out by the history of racial conflict in America and in many other countries. And many of the drawbacks of racial affirmative action are enhanced by the conspicuous visibility of people's race. The stigma of having received preferential treatment is greatly enhanced if it is obvious at a glance. (Even a minority student admitted on the merits, without any preference, might be assumed by others to have received preference and will know that others are making this assumption.) For the same reason, the stigma of race preference may persist throughout a person's professional life. And segregation, including self-segregation, is facilitated by obvious physical distinctions.

Beneficiaries of class preferences do not stand out in the same way: it is not so obvious that a particular student might have received class preference. Hence, there might not be the same stigma in one's student years or beyond. Moreover, affirmative action based on social class (rather than race) might be less corrosive of academic standards—at least if faculties and administrators are less prone to dilute standards in order to disguise the failure or poor performance of those receiving class preference. After all, students preferred by social class, rather than by race, might be less conspicuous and cohesive. And if they succeed less well than their academically better-prepared fellows, then at least it would not replicate the painful American history of race discrimination, with the scarcely tolerable spectacle of such a racial group being once again at the bottom.

Class preferences also have the virtue of preferring the less privileged. Racial affirmative action, by contrast, often means preferential treatment for the children of middle-class, or even wealthy and prominent, minority families. This is especially true given the minority "applicant pool" at elite colleges, universities, and professional schools: that is, given that the minority applicants with the strongest academic qualifications—although they still might not be admitted without preferential treatment—are often children of prosperous homes. Realistically, if today's racial affirmative action "goals" can be satisfied by admitting minority applicants with the best academic qualifications, even if these are the most prosperous minority applicants, then colleges and universities are apt to do so, just as there is an obvious incentive to admit minority applicants who can afford to pay high tuition rates. Insofar as affirmative action is meant to help the less privileged, class preferences would surely be a more direct and a more consistent way of achieving it.[7]

On the other hand, the moral urgency for class preference is far less clear than for racial affirmative action. The legacy of slavery and the history of racial segregation and discrimination in America are known to everyone: they are rightly sources of national regret. Today there is broad national consensus for racial equality, for "equal justice under law," and for the moral claims of the civil rights movement: hence the stature of Martin Luther King, Jr., as a national hero. There is also a widely shared belief that racial stratification, with dramatically better or worse conditions of life depending on race, is dangerous for society, sowing the seeds of racial conflict. Whether preferential affirmative action is a just way toward racial equality and integration, or even whether it leads to these goals at all, is controversial. But as recompense for undeniable racial injustice, and as a means to racial integration, the case for affirmative action is on its strongest ground.

As to class, by contrast, there is reason to feel that America has less to atone for, and possibly less to worry about for the future, than where race is concerned. Unlike many European countries, the United States has no hereditary aristocracy. Historically, class distinctions have been fewer and less rigid in America. Instead, America has been known—sometimes even disparaged—for its emphasis on upward mobility and its cult of success. This is not to suggest that America has ever been a "classless society." Such a thing may not exist in nature. But America has been more a land of opportunity than most, a chosen destination for immigrants throughout the centuries. Has social mobility now slowed in America? Are there fewer opportunities today for those who start life without hereditary advantages? These are controversial questions that may be impossible to answer conclusively. There are academic studies—and widespread media reports—suggesting that *relative* mobility has diminished in America in recent years or decades: that there is less mobility than in the past between lower, middle, and upper income ranges.[8] Unsurprisingly, there is also criticism of the statistical methods, and even of the tacit biases, of these studies, and some evidence that even *relative* class mobility has not grown or shrunk—or at least not very much—over recent decades.[9] There is less controversy that *absolute* incomes have continued to rise on average in recent decades, despite periodic economic downturns such as that beginning in 2008. The rich may have gotten richer, as they proverbially do; but the poor have gotten richer too, albeit at a lesser rate than the rich. (Historically, when the rich get richer more slowly, the poor often do not get richer at all.) In short, there has been considerable—if far from perfect—class mobility in America in the past, and there is considerable economic and social opportunity in America today, with standards of living that continue to rise on average.[10]

The rates of legal and illegal immigration to the United States, and the eagerness with which many more seek to come, also suggest that there is no present crisis of social opportunity in America, however controversial the question of income and wealth inequality may be as a political issue. Impressive numbers of people have "voted with their feet" that they can achieve a better life for themselves and their children in the United States, despite arriving with few hereditary advantages of wealth, status, or position.

If the sense of moral and social urgency for class affirmative action is less pressing than that for racial affirmative action, the costs and dangers of class preferences, while perhaps less obvious than for race preferences, are still considerable and for some of the same reasons.

Racial conflict is socially incendiary in any country unlucky enough to have it, but class conflict is scarcely less so. In various countries that have experimented with class preferences in education, these preferences have not only reflected but also aggravated class division and animosity. Perhaps the least edifying examples of class affirmative action in the twentieth century were in the USSR and in China under Mao Tse-Tung. Universities were required to favor applicants with "good"— worker or peasant—class backgrounds and to disfavor or exclude applicants with "bad" class origins. These policies contributed to the thorough politicization of Communist universities and to sharply declining academic and intellectual standards. In China, during Mao's Cultural Revolution, there was wholesale persecution of "bad classes," and sons and daughters of alleged "landlords" were beaten to death on campuses.[11] Even before the Cultural Revolution, class was pervasive in selecting and indoctrinating students in China, at great cost to any possible academic integrity.[12] In Stalin's Soviet Union, not only were "workers' children" given preferential acceptance at institutes of higher education, but camp guards in the gulags who volunteered to work in especially undesirable concentration camps were offered the chance to have their children reclassified as "children of workers" for this purpose.[13]

India is another discouraging example. For many decades, India has had extensive preferences for lower-caste applicants, in higher education as well as for various government jobs and benefits. Caste in India is not quite the same, to be sure, as class in other countries. Caste is rigidly hereditary; traditionally it reflected and determined one's occupation and social status. Upper castes also tend to be lighter-skinned and more Aryan, so there is something of a racial aspect too. Perhaps it is fairest to think of caste as being somewhere on a spectrum between race and class. In any event, caste affirmative action in India has been incendiary in the most literal sense: there have been cases of disfavored upper-caste university applicants publicly burning themselves to death in protest. Caste preferences are widely acknowledged to have contributed to sharply declining academic standards, as well as to reinforcing caste enmity, which erupts in frequent and deadly riots, sometimes verging on caste warfare, in various parts of India.[14]

The United States is not India or China, to be sure. But there is little reason to think that class preferences in the United States would not promote class animosities, just as Indian caste preferences do, and just as race preferences in America may already tend to aggravate racial ill will.

Moreover, systematic class preferences on campus would create pressures to dilute academic standards, even if not to the same degree or, at least, not in quite the same way as race preferences. With academically weaker students, classroom standards are almost inevitably lower. Class preferences weaken the academic ethos—the commitment of the institution and its faculty to academic seriousness—in more subtle ways as well. Preferences, at a minimum, convey a message that academic standards are not paramount for the college or university in question. Moreover, maintaining rigorous standards would tend to mean that students admitted with class preferences would cluster at the bottom of the class or fail entirely. Faculty and administrators might find this an unattractive prospect, even if not quite so unattractive as when the same thing happens with racial preferences. Diluting standards, here too, would be an easy solution. And students admitted with class preferences would have reason to band together as a kind of "victim" group, if only to press for looser standards under which they would not always tend to be at the bottom.

It is sometimes suggested that preferences do not really sacrifice academic merit, because applicants who are given a preference—whether on account of race or class—have more potential than their academic qualifications suggest: social deprivation accounts for their lower entering grades and test scores, and given a chance in college or in graduate school, they will do better than predicted. Would that it were so. Studies of minority students show that they do not perform better—if anything, they perform somewhat less well—than their qualifications would predict. Minority students, that is, receive grades in college or in graduate school that are no better than their entering credentials would predict; in fact, their grades after admission are slightly worse, on average, than those received by non-minority students with the same entering grades and test scores.[15] The "validity" of the SAT, especially when combined with high school grades—that is, the correlation between SAT scores and high school grades on the one hand, and subsequent college grades on the other—is strong, both for minority and for non-minority students.[16]

There is no evidence that tests like the SAT, or equivalent tests for graduate and professional schools, underpredict the academic performance of lower-class applicants any more than they do for minority students. Richard Kahlenberg, an advocate of class preferences, concedes that there could only be "a very minor" class preference if the preference were merely designed to correct, as he puts it, "the degree (if at all)" that entering academic credentials fail to predict the academic success of underprivileged students.[17]

In short, preferring academically weaker university applicants because of their class backgrounds would mean academically weaker university students.

The extent to which class preferences would compromise academic quality depends, in part, on the scale of the preferences. Are there minimum credentials below which no one would be admitted? If so, how low or high is the minimum for disadvantaged applicants? How large a boost would there be for being disadvantaged? What proportion of the entering class will be admitted with a preference: that is, how many disadvantaged students will be admitted who would not have been admitted on their merits? Once a widespread program of class preferences gets under way, it is unlikely that it would be restricted to a small number of the "most disadvantaged." There are proportionally few children of radically disadvantaged homes who could qualify, even by very relaxed preferential standards, for admission to elite or near-elite universities or graduate schools. Moreover, if the most disadvantaged are admitted on a lower standard, but there is no academic concession for the next-most disadvantaged, then the most disadvantaged are apt to be admitted at the expense of the somewhat disadvantaged: at the expense of applicants whose qualifications are somewhat lower, on average, than those of "privileged" applicants but who are receiving no preference.

To avoid the apparent injustice of any such "cutoff" in preferences, there would be great pressure to have a sliding scale of preferences for degrees of disadvantage. Moreover, preferences might seem more palatable politically if they were available to a broader range of applicants: the bottom half of the socio-economic ladder, say, rather than the bottom 10 percent. After all, an argument can be made that the "injuries of class" affect all families below the median, not just the poorest in society. (Indeed, 90 percent of Americans are not in the country's top 10 percent.) In practice, the very poorest would mostly not be qualified on any standard, so that a viable program of class preferences in higher education would mean preferences for the more moderately disadvantaged: a larger class of beneficiaries. Accordingly, when UCLA School of Law adopted a class-preference policy shortly after Proposition 209 went into effect in California in the late 1990s, more than half the law school class were admitted with such preferences.[18] Richard Kahlenberg, too, advocates a preference for any applicant below the socio-economic median: the median of the institution's applicants, in fact, not the national median. He would therefore give class preferences to solidly middle-class applicants, especially at elite universities where the average applicant is well off.[19]

The effect on academic standards might therefore be substantial. Preferences mean admitting academically weaker students. Racial preferences have some natural limit: the proportion of preferentially admitted minority students is unlikely to be greater, roughly, than the size of the minority in society. Class preferences have no such natural limit. If a university admits half or more of its students on a lower academic standard because of their "class origins," the academic life of that university will almost inevitably suffer, relative to what it would have been with students admitted on their academic merits.

Racial and ethnic affirmative action is already strongly institutionalized on many campuses, at least where laws like California's Proposition 209 do not limit it. Class preferences are sometimes presented as an alternative to racial preferences. Richard Kahlenberg urges straightforwardly that class preferences should substitute for racial ones, both on the moral ground that preferences should be directed to the disadvantaged and on the prudential ground that class preferences are politically and legally more palatable than racial ones. Carol Swain and other advocates of class-based affirmative action have taken much the same view.[20] Supporters of racial affirmative action, however, respond that class preferences are no substitute: most of America's "disadvantaged" are not minority, and if class preferences replace racial ones, black applicants in particular will fare much worse than they do when there are implicit or explicit numerical "goals"—and preferential standards—based on race. There ought to be class preferences in addition to the racial ones, not instead of them, insist many defenders of affirmative action—including William Bowen, coauthor with Derek Bok of *The Shape of the River*, a standard text in support of affirmative action.[21]

Class preferences, in fact, would probably reinforce racial preferences rather than replace them in most states. After all, there is stronger moral and historical justification for affirmative action by race than by class. It is one thing to adhere to a principle that colleges and universities should judge applicants on their academic merits: that preferential treatment is corrosive and wrong. But, once it is conceded that class preferences are desirable, it would be difficult or impossible to resist the claims that racial affirmative action should continue as well, wherever it is permitted by law. America's racial history gives these claims special resonance, and there is well-organized support for the existing preferences, especially on campuses. Any systematic program of preference tends to erode the principle of making academic judgments on an academic basis. If higher education is to have widespread preferential treatment by social class, it will probably be in addition to the already institutionalized racial and ethnic affirmative-action programs, not as a substitute for them.

CLASS PREFERENCES AND OPEN BORDERS

Preferential treatment for college and university applicants from "less privileged" families raises an obvious question of social fairness: What about immigrants and their children?

As of 2019, about 45 million foreign-born people lived in the United States, representing around 13.5 percent of the population.[22] Of these, about 20 million, roughly 45 percent, are naturalized American citizens.[23] As many as 11 million are estimated to be "unauthorized residents" illegally present in the United States.[24]

In states such as California, New York, Texas, and Florida, where over half the foreign-born live, there is a high concentration of immigrant families.[25] One in every four people in California and more than one in five in New York and New Jersey were born in another country.[26] There are growing numbers of immigrants in other regions of the country as well. The foreign-born population increased by over 100 percent in Kentucky, Tennessee, and Wyoming from 2000 to 2014, and the numbers of the foreign-born increased by at least 80 percent in seven other states during the same period.[27]

The levels of education and income among the foreign-born are rather polarized. Nearly 24 percent of the foreign-born over twenty-five years of age never completed high school, compared to just 7 percent of native-born Americans; yet 14 percent of the foreign-born have advanced graduate degrees, which is greater than the 13 percent of native-born Americans who have such degrees.[28] The median annual earnings of the foreign-born are 68 percent of the earnings of natives, and non-citizens' earnings are lower still, while 21 percent of foreign-born individuals lived in households earning less than $22,350 in 2011, compared with 16 percent of natives.[29]

People with incomes less than twice the official poverty rate are often called the "near poor." Approximately 31 percent of the American-born live "in or near poverty"; but 45 percent of immigrants and their minor children live in such households.[30]

Immigrants and their children, in short, make up a significant and disproportionate share of the "underprivileged" in America, almost regardless of how "underprivilege" is defined. In states like California and New York, immigrants may be a third or more of the "underprivileged." This should not be surprising and has undoubtedly been true throughout American history. Newcomers are obviously less apt to be "established" than families long settled in this country. And while immigrants are often ambitious people, they are typically without wealth or privilege: Otherwise, why emigrate?

America has attracted immigrants since the nation became independent, and even before, by offering something like equal opportunity. Not perfect equality: the foreign-born can never be president or vice president, and there have always been more workaday handicaps as well. But America has traditionally offered immigrants a fair chance to live and work, to be educated, and to compete and to succeed economically on substantially equal terms with natives. Americans generally accept that this is fair, and immigrants have come willingly—even eagerly and in extraordinary numbers—on these terms.

If the "underprivileged" are to receive preferential treatment in college and university admissions, and immigrants and their children are a substantial fraction of the "underprivileged," there will be acute questions about who should receive these preferences.[31] Affirmative action is typically seen, at least in part, as a policy to compensate for past injustices. Immigrants or their ancestors may have suffered injustice, but not in—or generally at the hands of—the United States. Throughout American history, immigrants and their children assimilated, and in many cases succeeded, without preferential treatment: indeed, in spite of headwinds, since they often faced social barriers of various kinds. Hence, American-born families might reasonably think it perverse now to give preferential treatment to immigrants and their children: "Immigrants come seeking equal treatment, and that's fair enough. But why penalize my child for the social capital our family has built up in America? If my children earn better grades and scores, why should they be rejected in favor of less qualified newcomers?"

In theory, various categories of people might be excluded from preference, but such discrimination would not necessarily be very palatable or even very practicable. Illegal immigrants would be obvious candidates for ineligibility. But enforcement would require scrutiny, presumably by college and university officials, of whether college applicants are lawful residents. In many American cities, even the police are reluctant to police compliance with the immigration laws.[32] In California, the state higher education law explicitly provides for illegal aliens who have attended three years of high school in California to be treated as state residents, who pay substantially less for public higher education than "out of state" American citizens and legal residents.[33] Sixteen other states make similar allowance for illegal aliens in higher education.[34] Given such trends, it is difficult to imagine how universities could or would identify illegal aliens and disqualify them from preferences for the underprivileged. As for reserving class preferences exclusively for citizens of the United States, discriminating between citizens and lawful residents would seem even more invidious than discriminating against illegal aliens, and discriminating against lawful residents would almost certainly violate a variety of federal and state civil-rights laws.[35]

Moreover, what about the children of the foreign-born? Proportionally to their numbers, perhaps few illegal residents themselves seek higher education, although some surely do. Among the foreign-born in general, there are fewer young people of high school age—the age of the typical college applicant—than among the native-born: only 7 percent of the foreign-born are under eighteen, compared to 27 percent of the American-born.[36] But children born in the United States, even to illegal aliens, are American citizens. The birth rate, in fact, is higher among the foreign-born in America than among natives.[37] If there is to be preferential treatment for the children of underprivileged homes, one or both parents in a substantial fraction of such homes are apt to be immigrants, legal or otherwise.

Immigration policy is a volatile topic in America today, as it often has been in the past. Many Americans would want, in principle, to take a welcoming attitude toward immigration: "Send these, the homeless, tempest-tossed to me; I lift my lamp beside the golden door!"[38] But the numbers of illegal immigrants have increased dramatically in recent decades, and the major political parties are increasingly divided about immigration policy, especially where illegal immigration is concerned. If significant numbers of immigrants, or their children, are known to receive preferential treatment in college and university admissions on grounds of "underprivilege," it is surely foreseeable that opposition to immigration—and ill will toward immigrants—would be strengthened, and a liberal public policy toward immigration would be even less politically viable than it is today.

PREFERENCE FOR WHOM? THE ELUSIVE DEFINITION OF CLASS

If applicants of lower social class are to receive preference in college and university admissions, social class will have to be defined in order to decide who is eligible. Racial affirmative action confronts this problem too, but in most cases there is broad agreement in America about who meets the rough-and-ready standards of being white, African American, or Hispanic. About 2.9 percent of Americans identified themselves as multiracial in the 2010 census.[39] The multiracial category is growing quickly, and nearly 8 percent of married couples are now interracial;[40] racial intermarriage is growing especially quickly among better-educated Americans.[41] But as of today, more than 90 percent of whites and blacks are still married within their groups.[42] Throughout American history, there have been individuals who have "passed" as members of another race, but there are still relatively few white college applicants who could plausibly claim to be black; and while there are more "borderline" cases of who is Hispanic, in the great majority of cases—at least up to now—there is no dispute.

At first blush, it might be thought that social class could equally easily be defined by family income: a college or university applicant would be entitled to class preference if the applicant's family income were below a certain threshold. (If a sliding scale were wanted, there might be a greater preference—a more relaxed standard of admissions—the lower the income.) But for various reasons—some of them cogent—supporters of class preferences do not wish to define class simply and straightforwardly by income.

For one thing, average cash incomes differ depending on geographic location. A given income might seem "underprivileged" in an expensive urban area, less so in a smaller city, and positively middle-class in a rural area. This would be an obvious problem for universities with applicants from across America; but even for institutions drawing primarily from a particular state, there are wide intra-state variations in the standards of living that a given income might represent in different areas.

Average incomes also vary by age: most people's income rises as they get older, then falls when they retire. If class preferences were based purely on parents' income, applicants with younger parents would have an arbitrary advantage over those whose parents are older and hence earning more, regardless of anything else about the applicants' family lives. By the same token, if income were the only criterion, children whose parents are retired would also tend to be preferred.

It is also quite possible to have a modest income but substantial capital. A family living on the return from private capital might have the same income as a working family, without being of the same social class by any reasonable standard. Indeed, if college admission standards depended only on income, it might be worthwhile for parents with private capital to decrease their earnings deliberately, by shifting temporarily to investments with lower yield but higher long-term gain.

There are also problems of disclosure and fraud, which may be particularly acute if class is measured—and preference granted—on any single criterion, such as income. For example, a family might fairly easily defer or hide income, whereas the family's social class, judged on a wider array of criteria, would not at all correspond to the disclosed income.

In fact, it is a commonplace that money and social class are not necessarily the same thing. In the 1930s, George Orwell wrote:

> [T]he essential point about the English class system is that it is not entirely explicable in terms of money. Roughly speaking, it is a money-stratification, but it is also interpenetrated by a sort of shadowy caste system; rather like a jerry-built modern bungalow haunted by medieval ghosts. . . . Perhaps there are countries where you can predict a man's opinions from his income, but it is never quite safe to do so in England; you have always got to take his traditions into consideration as well. A naval officer and his grocer very likely have the same income, but they are not equivalent persons and they would only be on the same side in very large issues such as war or a general strike—possibly not even then.[43]

The particulars of class differences in 21st-century America are not what they were in Orwell's England. But if class is a measure of unearned hereditary advantage (or its absence), there probably has to be more nuance about it than mere cash income. At a minimum, one would want to take capital into account—savings, investments, property holdings, trust funds, and so on—as well as income.

More broadly, as Orwell suggests, money is only one element of hereditary good or bad fortune. In America, as in every society, class is a subtle and many-faceted (if not many-splendored) thing, which is why it is so inexhaustible a topic in literature. A privileged or underprivileged childhood might depend not only on one's parents' income and capital, but also on their education and culture, their occupational status, whether they were married and stayed married, what sort of home and neighborhood one grew up in, and what sort of schools one attended. And this is to consider only the more tangible, and hence potentially measurable, elements of class: it leaves aside one's parents' values, tastes, and connections, which might be important elements too, but which are scarcely quantifiable at all.

Colleges and universities that have experimented with class preferences have actually considered some of the more tangible factors, and advocates of class preference urge that they do so. UCLA School of Law, for example, has questioned applicants about their fathers' and mothers' level of education, income, and net worth and the applicants' home address while in high school. (No applicant was required to answer these questions, but class preference was available only to those who did.) In calculating preferences, the law school considered the proportion of single-parent households in the applicant's home neighborhood; the proportion of families in the neighborhood receiving welfare; and the proportion of adults who had not graduated from high school.[44] Richard Kahlenberg urges that seven factors be taken into account: parents' education; parents' income; parents' net wealth; parents' occupation; the family structure (whether the parents were married; whether they divorced; mother's age when the applicant was born); the quality of the schools the applicant attended; and the quality of the applicant's neighborhood.[45]

The emphasis on home neighborhood as a criterion of class may be motivated, in part, by the fact that blacks and Hispanics, in particular, tend to live in neighborhoods that are "worse"—in terms of numbers of single-parent households, families receiving welfare, and so forth—than whites with similar incomes; and a desire on the part of the advocates and designers of class preferences to include as many blacks and Hispanics as possible among those who will benefit from the preferences.[46] Deliberate racial gerrymandering of these criteria, to be sure, would violate the provisions of laws like Proposition 209 in California that forbid racial preferences by state institutions and authorities.

It will be noticed, of course, that there are a variety of criteria of class here that might or might not be taken into account. UCLA School of Law did not take account of parents' occupation, family structure, or quality of the applicant's secondary school, for example, although Richard Kahlenberg urges that these should be considered. Some of the criteria require further decisions about what should be considered: for example, "family structure" might or might not include whether the applicant's parents were married and at what age, whether they divorced, whether a single mother was divorced or instead had never married, and so forth. Other criteria would also call for detailed judgment: for example, how to rank parents' occupations, how to rank the quality of an applicant's secondary school, and how to rank the quality of parents' education (if the status of the parents' schools or colleges, for example, were to be considered, not just how many years of schooling they had).

Choosing criteria of class, in short, entails a lot of discretion: far more discretion than deciding who is eligible for racial preferences, at least so long as most people's racial identification is easily settled. Moreover, there is further discretion in deciding how much weight to give each of the criteria once they are chosen. For example, to score an applicant's class, what relative importance should be given to parents' income, parents' net wealth, parents' education, the neighborhood where the family lives, and so forth? Class is a nebulous enough concept that there is no uniform standard of how to define it, nor is it easy to imagine how there could be.

UCLA School of Law's emphasis on neighborhood is probably an example of choosing a criterion—and giving it a lot of weight—in order to steer class preferences in a particular direction: in this case, to racial minorities. If so, it may violate the provisions of Proposition 209 in California. But other plausible criteria might be chosen, or given more weight, if one wanted to favor rural applicants, labor union families, Evangelicals, or other groups. Almost any change in the criteria, or variation in how they are weighted, will change the profile of those eligible for preferential treatment. Faculties and administrators could adapt and change the criteria over time, depending on the results from a particular formula. For example, there have not only been different formulas for class preferences at different campuses of the University of California, but different formulas at various schools and programs on the same campuses; the formulas have also changed from year to year.

It might be said that colleges and universities make discretionary decisions all the time: about whom to hire as faculty, whom to admit as students, what to teach, how to teach it, and so on. What is so special about their defining social class and granting preferences accordingly?

But these other discretionary decisions are, at least in principle, academic decisions, decided on academic criteria. That colleges and universities have academic expertise is—or was, until recently—generally accepted: hence the acceptance and respect accorded to academic degrees conferred by these institutions. It is less obvious that academic institutions have any particular expertise in social engineering, or in deciding which individuals or groups should receive preferential treatment on grounds of class or hereditary disadvantage.

The discretion involved in defining class and disadvantage would be open to political pressures of various kinds. Depending on what criteria a college or university uses—and how it weights these criteria—different racial and ethnic groups would receive greater or lesser preference, for example. At state universities, which are controlled by the state legislatures, well-organized ethnic groups would be in a position to lobby for criteria that would favor them. Private universities receiving public funds would be open to similar lobbying pressures, as well as to pressures from private donors who might be interested in promoting the interests of one group or another.

Deciding who is to receive how much preference would also be open to ideological favoritism. This might simply take the form of ideological preference for some minority groups over others. It might also take the form of shading the criteria in order to give a boost to applicants with particular political views. American colleges and universities are already widely recognized to have become more politicized in recent decades. Studies of university faculties and administrators reveal a heavy tilt to the political left, very disproportionately to the country as a whole and amounting to virtual unanimity on many campuses.[47] Consciously or otherwise, faculties and administrators might be inclined toward definitions of class disadvantage that would maximize admissions preferences for students with congenial political views—at the expense, for example, of rural or Evangelical applicants whose views might, on average, be less congenial.

Thus, when UCLA School of Law created a preference program based on class, the school was evidently concerned that preferences should not go to "highly talented applicants" with low family incomes who might be the children of "highly educated missionaries."[48] This might reflect a legitimate judgment that missionaries' children are not unlucky by birth or upbringing, but it might also reflect political and religious prejudice. Along the same lines, Richard Kahlenberg, probably the most widely read supporter of class preferences, explicitly sees preferences as a step that will "help reforge the coalition required to sustain much-needed social programs"—in other words, as a way to strengthen the political left.[49]

In the absence of any uniform definition of class or of social disadvantage, then, each college or university giving class preferences would be free—indeed, obliged—to fix its own definition. Class preferences, accordingly, would confer great power and discretion on the faculties and administrators undertaking to bestow them. The decisions about preferential treatment would not be made on academic criteria, which is where these institutions' expertise is claimed to be: preferences are avowedly a departure from such criteria. Moreover, since colleges and universities are protective of the confidentiality of their admissions decisions, the precise criteria of class disadvantage—and especially the all-important weightings of these criteria—would certainly not be made public. Indeed, no institution thus far that has adopted such preferences has revealed this information. Without public transparency, such preferences would be open to political pressures of various kinds. They would be open to ideological gerrymandering as well. Perhaps "class" admissions preferences would be attractive if colleges and universities were widely trusted to make non-academic social policy decisions and if preferential treatment were the only way to expand educational opportunity. Neither is the case.

OPENING THE DOORS WITHOUT PREFERENTIAL TREATMENT

In recent decades, economic barriers to educational opportunity have grown in at least two ways. First, the cost of higher education has risen sharply, both at private and at public institutions, far ahead of the rate of inflation.[50] Second, there has been a movement away from need-based scholarships toward merit scholarships, regardless of need.[51] Moreover, reflecting federal aid policies, colleges and universities have moved away from scholarship grants in general toward student loans: students relying on what is now offered as "financial aid" must often incur very substantial debt.[52]

The movement away from need-based scholarships is easily explained. Colleges and universities compete for the most highly qualified students. Enrolling such students is an important factor in widely publicized rankings of colleges and universities, such as in *U.S. News & World Report*, which in turn affect the prestige and competitive standing of these institutions. Many institutions therefore offer scholarship grants to applicants with the very highest test scores and other credentials, regardless of need, instead of directing their aid budgets toward other fully qualified, but needier, applicants.[53]

The dramatic rise in tuition costs in recent decades is less easily explained. Colleges and universities surely enjoyed a strong market position during much of this time, with higher education much in demand, especially given the apparent economic advantages of being a graduate. Various fixed costs to the institutions may have risen during these years, perhaps outpacing the rate of inflation. But it is also clear that expenditure on administration rose sharply on campus in recent decades. This was due in part to government compliance demands, in part to pressures for student services, in part to a shriveling of faculty governance that has come with the fragmentation of university curricula and the growing emphasis on publication and individual grant-seeking, and in part to higher education's bureaucratic preoccupation with "diversity and inclusion."[54]

Along with the growth in the number and expense of administrators, faculty salaries have risen for senior, tenured faculty, although much teaching is increasingly devolved to ill-paid adjuncts. In 2018, the average salary for full professors was over $100,000, taking into account more than one thousand universities and colleges, including community colleges.[55] At the more prestigious institutions, and on the faculties of professional schools, the average salaries for full professors are much higher still.

If the goal is to increase educational opportunity, a straight-forward way of doing it would be to ensure that scholarship aid is offered on the basis of need—to applicants admitted on their merits—rather than to bid for "star" students regardless of need. The academic cost to the college or university of a "need-based" policy would be minimal, although it might indeed preclude a certain amount of jockeying for position in the *U.S. News* rankings.

More controversially, if higher education is to be more accessible to poorer families, greater effort could be made to control costs. This might mean some sacrifice by tenured professors by way of how much their salaries rise or in terms of their teaching loads. It might mean fewer academic administrators or less lavish buildings. But it would not entail the compromise of academic quality and integrity that is inherent in preferential lowering of standards based on students' class origins.

Perhaps it is understandable that senior professors, including those who express the most fervent commitment to educational equity, might not wish to make any sacrifice in their salaries or teaching loads; that institutions prefer to use scholarship grants to enhance their rankings, rather than to aid needy students; and that controlling costs is not a priority when market forces do not compel it. Social-class affirmative action, by contrast, requires no sacrifices along these lines, whatever its costs in academic integrity; indeed, such affirmative action would only increase the power and prerogatives of faculty and administrators, deciding at their discretion who is to receive preferential treatment.

The mystique of affirmative action, moreover, is very strong among academic faculty and administrators. With the passage of Proposition 209 in California and similar initiatives and laws elsewhere, and with the ever-looming possibility that the Supreme Court might someday declare racial preferences unconstitutional in public colleges and universities, "class" affirmative action may have won academic adherents on the basis that "we are committed to preferences, and if we can't do it by race then let's do it by class." The affirmative-action outlook, by its very nature, tends to be inimical to impartial academic standards and to view preferential treatment not as a last resort but as something nearer to a first resort.

There is surely good reason to be concerned about educational equity in America and about making careers genuinely open to talent. Everyone knows that life is not a level playing field. Accidents of birth and upbringing differentiate people and their prospects in life, including their educational prospects. But there are reasonable things that can be done to mitigate educational inequality. If primary and secondary public education were more academically rigorous, it would reduce the competitive advantage of growing up in a cultured and well-read home. More immediately, colleges and universities could choose to allocate their scholarship budgets on the basis of need. And they could make greater efforts to control their tuition costs.

Class preferences, by contrast, tend to corrode the quality of higher education, to introduce a new element of arbitrariness and unfairness, and to mark a quantum jump in politicizing academic life in the United States. In a world economy in which prosperity and growth depend increasingly on education and knowledge—and social mobility, in turn, depends on prosperity and growth—burdening American higher education in this way tends to threaten social mobility rather than promote it. Some cures are worse than the disease. Perhaps class preference might be justifiable as a last resort. There are many first resorts that ought to be resorted to first.[†]

[†] An earlier version of this essay appeared in the *San Diego Law Review*.

ACKNOWLEDGMENTS

Thanks to Will Baskin, Amanda DeMatto, Will DeRooy, Alex Heideman, Roger Kimball, Dan Morenoff, Alison Somin, Mary Spencer, Wenyuan Wu, Lois Zvolensky, and especially Carissa Mulder for all their help in making this volume possible.

CONTRIBUTORS

JOHN M. ELLIS is Distinguished Professor Emeritus of German Literature at the University of California, Santa Cruz, and was its dean of graduate studies and research 1977–86. He is chair of the board of directors of the California Association of Scholars and was its president 2007–2013. He is the author of ten books on German literature, theory of language, and academic reform, most recently *The Breakdown of Higher Education: How It Happened, the Damage It Does, and What Can Be Done.*

GAIL HERIOT is a professor of law at the University of San Diego and a member of the U.S. Commission on Civil Rights. She sits on the board of directors of the American Civil Rights Project, Californians for Equal Rights, the National Association of Scholars, and its state affiliate, the California Association of Scholars. She was co-chair of both the campaign for California's Proposition 209 in 1996 and the successful campaign to prevent its repeal in 2020. She blogs at Instapundit and the Volokh Conspiracy.

LANCE IZUMI is senior director of the Center for Education at the Pacific Research Institute. He is the author of numerous books on education reform. He served as president of the board of governors of the California Community Colleges and as a commissioner on the California Postsecondary Education Commission. He served as director of writing and research for California governor George Deukmejian and as speechwriter for

Attorney General Edwin Meese III in the Reagan administration.

ROWENA M. ITCHON is senior vice president at the Pacific Research Institute, where she oversees research, marketing, and operations. She has edited more than 100 studies and books published by the institute, as well as produced videos and films. Her experience in public policy and government includes the speechwriting offices of former California governor Pete Wilson and President Ronald Reagan.

PETER N. KIRSANOW is a partner at Benesch, Friedlander, Coplan & Aronoff, a former member of the National Labor Relations Board, and a member of the U.S. Commission on Civil Rights. He received his BA from Cornell University and his JD from Cleveland State University. He has been published in dozens of magazines, newspapers and online sites.

HEATHER MAC DONALD is the bestselling author of *The Diversity Delusion* and *The War on Cops: How the New Attack on Law and Order Makes Everyone Less Safe.* She is the Thomas W. Smith Fellow at the Manhattan Institute and a contributing editor of *City Journal.* She has received numerous awards for her writing; she testifies frequently before Senate and House Committees. She has degrees in English from Yale and Cambridge Universities and a JD from Stanford.

CARISSA MULDER is an attorney in Washington, DC, and the special assistant to Commissioner Peter Kirsanow of the U.S. Commission on Civil Rights. She received her BA from Grand Canyon University and her JD from the University of Notre Dame.

MAIMON SCHWARZSCHILD is a professor of law at the University of San Diego and an affiliated professor at the University of Haifa. He is a member of the California State Advisory Committee to the U.S. Commission on Civil Rights. He is a member of the editorial board of the *Journal of Law & Philosophy*. He is an English barrister and has been a visiting professor at the University of Paris/Sorbonne and the Hebrew University in Jerusalem.

PETER W. WOOD is president of the National Association of Scholars. He served as provost of The King's College in New York City and as the president's chief of staff at Boston University, where he was also a tenured member of the anthropology department. He is the author of *1620: A Critical Response to the 1619 Project*.

NOTES

STARTING DOWN THE SLIPPERY SLOPE

1 These federal grant programs were administered by the Department of Health, Education, and Welfare (as it was then known), and later the Department of Education, under the auspices of Title VI of the 1964 Civil Rights Act, 42 U.S.C. §§2000-2000d-7.

A DUBIOUS EXPEDIENCY

1 18 Cal. 3d 36, 62-63 (1976).

2 The justifications that were thought appealing in the past are sometimes forgotten. For example, in the decades following the American Civil War, anti-Chinese mobs in California used both physical and political force against Chinese laundry businesses. *See, e.g.,* Yick Wo v. Hopkins, 118 U.S. 356 (1886). It was apparently their view that Chinese laundry businesses, of which there were many, were unfairly depriving white women, particularly widows, from earning a respectable living as laundresses and disrupting families by taking over traditional women's work. *See* David Bernstein, *Lochner, Parity, and the Chinese Laundry Cases*, 41 WM. & MARY L. REV. 211, 224 (1999); Paul Ong, *An Ethnic Trade: The Chinese Laundries in Early California*, J. ETHNIC STUD. 95, 96 (Fall 1981).

3 ALLAN SINDLER, BAKKE, DEFUNIS AND MINORITY ADMISSIONS: THE QUEST FOR EQUAL OPPORTUNITY (1978).

4 *Id.* at 64.

5 Harriet Chiang & Bob Egelko, *Stanley Mosk, 1912-2001, State Supreme Justice Dies at 88*, S.F. CHRON., June 20, 2001.

6 438 U.S. 265 (1978).

7 *See* Peter Schmidt, *U. of Colorado at Boulder Is Criticized for Its Diversity Expenditures*, CHRON. HIGHER ED. (Jan. 17, 2007) (citing a report that states that "of the $21.8-million that the campus has reported spending on diversity programs, just $4-million goes toward student scholarships" and noting that "Chancellor Peterson has acknowledged that the $21.8-million figure is 'not even close' to a full total for the campus's diversity expenditures."), https://www.chronicle.com/article/u-of-colorado-at-boulder-is-criticized-for-its-diversity-expenditures. *See also* Heather Mac Donald, *Multiculti U:*

The Budget-Strapped University of California Squanders Millions on Mindless Diversity Programs, CITY JOURNAL, Spring 2013, https://www.city-journal.org/html/multiculti-u-13544.html.

8 Grutter v. Bollinger, 539 U.S. 306 (2003).

9 *See, e.g.,* STEPHEN COLE & ELINOR BARBER, INCREASING FACULTY DIVERSITY: THE OCCUPATIONAL CHOICES OF HIGH ACHIEVING MINORITY STUDENTS (2003); Frederick L. Smyth & John J. McArdle, *Ethnic and Gender Differences in Science Graduation at Selective Colleges with Implications for Admission Policy and College Choice*, 45 RES. HIGHER EDUC. 353 (2004); Richard H. Sander, *A Systemic Analysis of Affirmative Action in American Law Schools*, 57 STAN. L. REV. 367 (2004); Rogers Elliott, A. Christopher Strenta, Russell Adair, Michael Matier & Jannah Scott, *The Role of Ethnicity in Choosing and Leaving Science in Highly Selective Institutions*, 37 RES. HIGHER EDUC. 681 (1996).

10 Things are evidently not very different in medical schools. This is consistent with the results of a 1994 JAMA study, which reported that an astonishing 51.1% of African American medical students failed the Part I exam, as contrasted with only 12.3% of white medical students. *See* B. Dawson, C.K. Iwamoto, L.P. Ross, R.J. Nungester, D.B. Swanson & R.L. Volle, *Performance on the National Board of Medical Examiners Part I Examination by Men and Women of Different Race and Ethnicity*, 272 JAMA 674 (Sept. 7, 1994). Racial preferences almost wholly accounted for the gap. When African American medical students competed against white exam takers with similar academic credentials, they fared about the same.

 R.C. Davidson & E.L. Lewis, *Affirmative Action and Other Special Consideration Admissions at the University of California, Davis, School of Medicine*, 278 JAMA 1153 (Oct. 8, 1997), has been touted by its authors as proof that relaxing academic standards in medical school admissions to admit more African American and Hispanic students is harmless—that it does not affect the quality of the doctors who graduate. The actual data, however, support the opposite conclusion. *See* Gail Heriot, *Doctored Affirmative Action Data*, WALL ST. J., Oct. 15, 1997.

11 Sander, *supra* note 9, at 427.

12 *Id.* at 431.

13 *Id.*

14 *Id.* at 427-36, Tables 5.1, 5.3 & 5.4.

15 *See* Ian Ayres & Richard Brooks, *Does Affirmative Action Reduce the Number of Black Lawyers?*, 57 STAN. L. REV. 1807, 1807 (2005) ("Richard Sander's study of affirmative action at U.S. law schools highlights a real and serious problem: the average black law student's grades are startlingly low").

16 WILLIAM G. BOWEN & DEREK BOK, THE SHAPE OF THE RIVER: LONG-TERM CONSEQUENCES OF CONSIDERING RACE IN COLLEGE AND UNIVERSITY ADMISSIONS 72 (1998). The figures presented in Bowen & Bok for elite undergraduate institutions are not quite so alarming as the figures for law

schools. But there are two ways in which they understate the problem. First, they report the average GPA for African Americans and not for African Americans who needed a preference to attend the school they attended. Second, the lack of a common undergraduate curriculum makes comparisons misleading. Minority students are less likely to choose tough majors like physics and chemistry, which are notorious for both their competitiveness and their low curve. *See* Peter Arcidiacono, Esteban Aucejo, & Ken Spenner, *What Happens After Enrollment? An Analysis of the Time Path of Racial Differences in GPA and Major Choice*, 1 IZA J. LAB. & ECON. art. 5 (2012). This artificially inflates performance. Despite this, the authors found that the average African American student's grades at the elite schools they studied was in the 23rd percentile and characterized the grades gap as "very large when seen in the context of the overall distribution of grades." BOWEN & BOK at 72. Some attempt to explain the poor grades of the typical African American student as something other than just poor performance. African American students as a group simply do not test well, some say. But where evidence is available, it tends to demonstrate otherwise. In law schools, for example, the black-white gap is at least as great in legal writing classes as it is in classes that are graded by a traditional examination. Sander, *supra* note 9, at 427.

17 *See, e.g.*, THOMAS SOWELL, INSIDE AMERICAN EDUCATION: THE DECLINE, THE DECEPTION, THE DOGMAS (1993).

18 Being the most gifted student in the class can pose similar mismatch problems. Such a student may learn less than she would have in a class with students more like herself, in part because she knows she can get the A without much effort. Put simply, it is best for a student to be challenged but not *too* challenged.

19 *See* Esther Duflo, Pascaline Dupas & Michael Kremer, *Peer Effects, Teacher Incentives, and the Impact of Tracking: Evidence from a Randomized Evaluation in Kenya*, 101 AM. ECON REV. 1739 (2011) ("To the extent that students benefit from high-achieving peers, tracking will help strong students and hurt weak ones. However, all students may benefit if tracking allows teachers to present material at a more appropriate level. Lower-achieving pupils are particularly likely to benefit from tracking if teachers would otherwise have incentives to teach to the top of the distribution.").

20 Peter Arcidiacono & Cory Koedel, *Race and College Success: Evidence from Missouri*, 6 AM. ECON. J. APPLIED ECON. 20 (2014) (finding no mismatch effect resulting from race-preferential admissions in a dataset consisting of information from several Missouri state institutions).

21 In general, when I refer to science and engineering in this article, I mean to include science, technology, engineering, and mathematics, which are collectively referred to as "STEM" by some career experts. Because I cannot bring myself to use such jargon, I use "science and engineering." The exception is when I discuss the findings of individual empirical studies. There I use terms as they are used in the particular study I am discussing.

22 Dana Milbank, *Education: Shortage of Scientists Approaches a Crisis as More Students Drop Out of the Field*, WALL ST. J., Sept. 17, 1990.

23 Richard Sander & Roger Bolus, Do Credentials Gaps in College Reduce the Number of Minority Science Graduates?, Working Paper 2 (Draft July 2009) (using data from 2003).

24 Elliott et al., *supra* note 9, at 695.

25 *Id.* at 700.

26 *See, e.g.*, Elliott et al., *supra* note 9; Smyth & McArdle, *supra* note 9.

27 *Status and Trends in the Education of Racial and Ethnic Groups*, NATIONAL CENTER FOR EDUCATION STATISTICS (Feb. 2019) (2017 figures), https:// nces.ed.gov/programs/raceindicators/indicator_RAA.asp; *Fast Facts: Degrees Conferred by Race and Sex*, NATIONAL CENTER FOR EDUCATION STATISTICS, Table 318.45 & Table 322.20, https://nces.ed.gov/programs/digest/d18/ tables/dt18_318.45.asp and https://nces.ed.gov/programs/digest/d18/tables/ dt18_322.20.asp. Figures are for degrees conferred on American citizens and resident aliens only.

28 Sander & Bolus, *supra* note 23, at 1. These figures are, in part, a reflection of the immigration of highly qualified individuals from abroad.

29 Beverly Gray, *Is There a "Docta" in the House?: Red Tape and a Lower Earning Potential Have Made a Career in Medicine Seem Unappealing to a Growing Number of Jews*, JEWISH JOURNAL (Sept. 4, 2003) (stating that 2% of the American population at the end of the 20th century was Jewish, but Jewish doctors made up 12% to 15% of the physicians), https://jewishjournal.com/ culture/health/8326/; Leon Bouvier, *Doctors and Nurses: A Demographic Profile*, Table 3.8, CENTER FOR IMMIGRATION STUDIES (Feb. 1998) (showing that 2% of physicians in the United States are ethnically Chinese, 1.1% are ethnically Cuban, and 3.9% are ethnically South Asian), http://www.cis.org/ articles/1998/DocsandNurses.html#3.7. All three of the percentages cited by Bouvier were in excess of the proportion of the American population for that ethnic group as recorded by the U.S. Census for either 2000 or 2010.

30 Regan Morris, *How Tippi Hedren Made Vietnamese Refugees into Nail Salon Magnates*, BBC NEWS, May 3, 2015, http://www.bbc.com/news/ magazine-32544343.

31 *See Meet the Jockeys of the 2019 Kentucky Derby*, BLOODHORSE, https://www. bloodhorse.com/horse-racing/articles/233335/meet-the-jockeys-of-the-2019- kentucky-derby.

32 DICK ROSANO, WINE HERITAGE: THE STORY OF ITALIAN-AMERICAN VINTNERS (2000); THOMAS PINNEY, A HISTORY OF WINE IN AMERICA (1989).

33 JOHN P. HEINZ, URBAN LAWYERS: THE NEW SOCIAL STRUCTURE OF THE BAR (2005) (using data from Chicago).

34 Stephen R. Baker, Humaira Chaudry & Gauri S. Tilak, *Indian Radiologists in the United States: Hierarchical Distribution and Representation*, 4 J. AM. COLL. RADIOLOGY 234 (2007).

35 Elizabeth Culotta & Ann Gibbons, *Minorities in Science: Two Generations of Struggle: Special Report Overview*, 258 SCIENCE 1176, Nov. 13, 1992.

36 Calvin Sims, *What Went Wrong: Why Programs Failed*, 258 SCIENCE 1185, 1185, Nov. 13, 1992.

37 *Id.* at 1187.

38 Milestones in MESA History—1997, MESA, https://mesa.ucop.edu/timeline.

39 MESA by the Numbers, MESA, https://mesa.ucop.edu.

40 Sims, *supra* note 36, at 1187.

41 Elliott et al., *supra* note 9, at 689. When Dartmouth College psychology professor Rogers Elliott and his co-investigators looked at a sample of 4,687 students enrolling at four elite colleges and universities in 1988, they found that 55% of Asian, 44.2% of African American, 44% of Hispanic, and 41.4% of white students were initially interested in majoring in science. Similarly, Richard Sander & Roger Bolus, in analyzing all students enrolling in the University of California between 2004 and 2006, found that 57.1% of Asian, 40.5% of African American/Hispanic, and 34.7% of white students declared an intention to major in science or engineering. Sander & Bolus, *supra* note 23, at 3. Sander and Bolus also report that among the University of California students enrolling from 1992 to 2006, 52.6% of Asians declared an intention to major in science and engineering, as did 37.5% of blacks/Hispanics and 34.7% of whites. *See* Arcidiacono et al., *supra* note 16, at 1-3, 5, 12; Smyth & McArdle, *supra* note 9, at 357 (calling this finding "consistent" and citing a number of studies dating back to the late 1970s).

42 Alexander W. Astin & Helen S. Astin, *Undergraduate Science Education: The Impact of Different College Environments on the Educational Pipeline in the Sciences* 3-9, Table 3.5 (1993), https://files.eric.ed.gov/fulltext/ED362404.pdf.

43 Elliott et al., *supra* note 9, at 694; Arcidiacono et al., *supra* note 16, at 1-3, 12; Smyth & McArdle, *supra* note 9, at 361-63. *See also* National Science Foundation, *Women, Minorities, and Persons with Disabilities in Science and Engineering* (NSF Report 99-338) (1999); National Science Foundation, *Future Scarcities of Scientists and Engineers: Problems and Solutions* (1990) (finding persistence rates of 43% for majority students and 21% for minority students); T.L. Hilton, J. Hsia, D.G. Solorzano & N.L. Benton, *Persistence in Science of High Ability Minority Students*, EDUCATIONAL TESTING SERVICE (1989) (reporting that 54% of Asian, 44% of white, 36% of black, and 29% of Latino high school seniors who had intended to attend college and major in science or engineering were doing so two years later).

44 Astin & Astin, *supra* note 42, at 3-9, Table 3.5; Elliott et al., *supra* note 9, at 694; Smyth & McArdle, *supra* note 9, at 357; Sander & Bolus, *supra* note 23.

45 *See* Elliott et al., *supra* note 9; Smyth & McArdle, *supra* note 9; Sander & Bolus, *supra* note 23.

46 Elliott et al., *supra* note 9, at 700 (emphasis in original).

47 Elizabeth Culotta, *Black Colleges Cultivate Scientists*, 258 SCIENCE 1216, Nov. 13, 1992.

48 *See, e.g.,* National Science Foundation, J. Burrelli & A. Rapoport, *InfoBrief, Role of HBCUs as Baccalaureate-Origin Institutions of Black S&E Doctorate Recipients* 6, Table 2 (2008); American Association of Medical Colleges, *Diversity in Medical Education: Facts & Figures* 86, Table 19 (2012). Both sources were cited by Justice Clarence Thomas in his concurrence in Fisher v. Univ. of Texas, 133 S. Ct. 2411, 2422, 2432 n.5 (2013) (Thomas, J., concurring).

49 Culotta, *supra* note 47, at 1218.

50 Smyth & McArdle, *supra* note 9.

51 Sander & Bolus, *supra* note 23. *See also* Marc Luppino & Richard Sander, *College Major Competitiveness and Attrition from the Sciences* (2012), https:// papers.ssrn.com/sol3/papers.cfm?abstract_id=2167961.

52 Eleanor Wiske Dillon & Jeffrey A. Smith, *The Consequences of Academic Match Between Students and Colleges,* J. HUMAN RESOURCES (2019), http://jhr. uwpress.org/content/early/2019/11/07/jhr.55.3.0818-9702R1.abstract.

53 133 S. Ct. 2411 (2013).

54 Arcidiacono et al., *supra* note 16.

55 *See A Message from Administrators Regarding New Study,* DUKE CHRON., Jan. 17, 2012, http://www.dukechronicle.com/articles/2012/01/18/message-administrators-regarding-new-study#.VJdF4AC3A.

56 2019 College Admissions Bribery Scandal, WIKIPEDIA, https://en.wikipedia. org/wiki/2019_college_admissions_bribery_scandal.

57 Susan Berfield & Anne Tergson, *I Can Get Your Kid into an Ivy: Michele Hernandez Boasts that 95% of Her Teenage Clients Are Accepted by Their First-Choice School. Her Price: As Much as $40,000 a Student,* BUS. WEEK, Oct. 22, 2007, https://www.bloomberg.com/news/articles/2007-10-21/i-can-get-your-kid-into-an-ivy.

58 James Davis, *The Campus as a Frog Pond: An Application of the Theory of Relative Deprivation to Career Decisions of College Men,* 72 AM. J. SOCIO. 17 (1966).

59 *Id.* at 30-31.

60 *See* LINDA CHAVEZ, AN UNLIKELY CONSERVATIVE: THE TRANSFORMATION OF AN EX-LIBERAL (2002); DONALD ALEXANDER DOWNS, CORNELL '69: LIBERALISM AND THE CRISIS OF THE AMERICAN UNIVERSITY (1999); THOMAS SOWELL, BLACK EDUCATION: MYTHS AND TRAGEDIES 135 (1972).

61 SOWELL, *supra* note 60.

62 *See* text and note *supra* note 60.

63 Clyde Summers, *Preferential Admissions: An Unreal Solution to a Real Problem,* 1970 U. TOLEDO L. REV. 380, 384 (1970).

64 Michel Marriott, *White Accuses Georgetown Law School of Bias in Admitting Blacks,* N.Y. TIMES, Apr. 15, 1991, https://www.nytimes.com/1991/04/15/us/ white-accuses-georgetown-law-school-of-bias-in-admitting-blacks.html.

65 These figures came from data from the three-year period from July 1988 to February 1991. An LSAT score of 43 was in the 94.49th percentile. An LSAT

score of 36 was in the 70.73th percentile. Data furnished by Philip Handwerk, Institutional Researcher at the Law School Admission Council, via email on November 1, 2010.

66 *Georgetown University*, PUBLIC LEGAL, https://www.ilrg.com/rankings/law/view/44.

67 Saundra Torry, *GU Law Student Stands by Article*, WASH. POST, Apr. 18, 1991 [hereinafter Torry, *GU Law Student*], https://www.washingtonpost.com/archive/local/1991/04/18/gu-law-student-stands-by-article/6b787d93-15d5-4871-9555-baabf0a64847; Saundra Torry, *Black Law Students Assail Author of Article on GU Law Admissions*, WASH. POST, Apr. 16, 1991 [hereinafter Torry, *Black Law Students*], https://www.washingtonpost.com/archive/local/1991/04/16/black-law-students-assail-author-of-article-on-gu-law-admissions/358cf9f5-b45f-4cb3-bef9-112c4ac7a5b9; Clarence Page, *Law Student's Charges Don't Pass the Fairness Test*, CHI. TRIB., Apr. 24, 1991, https://www.chicagotribune.com/news/ct-xpm-1991-04-24-9102060343-story.html.

68 Page, *supra* note 67.

69 Marriott, *supra* note 64.

70 Saundra Torry, *Affirmative Action a Flash Point at GU; Law Students Jam Meeting to Decry Article as Racist*, WASH. POST, Apr. 17, 1991, https://www.washingtonpost.com/archive/local/1991/04/17/affirmative-action-a-flash-point-at-gu/16ce1388-7756-4712-b9e3-f831d93dfe38.

71 *Id.*

72 *Id.*

73 *Id.*

74 Editorial, *A Numbers Game at Georgetown Law*, N.Y. TIMES, Apr. 18, 1991, A24, https://www.nytimes.com/1991/04/18/opinion/a-numbers-game-at-georgetown-law.html.

75 *See also, e.g.*, Colman McCarthy, *Tests Measure Small Portions of One's Ability*, ST. PETERSBURG TIMES, Apr. 26, 1991.

76 Silence has its costs. *Cf.* Peter Arcidiacono, Esteban M. Aucejo, Hanming Fang & Kenneth I. Spenner, *Does Affirmative Action Lead to Mismatch? A New Test and Evidence*, 2 QUANT. ECON. 303 (2011) (discussing how asymmetrical access to information can lead preference beneficiaries to attend the more elite school that has offered them admission rather than the school at which they would have a greater chance of success).

77 Torry, *Black Law Students, supra* note 67; Torry, *GU Law Student, supra* note 67. Dean Areen's complaint that Maguire's sample was not necessarily random was not without merit. His sample was indeed inadequate to prove the size of the credentials gap with certainty. There was no way to know whether the files in the pile he examined were placed together for a reason or not. But Maguire's highly suggestive findings were the only evidence available for anyone on the outside of a college or university admissions office. Race-based admissions policies ordinarily operated beneath the radar screen, and for once the public was getting some information. The fact that

Areen declined to furnish the actual figures made Maguire's seem all the more credible. It was only after the Cornblatt memorandum came to light that it became clear that Maguire's figures more likely understated than overstated the credentials gap.

78 Torry, *GU Law Student, supra* note 67.

79 Charles Krauthammer, . . . *Secrecy and Conformity*, WASH. POST, Apr. 16, 1991, https://www.washingtonpost.com/archive/opinions/1991/04/26/secrecy-and-conformity/8874d4ed-9f9e-4c3f-9fbe-0622c4cf4d1a; *Student Faces School Charges for His Position*, LUDINGTON DAILY NEWS, Apr. 29, 1991.

80 Nathan McCall, *Reprimand 'Vindicates Me,' Georgetown Law Student Says*, WASH. POST, May 22, 1991, https://www.washingtonpost.com/archive/local/1991/05/22/reprimand-vindicates-me-georgetown-law-student-says/056782c4-8d8c-4cdd-ba16-bbebdcd61154.

81 Gabriel Escobar, *At GU Law Center, Silence Speaks in Protest; Green Ribbons, Placards Replace Angry Words as Author of Race Article Receives Degree*, WASH. POST, May 28, 1991.

82 *See* George M. McCarter, *The New Jersey Supreme Court Committee on Character (Or Who Will Guard the Guardians?)*, www.mccarterhiggins.com/Maguire.html (short essay by Maguire's attorney in those proceedings).

83 Althea Nagai, *If California Restores Race Discrimination: Implications for Higher Education*, CENTER FOR EQUAL OPPORTUNITY (Sept. 8, 2020), http://www.ceousa.org/attachments/article/1374/California Project.Final-Embargoed_9-9-20.pdf.

84 *Id.* at 16.

85 Althea K. Nagai, *Racial and Ethnic Preferences in Undergraduate Admissions at the University of Michigan*, CENTER FOR EQUAL OPPORTUNITY (Oct. 17, 2006), http://www.ceousa.org/attachments/article/548/UM_UGRAD_final.pdf.

86 Althea Nagai, *Admissions Discrimination at Virginia Public Universities*, CENTER FOR EQUAL OPPORTUNITY (Sept. 10, 2019), http://www.ceousa.org/affirmative-action/1331-admissions-discrimination-at-virginia-public-universities.

87 Althea Nagai, *Racial and Ethnic Preferences in Undergraduate Admissions at the University of Wisconsin-Madison*, CENTER FOR EQUAL OPPORTUNITY (Sept. 13, 2011), https://www.ceousa.org/attachments/article/546/U.Wisc.undergrad.pdf.

88 *See* Statement of Commissioner Gail Heriot, U.S. Commission on Civil Rights, AFFIRMATIVE ACTION IN AMERICAN LAW SCHOOLS 175-184 (2007).

89 The academic index used by Sander is computed in this manner: Academic Index + 0.4 (UGPA) + 0.6 (LSAT), with both UGPA and LSAT normalized into a one-thousand-point scale. Most, if not all, law schools use such an index. The particular formula used by Sander is fairly typical. Sander, *supra* note 9, at 393. As for the size of the gap, *see* Sander at 416, Table 3.2.

90 Althea K. Nagai, *Racial and Ethnic Preferences in Admission at the University of*

Nebraska College of Law, CENTER FOR EQUAL OPPORTUNITY (Oct. 8, 2008), http://www.ceousa.org/attachments/article/544/NE_LAW.pdf. According to the report, in 2006, the median LSAT score for African American admittees was 146, with the 75th percentile score at 152 and the 25th percentile score at 142. For Hispanics, the median was 151, and the 75th and 25th percentile scores were 153 and 148. For whites, the corresponding figures were 158, 160, and 155. The preference given to under-represented minorities swamped the preference given to Nebraska citizens. All other things being equal, an African American out-of-stater was much more likely to be admitted than a white Nebraskan.

91 Althea K. Nagai, *Racial and Ethnic Preferences in Admission at University of Utah College of Law*, CENTER FOR EQUAL OPPORTUNITY (August 2013), https://www.ceousa.org/attachments/article/880/Utah%20Law%20School.pdf.

92 Robert Lerner & Althea K. Nagai, *Preferences in Medical Education: Racial and Ethnic Preferences in Admissions at Five Public Medical Schools*, CENTER FOR EQUAL OPPORTUNITY (Jun. 14, 2001), https://www.ceousa.org/attachments/article/659/multimed.pdf; Althea K. Nagai, *Racial and Ethnic Preferences in Admission at the University of Michigan Medical School*, CENTER FOR EQUAL OPPORTUNITY (Oct. 17, 2006), https://www.ceousa.org/attachments/article/543/UMichMedFinal.pdf.

93 Editorial, *The Facts About Affirmative Action*, N.Y. TIMES, Sept. 14, 1998, https://www.nytimes.com/1998/09/14/opinion/the-facts-about-affirmative-action.html.

94 Ellis Cose, *Cutting Through Race Rhetoric*, NEWSWEEK, Sept. 28, 1998.

95 Cynthia Tucker, *Affirmative Action Backers on Solid Ground*, ATLANTA JOURNAL-CONSTITUTION, Sept. 13, 1998.

96 Nathan Glazer, *A Place for Racial Preferences*, WASH. POST, Nov. 24, 1998.

97 Editorial, *Affirmative Evidence, Racial Preferences Help, Not Harm, Black Students*, PITTS. POST-GAZETTE, Sept. 12, 1998.

98 Some enrolled in 1951. Since affirmative action was not practiced in 1951, no purpose could have been served by including those who enrolled in 1951 in the parts of the study that are relevant to mismatch, and it does not appear that they were included. Given that, the 80,000-person count may be overstated.

99 *See* Stephan Thernstrom & Abigail Thernstrom, *Reflections on The Shape of the River*, 46 U.C.L.A. L. REV. 1583, 1590 (1999).

100 BOWEN & BOK, *supra* note 16, at 47 (using 1992 figures furnished by economist Thomas Kane derived from the National Longitudinal Study and defining low-income families as those with incomes of $20,000 or less).

101 *See* text and note, *supra* at note 16.

102 BOWEN & BOK, *supra* note 16, at 143, Table 5.1.

103 *Id.* at 144.

104 This seems strange for supporters of race-based admissions policies. Supporters frequently argue that standardized tests scores shouldn't be

regarded as the measure of a man or woman, and of course they are right. There are a large number of factors a college or university might legitimately take into account. High school rank looms very large for nearly all selective schools—larger than standardized test scores. And some schools may want to take other things into account—from musicianship to military service to an interest in the welfare of small children. Private schools may wish to take religion or even commitment to a particular political ideology into consideration. The point opponents make is simply that race shouldn't be among them.

105 Gail Heriot, *The Sad Irony of Affirmative Action*, NATIONAL AFFAIRS 89 (Winter 2013), http://www.nationalaffairs.com/doclib/20130102_Heriot.pdf.

106 BOWEN & BOK, *supra* note 16, at 143, Table 5.1.

107 *Id.* at Appendix D.5.4 and Appendix D.5.5.

108 *See* U.S. News & World Report's College Rankings (2011). The average combined SAT score for Pennsylvania State University students is reported to be 1090 at the 25th percentile and 1300 at the 75th percentile. Note that I am using SAT scores from the 2011 edition of *U.S. News & World Report* rather than the scores that would have been applicable at the time the students studied by Bowen & Bok would have been in college. There are two reasons for this. First, they will seem more familiar to most readers. In 1995, the SAT was re-centered in a way that makes what used to be an excellent score seem less so. There was a time, for example, when a score of 1400 would have been more than sufficient to get an applicant into any school in the country (with the possible exception of Caltech). Under the 1995 adjustments, that was no longer the case. Second, *U.S. News & World Report* currently publishes SAT scores for each institution at the 75th and 25th percentiles. That makes it easier to estimate whether a particular student with scores in the bottom quarter of a particular Tier 1 school would be in the top quarter of a particular Tier 3 school. In 1978, one of the years that many of the students in the Bowen & Bok study would have been in college, the average SAT score for each school would have been as follows (old scale): Pennsylvania State University (1038), Princeton University (1308), University of North Carolina (Chapel Hill) (1080), and Yale University (1360). *See* Stacy Berg Dale & Alan B. Krueger, *Estimating the Payoff to Attending a More Selective College: An Application of Selection on Observables and Unobservables*, Q. J. ECON. 1491, 1525 (appendix 1) (2002) (using HERI figures).

109 *See* U.S. News & World Report's College Rankings (2011), *supra* note 108. The average combined SAT score for Princeton students was reported to be 1390 at the 25th percentile and 1580 at the 75th percentile.

110 *See id.* The average combined SAT score for Yale students was reported to be 1400 at the 25th percentile and 1580 at the 75th percentile. The corresponding figures for the University of North Carolina were 1210 and 1410.

111 The study that this more closely resembles is Linda Datcher Loury & David Garman, *Affirmative Action in Higher Education*, 83 AM. ECON. REV. 99 (1993) ("those who attend the most selective colleges and perform less well because of mismatching would have had higher earning if they had attended the somewhat less selective group of schools").

112 Compare Peter Arcidiacono, Esteban Aucejo, Patrick Coate & V. Joseph
Hotz, *Affirmative Action and University Fit: Evidence from Proposition 209*,
National Bureau of Economic Research Working Paper 18523 (2012) (finding
a mismatch effect on graduation rates), https://www.nber.org/papers/w18523.
pdf; Audrey Light & Wayne Strayer, *Determinants of College Completion:
School Quality or Student Ability*, 35 J. HUMAN RESOURCES 299 (2000) ("We
find that students of all abilities have higher chances of graduation if the
quality level of their college 'matches' their observed skill level"); and Linda
Datcher Loury & David Garman, *Affirmative Action in Higher Education*, 83
AM. ECON. REV. 99 (1993) ("With higher required levels of performance and
smaller offsetting increases in actual performance, [mismatched] blacks at
more selective schools will have poorer grades, be less likely to graduate,
and choose less lucrative majors than if they had attended less selective
institutions") with Sigal Alon & Marta Tienda, *Assisting the "Mismatch"
Hypothesis: Differences in College Graduation Rates by Institutional Selectivity*,
78 SOCIOLOGY EDUC. 294 (2005) (finding no mismatch effect on graduation
rates) and Mary J. Fischer & Douglas S. Massey, *The Effects of Affirmative
Action in Higher Education*, 36 SOC. SCI. RES. 531 (2007) ("We find no
evidence for the mismatch hypothesis. If anything, individual students with
SAT scores below the institutional average do better than other students,
other things equal"). *See also* Eleanor Wiske Dillon & Jeffrey Andrew Smith,
The Consequences of Academic Match Between Students and Colleges, 55 J.
HUMAN RESOURCES 767 (2019) (finding a mismatch effect at the four-year
graduation rate, but not at the six-year rate). Each of these studies employed
a different methodology. For example, the Fischer & Massey analysis controls
for students' feelings of self-efficacy and self-esteem.

In 2012, Richard Sander and Stuart Taylor, Jr., criticized earlier studies of
graduation rates on the ground that they understate the mismatch effect by
failing to take into account the "unobservables" that separate students who
attend more elite schools from those who appear to have similar credentials
but who were not selected by such a school. RICHARD SANDER & STUART
TAYLOR, JR., MISMATCH: HOW AFFIRMATIVE ACTION HURTS STUDENTS IT'S
INTENDED TO HELP, AND WHY UNIVERSITIES WON'T ADMIT IT, 107 (2012).
Sander himself had studied law school graduation rates in a way that seems
to eliminate the "unobservable" problem. He compared African American
students who had gotten into their "first choice" law school but had passed it
up in order to attend a school that had originally been their second or lower
choice to all other African American students and to white students. The
reasons for the second choice could be a matter of geography or of financial
aid available. The interesting thing was that these students were much more
similar to white students than to other African American students in their
graduation rates. Indeed, once entering academic credentials were controlled
for, they were more likely to graduate than white students and much more
likely to graduate than other African American students. *See* Richard H.
Sander, *A Reply to Critics*, 57 STAN. L. REV. 1963 (2005).

113 COLE & BARBER, *supra* note 9, at 124 (citations omitted).

114 *Id.* at 30.

115 *Id.* at 249.

116 *Id.*

117 Robin Wilson, *The Unintended Consequences of Affirmative Action: A Controversial Study from Unlikely Sources Asks Why College Faculties Lack Diversity*, CHRON. HIGHER EDUC., Jan. 27, 2003, https://www.chronicle.com/article/the-unintended-consequences-of-affirmative-action.

118 Sander, *supra* note 9, at 370.

119 *See, e.g.*, Elie Mystal, *Racists' T-Shirts on Campus? Only If You Bother to Think About It*, ABOVE THE LAW (Nov. 22, 2013) (arguing that UCLA first-year students in Professor Sander's property class, who printed up "Team Sander" T-shirts to distinguish themselves from the students in the other Property small section, deliberately intended to send a racist message), https://abovethelaw.com/2013/11/racists-t-shirts-on-campus-only-if-you-bother-to-think-about-it.

120 Sander, *supra* note 9, at 428, Table 5.2. While thirty-five years earlier it had been common for preference supporters to argue that African American students would perform better than their entering credentials once they got into an elite school (and that, therefore, preferential treatment is justified), Sander's critics have argued just the opposite—that African American students will perform *even less well* then their entering credentials suggest. Their argument runs this way: Sander paints too rosy a picture of African American academic performance in law school. In fact, ending race preferences and letting African American students enroll in schools where their entering credentials match those of other students will not cause those African American students to pass the bar as often as their white or Asian peers. No matter what law school they attend, they will fail at higher rates than white and Asian American students with identical academic indices. Sander's belief that the problem can be remedied is, thus, overly optimistic—or so their argument goes. This is a very odd way to defend race-based admissions. The argument that was made thirty-five years ago was perfectly coherent: Hypothetically, an African American student from a poor background with a B average in high school might have overcome so much to achieve that B average that one could realistically expect him to "catch up" to his fellow students with an A average in elite schools. It, therefore, it made sense for an admissions officer to take a chance and admit him. Actual experience, however, did not bear out this theory. The argument made by Sander's critics today is that African American students with a B average should be admitted to law schools that would ordinarily require an A average but that they will probably perform below even the level their B average would suggest. This is an uncomfortable argument for a supporter of race-based admissions to have to make. Sander has replied to this criticism by showing that "all of the available evidence (including the large systematic study by Anthony & Liu) indicates that at least ninety percent of the black-white grade gap is attributable to racial preferences, not black underperformance." Richard H. Sander, *A Reply to Critics*, 57 STAN. L. REV. 1963, 1997 (2005). *See* Lisa C. Anthony & Mei Liu, Law School Admission Council, LSAT Technical Report 00-02, *Analysis of Differential*

Prediction of Law School Performance by Racial/Ethnic Subgroups Based on the 1996-1998 Entering Law School Classes 14–15 (2003) (finding only "very slight" underperformance (one-eighth of a standard deviation) by African American law students, controlling for preferences), https://files.eric.ed.gov/fulltext/ED479509.pdf. While it is possible that African Americans underperform their entering credentials by some tiny amount, this phenomenon is swamped by the racial preference effect. No one has disputed Sander's reply on this matter.

121 Sander, *supra* note 9, at 437, Table 5.5.

122 *Id.* at 439, Table 5.6. The other factors that seemed to matter were the ranking of the law school and part-time status. Both had overwhelmingly more importance than family income, which mattered only very slightly.

123 *Id.* at 442, Table 6.2.

124 *Id.* at 454.

125 Sander was not convinced that the greater attention to the bar exam by itself was important. *Id.* at 449. He noted that "[w]hen we control as best we can for the incoming credentials of student bodies, students at more elite schools have higher, not lower, success rates on the bar." *See id.* at 444, Table 6.1 & 449.

126 *Id.* at 473, Table 8.2. These calculations were drawn from data for matriculants in the year 2001 at ABA-accredited law schools.

127 *See*, e.g., Jesse Rothstein & Albert Yoon, *Affirmative Action in Law School Admissions: What Do Racial Preferences Do?*, 75 U. CHI. L. REV. 649 (2008).

128 *See* text and note, *supra* note 1.

129 2007 SALT Equalizer (Issue 1) 3 (Feb. 2007), https://scholars.law.unlv.edu/cgi/viewcontent.cgi?article=1006&context=salt.

130 Letter from SALT Co-Presidents Eileen Kaufman and Tayyab Mahmud to Gayle Murphy, Senior Executive for Admissions, State Bar of California 2, n. 4, (Jan. 15, 2007), http://www.seaphe.org/pdf/bar-proposal/letter_from_SALT.pdf. The letter states, "Once exam scores are allowed to be equated with how well applicants 'have learned the law' it is not unreasonable to assume the bar exam might metamorphize into a ranking mechanism. Should this occur, it would open the door to a host of legal challenges."

131 Memorandum from Bill Kidder, Special Assistant to the Vice President— Student Affairs, University of California Office of the President, to Gayle Murphy, Senior Executive for Admissions, Office of Admissions, State Bar of California 2 (Jan. 19, 2007), http://www.seaphe.org/pdf/bar-proposal/kidder_critique.pdf. Kidder also coauthored a response to Sander's initial "mismatch" article (see Sander, *supra* note 9) that was published by the *Stanford Law Review* as one of the responses to the Sander article. See David L. Chambers, Timothy T. Clydesdale, William C. Kidder & Richard O. Lempert, *The Real Impact of Eliminating Affirmative Action in American Law Schools: An Empirical Critique of Richard Sander's Study*, 57 STAN. L. REV. 1855 (2005). At the time he coauthored the Sander critique, Kidder was employed as a researcher with the Equal Justice Society, an organization whose legal strategy "aims to broaden

conceptions of present-day discrimination to include unconscious and structural bias by using cognitive science, structural analysis, and real-life experience." *About the Equal Justice Society*, EQUAL JUSTICE SOCIETY, https://equaljusticesociety.org/aboutus. More recently, Kidder has been employed as an administrative staff member at the University of California.

132 Sander v. State Bar of California, 58 Cal. 4th 300, 165 Cal. Rptr. 3d 250, 314 P.3d 488 (2013).

133 Sander v. State Bar of California, 237 Cal. Rptr. 3d 276 (Cal. Ct. App. 2018) (petition for review denied, Nov. 14, 2018).

134 Richard H. Sander & Jane Bambauer, *The Secret of My Success: How Status, Eliteness, and School Performance Shape Legal Careers*, 9 J. EMPIRICAL LEGAL STUD. 893 (2012).

135 Doug Williams, *Do Racial Preferences Affect Minority Learning in Law Schools?*, 10 J. EMPIRICAL LEGAL STUD. 171 (2013).

136 Peter Arcidiacono & Michael Lovenheim, *Affirmative Action and the Quality-Fit Tradeoff*, 54 J. ECON. LIT. 3, 20 (2016).

137 Richard H. Sander & Robert Steinbuch, *Mismatch and Bar Passage: A School Specific Analysis* (Sept. 2019 draft) (on file with the editors).

138 CAL. CONST. ART. I, § 31.

139 572 U.S. 291 (2014). *See* Gail Heriot, *The Parade of Horribles Lives: Schuette v. Coalition to Defend Affirmative Action, Integration and Immigrant Rights and Fight for Equality by Any Means Necessary*, 14 ENGAGE 15 (Oct. 2013), https://fedsoc.org/commentary/publications/the-parade-of-horribles-lives-schuette-v-coalition-to-defend-affirmative-action-integration-and-immigrant-rights-and-fight-for-equality-by-any-means-necessary.

140 Gail Heriot, *The Politics of Admissions in California*, ACAD. QUESTIONS 29 (Fall 2001).

141 Kenneth R. Weiss & Mary Curtius, *Acceptance of Blacks, Latinos to UC Plunges*, L.A. TIMES, Apr. 1, 1998.

142 *Coalition for Economic Equity v. Wilson*, 122 F.3d 692 (9th Cir. 1997).

143 Heriot, *supra* note 140.

144 *Id.*

145 *Id.*

146 UC-San Diego, Academic Performance Report 1, n. 1 (1999), quoted in Heriot, *supra* note 140, at 34.

147 *Id.*

148 SANDER & TAYLOR, *supra* note 112, at 146 (2012).

149 Arcidiacono et al., *supra* note 112.

150 Kevin Carey, *A Detailed Look at the Downside of California's Ban on Affirmative Action*, N.Y. TIMES, Aug. 21, 2020, https://www.nytimes.com/2020/08/21/upshot/00up-affirmative-action-california-study.html.

151 Zachary Bleemer, *Research and Occasional Paper: Affirmative Action, Mismatch and Economic Mobility After California's Proposition 209*, UC Berkeley Center for Studies in Higher Education (Aug. 2020), https://cshe.berkeley.edu/publications/affirmative-action-mismatch-and-economic-mobility-after-california's-proposition-209.

152 Richard Sander, *A Brief Commentary on Zachary Bleemer's August 2020 Paper*, Californians for Equal Rights (Sept. 4, 2020), https://californiansforequalrights.org/wp-content/uploads/2020/09/Sander-Rebuttal.pdf.

153 The Editorial Board, *Racial Thunder out of California*, Wall St. J., Nov. 4, 2020, https://www.wsj.com/articles/racial-thunder-out-of-california-11604533888.

154 *Stanley Mosk, 88, Long a California Supreme Court Justice*, N.Y. Times, June 21, 2001, https://www.nytimes.com/2001/06/21/us/stanley-mosk-88-long-a-california-supreme-court-justice.html.

155 347 U.S. 483 (1954).

156 Jerome Karabel, The Chosen: The Hidden History of Admission and Exclusion at Harvard, Yale and Princeton 496 (2005), *quoting* John C. Jeffries, Jr., Justice Lewis F. Powell, Jr. 2, 234, 172 (2001).

157 Powell's kindred spirit on the affirmative-action issue, Justice Sandra Day O'Connor, can also be described as a pragmatic accommodator, concerned, not wholly without cause, about the problems that can arise from a politically unpopular decision. A few weeks before O'Connor's decision for the 5-4 majority in *Grutter v. Bollinger* was handed down, she published a book that gave some useful insight into her pragmatic judicial philosophy. In it, she argued that courts cannot and should not lead the nation in a direction it isn't already going. Change, she wrote, must stem "principally from attitudinal shifts in the population at large." "Rare indeed is the legal victory—in court or legislature—that is not a careful by-product of an emerging social consensus." Sandra Day O'Connor, The Majesty of the Law: Reflections of a Supreme Court Justice 166 (2003).

158 It is interesting to note in that regard that another 20th-century jurist remembered by *Time* magazine as "the most doctrinaire and committed civil libertarian ever to sit on the court," William O. Douglas, was also a vocal opponent of race-preferential admissions policies. Four years prior to the *Bakke* decision, in *DeFunis v. Odegaard*, 416 U.S. 312 (1974), the indefatigable Douglas had protested the court's decision to dodge the issue of affirmative-action admissions at the University of Washington School of Law: "There is no superior person by constitutional standards. A DeFunis who is white is entitled to no advantage by reason of that fact; nor is he subject to any disability, no matter what his race or color. Whatever his race, he had a constitutional right to have his application considered on its individual merits in a racially neutral manner." *Id.* at 337.

DIVERSITY'S DESCENT

1 *Morgan Stanley Sued by Former Diversity Chief*, BARRONS, June 16, 2020, https://www.barrons.com/articles/morgan-stanley-sued-by-former-diversity-chief-51592352526.

2 I continue a long-standing practice of italicizing *diversity* wherever I refer to the modern ideology, as distinct from its other meanings.

3 438 U.S. 265 (1978).

4 539 U.S. 306 (2003).

5 570 U.S. 297 (2013).

6 136 S. Ct. 2198 (2016).

7 GLENN RICKETTS, PETER W. WOOD, STEPHEN H. BALCH & ASHLEY THORNE, THE VANISHING WEST 1964-2010: THE DISAPPEARANCE OF WESTERN CIVILIZATION FROM THE AMERICAN UNDERGRADUATE CURRICULUM (2018).

8 STANLEY KURTZ, THE LOST HISTORY OF WESTERN CIVILIZATION (2020).

9 Dion J. Pierre & Peter Wood, *Neo-Segregation at Yale*, NATIONAL ASSOCIATION OF SCHOLARS (Apr. 2019), https://www.nas.org/storage/app/media/Reports/NeoSeg%20at%20Yale/NeoSegregation_at_Yale.pdf.

10 PETER W. WOOD, DIVERSITY: THE INVENTION OF A CONCEPT (2003); PETER W. WOOD, DIVERSITY RULES (2019); HEATHER MAC DONALD, THE DIVERSITY DELUSION (2018).

11 PAMELA NEWKIRK, DIVERSITY, INC.: THE FAILED PROMISE OF A BILLION-DOLLAR BUSINESS 2, 6 (2019).

12 IBRAM X. KENDI, STAMPED FROM THE BEGINNING: THE DEFINITIVE HISTORY OF RACIST IDEAS IN AMERICA 5, 510-511 (2016).

13 IBRAM X. KENDI, HOW TO BE AN ANTIRACIST (2019).

14 MATTHEW JOHNSON, UNDERMINING RACIAL JUSTICE: HOW ONE UNIVERSITY EMBRACED INCLUSION AND INEQUALITY 204 (2020).

15 CYNDI KERNAHAN, TEACHING ABOUT RACE AND RACISM IN THE COLLEGE CLASSROOM: NOTES FROM A WHITE PROFESSOR 5, 9, 115, 171-172, 186 (2019).

16 DANIEL MARKOVITS, THE MERITOCRACY TRAP: HOW AMERICA'S FOUNDATIONAL MYTH FEEDS INEQUALITY, DISMANTLES THE MIDDLE CLASS, AND DEVOURS THE ELITE 60-62 (2019).

17 MELVIN I. UROFSKY, THE AFFIRMATIVE ACTION PUZZLE: A LIVING HISTORY FROM RECONSTRUCTION TO TODAY 452 (2020).

18 Michael Poliakoff, *How Diversity Screening at the University of California Could Degrade Faculty Quality*, FORBES, Jan. 21, 2020, https://www.forbes.com/sites/michaelpoliakoff/2020/01/21/how-diversity-screening-at-the-university-of-california-could-degrade-faculty-quality.

19 Abigail Thompson, *A Word From...*, 66 NOTICES OF THE AMERICAN MATHEMATICAL SOCIETY 1778 (2019), https://www.ams.org/journals/notices/201911/rnoti-p1778.pdf; Colleen Flaherty, *Diversity Statements as 'Litmus Tests,'* INSIDE HIGHER ED. (Nov. 19, 2019), https://www.

insidehighered.com/news/2019/11/19/mathematician-comes-out-against-mandatory-diversity-statements-while-others-say-they.

20 PETER WOOD, 1620: A CRITICAL RESPONSE TO THE 1619 PROJECT (2020).

21 Charles Kesler, *Call Them the 1619 Riots*, N.Y. POST, June 19, 2020, https://nypost.com/2020/06/19/call-them-the-1619-riots.

22 Allison Schuster, *Nikole Hannah-Jones Endorses Riots and Toppling Statues as a Product of the 1619 Project*, THE FEDERALIST, June 20, 2020, https://thefederalist.com/2020/06/20/nikole-hannah-jones-endorses-riots-and-toppling-statues-as-a-product-of-the-1619-project.

SEGREGATION NOW

1 *Ujamaa Residential College*, CORNELL HOUSING, https://scl.cornell.edu/residential-life/housing/campus-housing/upperlevel-undergraduates/ujamaa-residential-college.

2 For a thorough account of the Willard Straight takeover and the circumstances surrounding it by a professor who was, at the time, a member of the SDS at Cornell, *see* Tony Feis, *The Fog of Youth*, QUILLETTE, June 25, 2019, https://quillette.com/2019/06/25/the-fog-of-youth-the-cornell-student-takeover-50-years-on.

3 *Our History*, UJAMAA RESIDENTIAL COLLEGE, CORNELL UNIVERSITY, https://cornell.campusgroups.com/urc/home.

4 *Id.*

5 *Ujamaa's Mission, Vision, and Motto*, UJAMAA RESIDENTIAL COLLEGE, CORNELL UNIVERSITY, https://cornell.campusgroups.com/urc/home.

6 *Meet the Team!*, UJAMAA RESIDENTIAL COLLEGE, CORNELL UNIVERSITY, https://cornell.campusgroups.com/urc/leadership-team.

7 Catherine St. Hilaire, *Ujamaa Residents, Community Members Discuss the Black Male Experience in Education*, CORNELL DAILY SUN, Nov. 22, 2019, https://cornellsun.com/2019/11/22/ujamaa-residents-community-members-discuss-the-black-male-experience-in-education/.

8 *Asian & Asian American Center (A3C)*, STUDENT AND CAMPUS LIFE, https://scl.cornell.edu/identity-resources/asian-asian-american-center-a3c.

9 *Id.*

10 Janet Liao, *C.U. Reacts to Suicide Among Asian-Americans*, CORNELL DAILY SUN, Nov. 1, 2002, https://cornellsun.com/2002/11/01/c-u-reacts-to-suicide-among-asian-americans.

11 Krishna Ramanujan, *Health Expert Explains Asian and Asian-American Students' Unique Pressures to Succeed*, CORNELL CHRONICLE, Apr. 19, 2006, https://news.cornell.edu/stories/2006/04/health-expert-explains-asian-students-unique-pressures-succeed.

12 *Id.*

13 *Id.*

14 *Id.*

15 *Profile: Class of 2023*, CORNELL UNIVERSITY, http://irp.dpb.cornell.edu/wp-content/uploads/2019/08/Profile2019-Freshmen.pdf.

16 *Id.*

17 Alex Berg, *C.U. Grants Asian Center a Space*, CORNELL DAILY SUN, Mar. 3, 2009, https://cornellsun.com/2009/03/03/cu-grants-asian-center-space.

18 Caroline Hugh, *Recent Editorials/Articles*, CORNELL'S A3C BLOG (Mar. 6, 2009), http://a3c-cornell.blogspot.com/2009/03/recent-editorials.html.

19 Dion J. Pierre & Peter Wood, *Neo-Segregation at Yale*, NATIONAL ASSOCIATION OF SCHOLARS (Apr. 2019), https://www.nas.org/storage/app/media/Reports/NeoSeg%20at%20Yale/NeoSegregation_at_Yale.pdf.

20 Caroline Hugh, *A Brief History About A3C*, CORNELL'S A3C BLOG (Oct. 4, 2008), http://a3c-cornell.blogspot.com/2008/10/brief-history-about-a3c.html.

21 Caroline Hugh, *Action Items to Keep A3C Momentum Going!*, CORNELL'S A3C BLOG (Oct. 6, 2008), http://a3c-cornell.blogspot.com/2008/10/ideas-to-keep-a3c-momentum-going.html.

22 *Get Involved with the Asian & Asian American Center*, STUDENT & CAMPUS LIFE, https://scl.cornell.edu/identity-resources/asian-asian-american-center/get-involved-asian-asian-american-center.

23 R. Shep Melnick, *The Strange Evolution of Title IX*, NATIONAL AFFAIRS, Summer 2018, https://www.nationalaffairs.com/publications/detail/the-strange-evolution-of-title-ix.

24 *Ujamaa*, STANFORD RESIDENTIAL EDUCATION, https://resed.stanford.edu/residences/find-house/ujamaa.

25 *Id.*

26 *Id.*

27 *Id.*

28 *Id.*

29 *#BlackTransLivesMatter: Black Transgender Incarceration and Activism*, STANFORD RESIDENTIAL EDUCATION, https://resed.stanford.edu/sites/g/files/sbiybj10436/f/proposal11_5.pdf.

30 *Id.*

31 *Casa Zapata*, RESIDENTIAL EDUCATION, STANFORD UNIVERSITY, https://resed.stanford.edu/residences/find-house/casa-zapata.

32 *Id.*

33 *Id.*

34 *Dorm Diversity*, STANFORD DAILY, Jan. 12, 2010, https://www.stanforddaily.com/2010/01/12/dorm-diversity/.

35 *Casa Zapata*, *supra* note 31.

36 Elvira Prieto, *RF Letter—Casa Zapata*, STANFORD UNIVERSITY, Aug. 2018, https://rde.stanford.edu/studenthousing/3003.

37 *Id.*

38 Yusra Arub, *Three Positions Filled in Student Affairs*, STANFORD DAILY, May 17, 2019, https://www.stanforddaily.com/2019/05/17/three-positions-filled-in-student-affairs.

39 *Casa Zapata, supra* note 31.

40 *Id.*

41 Prieto, *supra* note 36.

42 *Id.*

43 *Luz Jimenez Ruvalcaba,* PEOPLE: SCHOOL OF HUMANITIES AND SCIENCES, STANFORD UNIVERSITY, https://mtl.stanford.edu/people/luz-jimenez-ruvalcaba.

44 Sam Wolfe, *Ethnic Theme Houses: Cultural Centers, Not Segregated Shelters,* STANFORD REV., Apr. 3, 2017, https://medium.com/stanfordreview/ethnic-theme-houses-cultural-centers-not-segregated-shelters-9c77a899f380.

45 Sierra Garcia, *What* The Review *Gets Wrong About Ethnic Theme Dorms,* STANFORD DAILY, May 2, 2017, https://www.stanforddaily.com/2017/05/02/what-the-review-gets-wrong-about-ethnic-theme-dorms.

46 Joe Gettinger, *Ethnic Dorms: A Double Edged Sword,* STANFORD REV., Sept. 25, 2010, https://medium.com/stanfordreview/ethnic-dorms-a-double-edged-sword-da62d4f52642.

47 Scott Borgeson, *"Respected and Safe": An Open Letter to Provost Drell,* STANFORD REV., Nov. 7, 2019, https://stanfordreview.org/respected-and-safe-an-open-letter-to-provost-drell.

48 Febe Martinez & Salvador Tello, *SCR: Your Hate Speech Is Not Welcome Here,* STANFORD DAILY, Nov. 20, 2019, https://www.stanforddaily.com/2019/11/20/scr-your-hate-speech-is-not-welcome-here.

49 *Id.*

50 Kara Zupkus, *Unhinged Stanford Leftists Vandalize Shapiro Posters, Mob Conservative Students,* YOUNG AMERICA'S FOUNDATION (Oct. 28, 2019), https://www.yaf.org/news/unhinged-stanford-leftists-vandalize-shapiro-posters-mob-conservative-students.

51 Leily Rezvani & Emma Talley, *Conservative Commentator Ben Shapiro Blasts Alt-Right, Radical Left, Identity Politics in MemAud Lecture,* STANFORD DAILY, Nov. 8, 2019, https://www.stanforddaily.com/2019/11/08/conservative-commentator-ben-shapiro-blasts-alt-right-radical-left-identity-politics-in-memaud-lecture.

Some flyers hung in dorms advertising Shapiro's talk were torn down or crumpled, sparking controversy on campus. One incident led to a confrontation at Latinx-themed dorm Casa Zapata.

According to Casa Zapata resident Kamilah Arteaga '22, SCR members attempted to put flyers in the residence hall on Oct. 18, but were denied under the dorm policy that flyers must be approved by staff. Arteaga claimed that SCR was "trying to antagonize residents" after they were not invited into the dorm.

SCR posted on its public Facebook page that dorms had "erected censorious flyering policies in an attempt to keep students from hearing conservative views."

"An aggressive mob of students heckled our members and spewed obscenities," SCR wrote. "When we returned a few days later to discuss the policy with staff, our group was laughably accused of 'targeting' the dormitory."

Following the incident, Provost Persis Drell hosted an open discussion with residents in the Zapata lounge on Oct. 22.

"These acts by SCR are specifically targeting Casa Zapata and its residents, making us feel unsafe on our own campus, at our school, in our homes," Arteaga said.

52 Walker Stewart, *Free Speech Suppression on the Farm: My Experience Flyering for the Ben Shapiro Event*, STANFORD REV., Nov. 6, 2019, https:// stanfordreview.org/free-speech-suppression-on-the-farm-my-experience-flyering-for-the-ben-shapiro-event.

Casa Zapata has banned flyers altogether after their residents harassed a group of SCR members. When I entered Zapata with flyers, a resident peeked at my flyers, and only after seeing they were for the Shapiro event did she mention that flyering was banned.

53 Martinez & Tello, *supra* note 48.

As first generation, low-income (FLI) Latinx students, we find it outrageous that we cannot be allowed to protect one of our few safe spaces on campus without being threatened and harassed. Our strict visitor policy is not unfounded and is based off of previous years, when Stanford students entered Zapata to write disgusting messages on community whiteboards, such as "Build The Wall" and #MAGA last winter and spring. In an ethnic-themed dorm such as Zapata, where many students and their families have been personally affected by issues of race and immigration, these messages were obviously and rightfully perceived as more than just an expression of free speech, and were recognized as being overtly targeted and racist.

54 John Rice Cameron, *Inclusion or Division? Why We Should Re-Think Ethnic Themed Dorms*, STANFORD REV., Apr. 3, 2017, https://medium.com/ stanfordreview/inclusion-or-division-why-we-should-re-think-ethnic-themed-dorms-749fdb2baaf7.

55 *Dorm Diversity*, STANFORD DAILY, Jan. 12, 2010, https://www.stanforddaily. com/2010/01/12/dorm-diversity.

56 *Mission Statement*, CHOCOLATE CITY, https://www.ccity.mit.edu.

57 *History*, CHOCOLATE CITY, https://www.ccity.mit.edu/history.

58 Kelvin Green II, Class of 2021, CHOCOLATE CITY, https://www.ccity.mit. edu/2021.

59 Kelvin L. Green II, https://www.linkedin.com/in/kelvingreenii.

60 Ronald Vaughan II, Class of 2023, CHOCOLATE CITY, https://www.ccity.mit. edu/2023.

61 MIT Chocolate City i3, 2019, at 2:38, https://www.ccity.mit.edu/i3-videos.

62 *APIDA Leaders Residential Floor*, UNIVERSITY OF SOUTHERN CALIFORNIA, https://apass.usc.edu/initiatives/apida.

63 Jeff Murakami, *APASS History*, University of Southern California, https://apass.usc.edu/about/history.

64 *Id.*

65 *Mission*, Asian Pacific American Students Services, https://apass.usc.edu/about/mission.

66 *Facts and Figures*, About USC, https://about.usc.edu/facts.

67 Russell Blair, *U.S. Civil Rights Commissioners Say UConn Dormitory Plan Promotes Racial Division*, Chi. Trib., Mar. 23, 2016, https://www.chicagotribune.com/hc-uconn-african-american-students-scholars-house-20160323-story.html; *Information About the Contribution Program*, Booth Ferris Foundation, http://fdnweb.org/boothferris.

   "The Booth Ferris Foundation was established in 1957 under the wills of Willis H. Booth and his wife, Chancie Ferris Booth. Since that time, approximately $281 million has been contributed from the Foundation to worthy organizations for a variety of charitable purposes. Grants are made to charitable organizations that are exempt from federal taxes under Section 501(c)(3) of the Internal Revenue Code and are not classified as private foundations."

68 *ScHOLA²Rs House*, University of Connecticut, https://lc.uconn.edu/schola2rshouse.

69 Letter from Gail Heriot & Peter Kirsanow, U.S. Commission on Civil Rights, to Susan Herbst, President, U. of Connecticut (Mar. 21, 2016), http://www.newamericancivilrightsproject.org/wp-content/uploads/2016/03/3.21LettertoUConnonRacialThemeHousing.pdf.

70 Lidia Ryan, *Members of Civil Rights Group Criticize UConn's African-American Housing*, CT Post, Mar. 23, 2016, https://www.ctpost.com/apple-business/article/Members-of-Civil-Rights-group-criticize-UConn-s-6983511.php.

71 *Learning Community Program*, University of Connecticut, https://lc.uconn.edu.

72 *Id.*

73 *UConn Scholars House*, UCTV News (Sept. 26, 2016), https://www.youtube.com/watch?v=wkyoH-bdVCc.

74 Joshua Rhett Miller, *Black Student Erupts over 'Too Many White People' at UVA Multicultural Center*, N.Y. Post, Feb. 14, 2010, https://nypost.com/2020/02/14/black-student-erupts-over-too-many-white-people-at-uva-multicultural-center.

75 *Id.*

76 *Multicultural Student Center*, University of Virginia, https://multicultural.virginia.edu/multicultural-student-center.

77 *Multicultural Consciousness Series*, MSC Programs & Signature Events, University of Virginia, https://multicultural.virginia.edu/msc-programs-signature-events.

78 42 U.S.C. § 2000d.

79 *Munk-skukum Indigenous Living-Learning Community*, Oregon State University, https://uhds.oregonstate.edu/housing/munk-skukum.

80 *Id.*

81 *Id.*

82 *Tyler Hogan Oral History Interview*, Oregon State University Cultural Centers Oral History Collection, 2013-2014, at 10-11, https://oregondigital.org/catalog/oregondigital:df724k56c#page/1/mode/1up.

83 *Paying It Forward to Benefit Native American Students*, Ecampus News, Oregon State University, https://ecampus.oregonstate.edu/news/2020/paying-it-forward-to-benefit-native-american-students [hereinafter *Paying It Forward*]; OSU's Native American Longhouse, Eena Haws (NAL) and Powwows Digital Display, https://www.flickr.com/photos/osuarchives/sets/72157627962377059.

84 *Paying It Forward, supra* note 83.

85 *Directory*, Diversity & Cultural Engagement, Oregon State University, https://dce.oregonstate.edu/directory.

86 Sharadha Kalyanam, *We Don't Live 'in' the Current System. It Lives on Top of Us Indigenous People, Says Luhui Whitebear, Activist and PhD Candidate in the WGSS Program*, Women, Gender, and Sexuality Studies, Oregon State University, https://liberalarts.oregonstate.edu/feature-story/we-don-t-live-current-system-it-lives-top-us-indigenous-people-says-luhui-whitebear-activist-and-phd-candidate-wgss-program.

87 *Id.*

88 Native American Longhouse Eena Haws, Oregon State University, https://dce.oregonstate.edu/nal [hereinafter Eena Haws].

89 Jessica Ruf, *How the U of Minnesota, Twin Cities Doubled Its Retention of Native American Students*, Diverse Issues in Higher Education, Apr. 12, 2020, https://diverseeducation.com/article/172353; Rachel Bryan, *Native American Student Success: The Effect of Tribal Colleges and Universities on Native American Student Retention*, CMSI Research Brief, Penn Graduate School of Education, https://cmsi.gse.rutgers.edu/sites/default/files/Native%20American%20Student%20Success.pdf.

90 Wendy Wang, *Interracial Marriage: Who Is 'Marrying Out'?*, Pew Research Center, June 12, 2015, https://www.pewresearch.org/fact-tank/2015/06/12/interracial-marriage-who-is-marrying-out.

91 Kristen Bialik, *Key Facts About Race and Marriage, 50 Years after Loving v. Virginia*, Pew Research Center, June 12, 2017, https://www.pewresearch.org/fact-tank/2017/06/12/key-facts-about-race-and-marriage-50-years-after-loving-v-virginia.

92 Kalyanam, *supra* note 86.

93 Eena Haws, *supra* note 88.

94 Richard Cockle, *Oregon Family at Heart of Sticky Issue: Does Intermarriage Threaten Native American Culture?*, Oregonian, Nov. 6, 2009, https://www.oregonlive.com/news/2009/11/oregon_family_at_heart_of_stic.html ("Marcus Luke, whose tribal heritage is Umatilla and Yakama, recognizes that he ignored his own father's advice. Marcus Luke, Sr., he says, often warned him: 'You can go with whoever you want. But if you marry outside

your own, I'll disown you.' Still, Luke married his college sweetheart. 'I followed my heart,' he says, adding that his father 'wasn't very nice' to his wife before he died nine years ago. Aunts and uncles still tease Luke, sometimes pointedly."); Tristan Athone, *Native American Intermarriage Puts Benefits at Risk*, NPR, Mar. 31, 2011 ("They have discussed marriage, kids, and the future, but here's the rub: LeClair is half Shoshone. If she has children with Diaz, their children will only be one-quarter Native American. That's the minimum amount of blood to be enrolled in the Shoshone tribe. Therefore, if their children marry someone nonnative as well, the grandchildren would technically not be Indians. It's an issue that troubles LeClair.").

95 *Id.* at 5.

96 *White Principal Fired for Post About 'Black Lives Matter'*, AP News, Oct. 19, 2020 ("[Riley] went on to write that while she wants to get behind Black Lives Matter, 'I do not think people should feel they have to choose Black race over human race.'"), https://apnews.com/article/race-and-ethnicity-vermont-media-social-media-school-boards-ddb8251472b5a7bf0817f aaa32010614; Jonathan Turley, *University of Massachusetts Nursing Dean Fired After Saying "Everyone's Life Matters" [Updated]*, JonathanTurley.org, July 2, 2020, https://jonathanturley.org/2020/07/02/university-of-massachusetts-nursing-dean-fired-for-saying-everyones-life-matters/.

BREAKING THE STEM

1 *ADVANCE: Organizational Change for Gender Equity in STEM Academic Professions (ADVANCE)*, National Science Foundation, https://www.nsf.gov/funding/pgm_summ.jsp?pims_id=5383.

2 *Id.*

3 Francis S. Collins, *Time to End the Manel Tradition*, National Institutes of Health (June 12, 2019), https://www.nih.gov/about-nih/who-we-are/nih-director/statements/time-end-manel-tradition.

4 UCLA scientist, email message to author, Jan. 16, 2018.

5 *Inclusion Across the Nation of Communities of Learners of Underrepresented Discoverers in Engineering and Science*, National Science Foundation, https://www.nsf.gov/funding/pgm_summ.jsp?pims_id=505289.

6 Erin Cech, *Rugged Meritocratists: The Role of Overt Bias and the Meritocratic Ideology in Trump Supporters' Opposition to Social Justice Efforts*, June 14, 2017, https://journals.sagepub.com/doi/10.1177/2378023117712395.

7 *E.g.*, Cancer Center Support Grants (CCSGs) for NCI-designated Cancer Centers, P30 Clinical Trial Option, PHS 398 Research Plan (Clinical Protocol and Data Management), Part III: Inclusion of Women and Minorities in Clinical Research (only required for Comprehensive and Clinical Cancer Centers), https://grants.nih.gov/grants/guide/pa-files/par-20-043.html. Relevant language follows:

> When women or minorities are substantially under-represented in relation to catchment area demographics, the adequacy of the institution's policies, specific activities and a corrective plan

become especially critical in convincing peer reviewers that the institution is serious about addressing the problem and is investing the appropriate effort to correct under-accrual. In addition, if the population of the catchment area of the Cancer Center has limited ethnic diversity, provide a discussion of the institution's efforts to broaden the ethnic diversity of its clinical trial accrual.

8   Stuart H. Hulbert, *Politicized External Review Panels as Unguided "Diversity" Missiles: California University Administrators Remain Ultra-slow Learners*, CENTER FOR EQUAL OPPORTUNITY, Sept. 13, 2017, https://www.ceousa.org/about-ceo/docs/1140-politicized-external-review-panels-as-unguided-diversity-missiles.

9   Erin Cech, *The STEM Inclusion Study: LGBTQ Professionals, Mechanisms of Disadvantage, and Tools*, AAAS ANNUAL MEETING, Feb. 18, 2018, https://aaas.confex.com/aaas/2018/meetingapp.cgi/Paper/21932.

10 Sharon Zhen, *Engineering School Introduces Associate Dean of Diversity and Inclusion*, DAILY BRUIN, Sept. 17, 2017, https://dailybruin.com/2017/09/17/engineering-school-introduces-associate-dean-of-diversity-and-inclusion.

11 *Lecturer – Environmental Conservation*, CAREERS AT UMASS AMHERST, Aug. 17, 2020, https://careers.umass.edu/amherst/en-us/job/505981/lecturer-environmental-conservation.

12 Paula Lemons, *Lecturer Position at University of Georgia*, CHEMICAL EDUCATION RESEARCH, https://cer.chemedx.org/mail-list/lecturer-position-university-georgia.

13 Rebecca Heald & Mary Wildermuth, *Initiative to Advance Faculty Diversity, Equity and Inclusion in the Life Science at UC Berkeley Year End Summary Report: 2018-2019*, https://ofew.berkeley.edu/sites/default/files/life_sciences_inititatve.year_end_report_summary.pdf.

14 Interview with electrical and computer engineering professor, July 27, 2012.

15 Maria Herrera Sobek, interview, July 18, 2012.

16 *Teaching to Increase Diversity and Equity in STEM (TIDES)*, ASSOCIATION OF AMERICAN COLLEGES AND UNIVERSITIES, https://www.aacu.org/tides; Kelly Mack, *Reconsidering STEM Faculty Professional Development: Daring Approaches to Broadening Participation in STEM*, ASSOCIATION OF AMERICAN COLLEGES & UNIVERSITIES, https://www.aacu.org/diversitydemocracy/2017/fall/mack; Inclusive Teaching @ Michigan: May 217 Series, Center for Research on Learning & Teaching, UNIVERSITY OF MICHIGAN, https://crlt.umich.edu/node?search=/grants&page=3; *STEM Program Evaluation & Research Lab*, YALE UNIVERSITY, https://stem-perl.yale.edu/hhmi-campus-grant.

17 Sylvia Hurtado & Victoria L. Stork, *Enhancing Student Success and Building Inclusive Classrooms at UCLA: Report to the Executive Vice Chancellor and Provost*, Dec. 2015, http://wscuc.ucla.edu/wp-content/uploads/2019/01/C5_16_Report_Enhancing_Student_Success-Building_Inclusive_Classrooms_at_UCLA_December_2015.pdf.

18 *A Practice-Based Approach to Designing Equitable Undergraduate Science*

Courses, UC STEM FACULTY LEARNING COMMUNITY (Jan. 26, 2018), https://youtu.be/vrR21DKl8MU.

19 Peter Arcidiacono, Esteban M. Aucejo & Ken Spenner, *What Happens After Enrollment? An Analysis of the Time Path of Racial Differences in GPA and Major Choice*, 1 IZA J. OF LABOR ECON. (Oct. 2012), https://link.springer.com/article/10.1186/2193-8997-1-5.

20 *Id.*

21 Karla F.C. Holloway (@ProfHolloway), TWITTER (Jan. 16, 2012, 1:37 PM), https://twitter.com/ProfHolloway/status/159011440831901697 ("#Duke authors' unpublished study of #race + #AffirmativeAction lacks academic rigor").

22 Timothy B. Tyson, *The Econometrics of Rwandan Pear Blossoms at Duke University*, MIKE KLONSKY'S BLOG (Jan. 27, 2012), http://michaelklonsky.blogspot.com/2012/01/econometrics-of-rwandan-pear-blossoms.html.

23 Duke Senior Academic Officials, *A Message from Administrators Regarding New Study*, CHRONICLE, Jan. 18, 2012, https://www.dukechronicle.com/article/message-administrators-regarding-new-study.

24 Jonathan Wai, Jaret Hodges & Matthew C. Makel, *Sex Differences in Ability Tilt in the Right Tail of Cognitive Abilities: A 35-Year Examination*, 67 INTELLIGENCE 76 (2018).

25 *Note to Employees from CEO Sundar Pichai*, GOOGLE BLOG (Aug. 8, 2017), https://www.blog.google/topics/diversity/note-employees-ceo-sundar-pichai.

26 Yonatan Zunger, *So, About This Googler's Manifesto*, MEDIUM, Aug. 5, 2017, https://medium.com/@yonatanzunger/so-about-this-googlers-manifesto-1e3773ed1788.

27 Physician-scientist, email message to author, Feb. 4, 2018.

THE SAUSAGE FACTORY

1 539 U.S. 306 (2003).

2 539 U.S. 244 (2003).

3 Plaintiff's Memorandum of Law in Support of Motion for Partial Summary Judgment on Liability, Gratz v. Bollinger, 122 F. Supp. 2d 811 (E.D. Mich. 2000) (No. 97-CV-75231-DT), https://web.archive.org/web/20140221121122/http://www.vpcomm.umich.edu/admissions/legal/gratz/gratsumj.html.

4 Althea K. Nagai, *Racial and Ethnic Preferences in Undergraduate Admissions at the University of Michigan*, CENTER FOR EQUAL OPPORTUNITY (Oct. 17, 2006), http://www.ceousa.org/attachments/article/548/UM_UGRAD_final.pdf.

5 570 U.S. 297 (2013).

6 136 S. Ct. 2198 (2016).

7 Gerald Gunther, *The Supreme Court 1971 Term—Foreword: In Search of Evolving Doctrine on a Changing Court: A Model for a Newer Equal Protection*, 86 HARV. L. REV. 1, 8 (1972).

8 539 U.S. at 328 (emphasis added).

9   339 U.S. 629 (1950).

10 339 U.S. 637 (1950).

11 347 U.S. 483 (1954).

12 Justice Thomas noted this in his concurrence in Fisher v. Univ. of Texas, 133 S. Ct. at 2424-28 (*Fisher I*).

13 Some of them may be harmless—like the notion that learning will be enhanced by painting mathematics classrooms blue or indigo and painting social studies classrooms orange, green, or brown. Others—as in the case of the extreme popularity of pedagogical methods that emphasize unguided or minimally guided student learning—can be disastrous. *See* William R. Daggett et al., *Color in an Optimum Learning Environment*, INTERNATIONAL CENTER FOR LEADERSHIP IN EDUCATION (2008) (classroom color); Paul A. Kirschner et al., *Why Minimal Guidance During Instruction Does Not Work: An Analysis of the Failure of Constructivist, Discovery, Problem-Based, Experiential, and Inquiry-Based Teaching*, 41 EDUC. PSYCHOLOGIST 75 (2006).

14 539 U.S. at 329 (emphasis added and internal quotation marks omitted).

15 Kent Greenawalt, *The Unresolved Problems of Reverse Discrimination*, 67 CAL. L. REV. 87, 122 (1979). *See* Brian Fitzpatrick, *The Diversity Lie*, 27 HARV. J.L. & PUB. POL'Y 385 (2003).

16 *See* Peter H. Schuck, *Affirmative Action: Past, Present, and Future*, 20 YALE L. & POL'Y REV. 1, 34 (2002) ("[M]any of affirmative action's more forthright defenders readily concede that diversity is merely the current rationale of convenience for a policy that they prefer to justify on other grounds."); Jed Rubenfeld, *Affirmative Action*, 107 YALE L.J. 427, 471 (1997) ("The purpose of affirmative action is to bring into our nation's institutions more blacks, more Hispanics, more Native Americans, more women, sometimes more Asians, and so on—period. Pleading diversity of backgrounds merely invites heightened scrutiny into the true objectives behind affirmative action."); Owen M. Fiss, *Affirmative Action as a Strategy of Justice*, 17 PHILOSOPHY & PUB. POL'Y 37 (1997) ("[T]wo defenses of affirmative action—diversity and compensatory justice—emerged in the fierce struggles of the 1970s and are standard today, but I see them as simply rationalizations created to appeal to the broadest constituency.... In my opinion, affirmative action should be seen as a means that seeks to eradicate caste structure by altering the social standing of our country's most subordinated group."); Daniel Golden, *Some Backers of Racial Preferences Take Diversity Rationale Further*, WALL ST. J., June 14, 2003 (quoting former University of Texas law professor Samuel Issacharoff: "'The commitment to diversity is not real. None of these universities has an affirmative-action program for Christian fundamentalists, Muslims, orthodox Jews, or any other group that has a distinct viewpoint.'").

Dean Erwin Chemerinsky has agreed that past discrimination is not just one among many objectives, but the "most frequently identified objective for affirmative action." Erwin Chemerinsky, *Making Sense of the Affirmative Action Debate*, 22 OHIO N.U. L. REV. 1159, 1161 (1996). Others have cited other arguments that are unlikely to win judicial approval. *See, e.g.,* James

D. Anderson, *Past Discrimination and Diversity: A Historic Context for Understanding Race and Affirmative Action*, 76 J. NEGRO EDUC. 204 (2007); Kim Forde-Mazrui, *Taking Conservatives Seriously: A Moral Justification for Affirmative Action and Reparations*, 92 CAL. L. REV. 683 (2004); Andrew Valls, *The Libertarian Case for Affirmative Action*, 25 SOC. THEORY & PRAC. 299 (1999).

17 Alan Dershowitz, *Affirmative Action and the Harvard College Diversity-Discretion Model: Paradigm or Pretext*, 1 CARDOZO L. REV. 379, 407 (1979).

18 Randall Kennedy, *Affirmative Reaction*, AM. PROSPECT (Mar. 1, 2003), https://prospect.org/features/affirmative-reaction.

19 *See, e.g.,* JOE R. FEAGIN, RACIST AMERICA: ROOTS, CURRENT REALITIES AND FUTURE REPARATIONS (2018); MICHELLE ALEXANDER, THE NEW JIM CROW: MASS INCARCERATION IN THE AGE OF COLORBLINDNESS (2012); EDUARDO BONILLA-SILVA, RACISM WITHOUT RACISTS: COLOR-BLIND RACISM AND THE PERSISTENCE OF INEQUALITY IN AMERICA (2009).

20 438 U.S. 265 (1978).

21 476 U.S. 267 (1986).

22 515 U.S. 200 (1995).

23 *Id.* at 239.

24 SUSAN WELCH & JOHN GRUHL, AFFIRMATIVE ACTION AND MINORITY ENROLLMENTS IN MEDICAL AND LAW SCHOOLS 80, Table 3.3 (1998).

25 DONALD E. HELLER, THE STATES AND PUBLIC HIGHER EDUCATION POLICY: AFFORDABILITY, ACCESS, AND ACCOUNTABILITY 145 (2001) (quoting Ward Connerly).

26 Jon Offredo & Jonathan Starkey, *NAACP, State Lawmakers: UD Is Lacking in Diversity*, NEWS JOURNAL, Feb. 10, 2015, https://www.delawareonline.com/story/news/education/2015/02/09/naacp-state-lawmakers-ud-lacking-diversity/23154215.

27 Paul Bowers, *Affirmative Action Comes to a Quiet End at College of Charleston*, POST AND COURIER, July 29, 2018, https://www.postandcourier.com/news/affirmative-action-comes-to-a-quiet-end-at-college-of-charleston/article_e89f0042-8b88-11e8-bbab-3f0dd42c81bb.html.

28 Paul Bowers, *College of Charleston Resumes Affirmative Action After 2-Year Hiatus,* POST AND COURIER, July 31, 2018, https://www.postandcourier.com/news/college-of-charleston-resumes-affirmative-action-after-2-year-hiatus/article_ddoecf68-9502-11e8-90c9-8fdfbaa98116.html.

29 Then there is the political pressure recently exerted by the University of California Board of Regents. In general, its members are (with a few exceptions) appointed by the governor; often they are simply wealthy donors to the governor's campaign. They are usually not academics and do not concern themselves with academic issues. But while the *Grutter* majority viewed the issue of race-preferential admissions as an issue calling for academic judgment, the regents, apparently, do not. In 2020, over the objection of the faculty senate, the regents voted to suspend use

of the SAT and ACT standardized tests precisely because, in their view, an insufficient number of African American and Latino students excel at them. Mikhail Zinshteyn, *UCs Ditch the SAT and ACT—Set Out to Make a "Fairer" Standardized Test,* CAL MATTERS, May 23, 2020, https://www.capradio. org/articles/2020/05/23/ucs-ditch-the-sat-and-act-set-out-to-make-a-fairer-standardized-test. Supporters of Ward Connerly's policies requiring race neutrality in admissions, passed by the University of California Board of Regents in 1995, implicitly agreed that the issue did not call for academic judgment. But, because those policies did not discriminate on the basis of race, they would not be subject to strict scrutiny in the first place.

In Rhode Island, it is the same. The Council on Postsecondary Education (the successor to the Board of Governors for Higher Education, which merged in 2014 into the Board of Education) is the body that long imposed affirmative-action requirements on that state's public colleges and universities. Its members are appointed by the governor. *See Affirmative Action and Equal Opportunity—Policy,* RHODE ISLAND BOARD OF GOVERNORS FOR HIGHER EDUCATION, http://www.ribghe. org/affirmativeactionpolicy.pdf; *Affirmative Action and Equal Opportunity Regulations,* RI OFFICE OF THE POSTSECONDARY COMMISSIONER, https:// www.riopc.edu/static/photos/2017/02/24/P3_affirmativeactionregs.pdf.

30 WELCH & GRUHL, *supra* note 24, at 80, Table 3.3.

31 John Ellis at 9.

32 John Ellis at 8 (discussing the "human cost" to supposed beneficiaries of preferential treatment who failed in their quest for a graduate degree). *See also* Public Health Service Act, Title VII, § 736, 42 U.S.C. § 293 (2011) (funding Centers of Excellence ("COE") programs in health professions education). HHS allocates funds appropriated for COE to schools of medicine, dentistry, pharmacy, and graduate programs in behavioral or mental health in part on the basis of whether those schools "have a significant number of URM [under-represented minority] students enrolled.").

33 *See, e.g.,* Daryl G. Smith et al., *Building Capacity: A Study of the Impact of the James Irvine Foundation Campus Diversity Initiative* (May 2006) (discussing a $29 million effort to assist California colleges and universities with strategically improving campus diversity), https://folio.iupui.edu/ handle/10244/51; *Briefing Room: Commitment to Diversity Leads to Gift,* MORITZ COLLEGE OF LAW (Apr. 5, 2012) (announcing gift by alumnus to Ohio State University), https://moritzlaw.osu.edu/briefing-room/alumni/ commitment-to-diversity-leads-to-gift.

34 Foundation grants from the Rockefeller Foundation were pivotal in the history of the earliest race-preferential "affirmative action" policies. Those early programs emphasized recruiting urban underclass students—without regard to traditional academic credentials or even whether the student had a high school diploma. Serious dissatisfaction with the results of these programs led to modern diversity policies, in which minority students from

upper-middle and upper-income families are much more likely to be the beneficiaries than are underclass students. *See* LINDA CHAVEZ, AN UNLIKELY CONSERVATIVE: THE TRANSFORMATION OF AN EX-LIBERAL 69-86 (2002); DONALD ALEXANDER DOWNS, CORNELL '69: LIBERALISM AND THE CRISIS OF THE AMERICAN UNIVERSITY 46-67 (1999); THOMAS SOWELL, BLACK EDUCATION: MYTHS AND TRAGEDIES 129-170 (1972).

35 *See* Peter Wood, *Mobbing for Preferences*, CHRON. HIGHER EDUC., Sept. 22, 2011, https://www.nas.org/blogs/article/mobbing_for_preferences.

36 Jaleesa Jones, *Colgate University Students Ask #CanYouHearUsNow*, USA TODAY, Sept. 24, 2014, https://www.usatoday.com/story/college/2014/09/24/colgate-university-students-ask-canyouhearusnow/37396699.

37 Samantha Tomilowitz & Sam Hoff, *UCLA Law Students Protest Lack of Diversity*, DAILY BRUIN, Feb. 10, 2014, https://dailybruin.com/2014/02/10/ucla-law-students-protest-lack-of-diversity.

38 Leah Libresco, *Here Are the Demands from Students Protesting Racism at 51 Schools*, FIVETHIRTYEIGHT (Dec. 3, 2015), https://fivethirtyeight.com/features/here-are-the-demands-from-students-protesting-racism-at-51-colleges.

39 Carlos Andres Lopez, *Students Demand More Diversity at New Mexico State University*, LAS CRUCES SUN-NEWS, Feb. 27, 2018, https://www.lcsun-news.com/story/news/local/2018/02/27/students-demand-more-diversity-new-mexico-state-university/378797002.

40 *Students Offer Fixes to Cal Poly's Diversity Problem, But 'They're Not Listening to Us,'* TRIBUNE, June 4, 2019, https://www.sanluisobispo.com/news/local/education/article230947963.html.

41 *See* Ben Flanagan, *Watch Alabama Students March for Diversity and Free Speech in Wake of Dean's Resignation*, AL.COM, Sept. 20, 2019, https://www.al.com/news/2019/09/watch-alabama-students-march-for-diversity-and-free-speech-in-wake-of-deans-resignation.html.

42 Holly Poag, *Students Demand Greater Diversity, Inclusion on Campus*, DAILY GAMECOCK, June 21, 2020, https://www.dailygamecock.com/article/2020/06/students-take-action-to-promote-diversity-and-inclusion-on-campus-poag-news; Devin Anderson-Torrez, *'Equity over Equality': MSU Students and Alumni March, Demanding University to Represent Their Community*, STATE NEWS, June 15, 2020, https://statenews.com/article/2020/06/equity-over-equality-msu-students-demand-changes-in-university.

43 78 F.3d 932 (5th Cir. 1996).

44 Tex. Educ. Code § 51.801 et seq.

45 Fisher v. Univ. of Texas, 136 S. Ct. 2198 (2016) (Alito, J., dissenting).

46 Gail Heriot, *Strict Scrutiny, Public Opinion, and Affirmative Action on Campus: Should the Courts Find a Narrowly Tailored Solution to a Compelling Need in a Policy Most Americans Oppose?*, 40 HARV. J. LEGIS. 217 (2003).

47 Frank Newport, *Americans on the Use of Race as a Factor in College Admissions*, GALLUP (Apr. 22, 2014), https://news.gallup.com/opinion/polling-matters/169358/americans-race-factor-college-admissions.aspx. (The two

alternative answers to the questions were rotated when the question was asked.) *See* Rasmussen Reports, *32% Favor Affirmative Action, 46% Oppose It,* July 13, 2010, https://www.rasmussenreports.com/public_content/politics/ general_politics/july_2010/32_favor_affirmative_action_46_oppose_it.

48 Frank Newport, *Affirmative Action and Public Opinion,* GALLUP NEWS (Aug. 8, 2020), https://news.gallup.com/opinion/polling-matters/317006/affirmative-action-public-opinion.aspx.

49 PAUL SNIDERMAN & THOMAS PIAZZA, THE SCAR OF RACE (1993).

50 *See, e.g.,* Thomas Wood, *Who Speaks for Higher Education on Group Preferences?,* 14 ACADEMIC QUESTIONS 31 (Spring 2001); Robert A. Frahm, *Debate Erupts over UConn Survey Poll: Professors Oppose Racial "Preferences,"* HARTFORD COURANT, Apr. 19, 2000; Carl A. Auerbach, *The Silent Opposition of Professors and Graduate Students to Preferential Affirmative Action Programs: 1969 and 1975,* 72 MINN. L. REV. 1233 (1988).

51 Bill Stall & Dan Morain, *Prop. 209 Wins, Bars Affirmative Action,* L.A. TIMES, Nov. 6, 1996, https://www.latimes.com/archives/la-xpm-1996-11-06-mn-62738-story.html.

52 *November 1998 General,* WASHINGTON SECRETARY OF STATE, ELECTIONS (Initiative 200, banning racial preferences, passed 58.2%-41.7%), https://www. sos.wa.gov/elections/results_report.aspx?e=10&c=&c2=&t=&t2=5&p=&p2 =&y=.

53 America Votes 2006, *Key Ballot Measures,* CNN (Proposal 2, banning racial preferences, was approved 58%-42%), https://www.cnn.com/ ELECTION/2006/pages/results/ballot.measures.

54 Election Center 2008, *Ballot Measures,* CNN (Initiative 424, banning racial preferences, was approved 58%-42%), https://www.cnn.com/ ELECTION/2008/results/ballot.measures.

55 Election Center 2010, *Ballot Measures,* CNN (Proposition 107, banning racial preferences, was approved 60%-40%), https://www.cnn.com/ ELECTION/2010/results/ballot.measures.

56 Election Center 2008, *Ballot Measures,* CNN (Amendment 46, banning racial preferences, lost 51%-49%), https://www.cnn.com/ELECTION/2008/results/ ballot.measures.

57 *November 5, 2019 General Election Results,* WASHINGTON SECRETARY OF STATE (Referendum 88, which would have repealed the state's ban on racial preferences, was defeated 50.56%-49.44%), https://results.vote.wa.gov/ results/20191105/State-Measures-Referendum-Measure-No-88_ByCounty. html.

58 *Best Colleges 2010,* U.S. NEWS & WORLD REPORT, https://web.archive.org/ web/20100914231058/http://colleges.usnews.rankingsandreviews.com/best-colleges/national-universities-rankings/page+2 [hereinafter *Best Colleges 2010*]; *2020 Best National University Rankings,* U.S. NEWS & WORLD REPORT, https://www.usnews.com/best-colleges/rankings/national-universities [hereinafter *2020 Best National University Rankings*].

59 U.S. News *Picks UC Berkeley as Top Public School Again*, UC BERKELEY NEWS, Aug. 18, 2006, https://www.berkeley.edu/news/media/releases/2006/08/18_rankings.shtml.

60 *Best Colleges 2010*, *supra* note 58; *2020 Best National University Rankings*, *supra* note 58.

61 *Best Colleges 2010*, *supra* note 58; *2020 Best National University Rankings*, *supra* note 58.

62 Samuel Weiss, *Baruch Chief Acknowledges Problem with Reaccreditation*, N.Y. TIMES, Apr. 18, 1990, https://www.nytimes.com/1990/04/18/nyregion/baruch-chief-acknowledges-problem-with-reaccreditation.html.

63 Harold Orlans, *Accreditation in American Higher Education: The Issue of "Diversity,"* 30 MINERVA 513 (Dec. 1992).

64 M. ALI RAZA, A. JANELL ANDERSON & HARRY GLYNN CUSTRED, JR., THE UPS AND DOWNS OF AFFIRMATIVE ACTION PREFERENCES 111-116 (1999).

65 *Id.*

66 Ben Wildavsky, *The Diversity Issue, Again: School Accreditation Becomes PC*, S.F. CHRON., Feb. 11, 1994.

67 *See* WELCH & GRUHL, *supra* note 24, at 80.

68 *See Appointment of LCME Members*, LCME, https://lcme.org/about/meetings-members.

69 Ad Hoc Survey Team, Report of the Secretariat Fact-Finding Survey of the University of Nevada School of Medicine 4, 9 (Apr. 1-3, 2012).

70 Ad Hoc Survey Team, Team Report of the Survey of Wright State University, Boonshoft School of Medicine 2-3 (Hopkins Letter), 38 (Mar. 22-25, 2009).

71 Ad Hoc Survey Team, Team Report of the Survey of University of South Alabama College of Medicine 2 (Moulton Letter) (Sept. 26-29, 2010).

72 These changes were a significant focus of discussion in a report by the U.S. Commission on Civil Rights. *See* U.S. Commission on Civil Rights, *Affirmative Action in American Law Schools* 90-137, 175-80 (2007) [hereinafter USCCR-AAALS Report], https://www.usccr.gov/pubs/docs/AALSreport.pdf.

73 Brief Amicus Curiae of the American Bar Association in Grutter v. Bollinger, 539 U.S. 306 (2003), No. 02-241, at 18-21 (filed Feb. 18, 2003) (initial caps reduced to lower case), https://www.americanbar.org/content/dam/aba/publications/individual_rights/grutter_v_bollinger.pdf.

74 Brief Amicus Curiae of the American Bar Association, Fisher v. Univ. of Texas, 133 S. Ct. 2411 (2003), No. 11-345, 20-29 (filed Aug. 13, 2012) ("Race-conscious admissions policies are essential to increasing minority representation in the legal profession") (original in all capitals), https://www.americanbar.org/content/dam/aba/administrative/crsj/Final%20Brief%20as%20filed.pdf.

75 *See* James T. Hammond, *Charleston School of Law: Fails to Win Accreditation So Students Can Take Bar*, THE STATE (Columbia, S.C.), July 12, 2006.

76 *Id.*; *College Notes: Charleston Law Taps Diversity Director*, THE STATE

(Columbia, S.C.), at B3, Aug. 13, 2006. *See also* David Barnhizer, *A Chilling Discourse*, 50 ST. LOUIS L.J. 361 (2006) (describing ABA influence on faculty diversity-hiring).

77 USCCR-AAALS Report, *supra* note 72, at 181.

78 *Id.* at 182.

79 *Id.* at 183.

80 *Id.*

81 *Id.*

82 *Id.*

83 Letter from Daniel D. Polsby, Dean, George Mason U. Sch. of Law, to Hulett H. Askew, Consultant on Legal Education, ABA (Jan. 3, 2008), http://www.newamericancivilrightsproject.org/wp-content/uploads/2014/05/Response-to-ABA-Site-Visit-Report-2.pdf.

84 *Id.* at 14.

85 *Id.*

RACE PREFERENCES AND DISCRIMINATION
AGAINST ASIAN AMERICANS IN HIGHER EDUCATION

1 *AIB2B Says NO to ACA-5*, L. A. POST, June 1, 2020, http://lapost.us/?p=25558.

2 *See Asian American History*, JAPANESE AMERICAN CITIZENS LEAGUE, http://jacl.org/asian-american-history.

3 John Aubrey Douglass, *California's Affirmative Action Fight: Power Politics and the University of California*, CENTER FOR STUDIES IN HIGHER EDUCATION, UNIVERSITY OF CALIFORNIA, BERKELEY, Mar. 2018, at 3, http://cshe.berkeley.edu/sites/default/files/publications/rops.cshe.5.2018.douglass.affirmativeactionuc.3.27.2018.pdf.

4 *Id.*

5 Michael Lynch, *Race-Based Admissions at University of California Medical Schools*, PACIFIC RESEARCH INSTITUTE, June 1995, at 8, *cited in* Lance T. Izumi, *Confounding the Paradigm: Asian Americans and Race Preferences*, 11 NOTRE DAME J.L.E.P.P. 121, 124 (1997), http://scholarship.law.nd.edu/cgi/viewcontent.cgi?article=1708&context=ndjlepp.

6 Lynch, *supra* note 5, at app. 2.

7 *Id.* at 8.

8 *Id.* at 8-12.

9 *Id.* at 15.

10 Douglass, *supra* note 3, at 15.

11 Nao Takasugi, Statement to the University of California Board of Regents, July 20, 1995, *cited in* Lance T. Izumi, *Confounding the Paradigm: Asian Americans and Race Preferences*, 11 NOTRE DAME J.L.E.P.P. 121, 124 (1997), http://scholarship.law.nd.edu/cgi/viewcontent.cgi?article=1708&context=ndjlepp.

12 *Black U.C. Regent Scores Liberal Racism*, HUMAN EVENTS, Aug. 4, 1995, at 3, *cited in* Lance T. Izumi, *Confounding the Paradigm: Asian Americans and Race*

Preferences, 11 Notre Dame J.L.E.P.P. 121, 124 (1997), http://scholarship.law.
nd.edu/cgi/viewcontent.cgi?article=1708&context=ndjlepp.

13 Cal. Const. Art. 1, § 31(a).

14 Jenna A. Robinson, *Did You Know? Eight States Ban Affirmative Action
    in College Admissions,* The James G. Martin Center for Academic
    Renewal (Oct. 24, 2019), http://www.jamesgmartin.center/2019/10/did-you-
    know-eight-states-ban-affirmative-action-in-college-admissions.

15 SCA-5, 2013-2014 Leg., Reg. Sess. (Cal. 2013) (Public education: student
    recruitment and selection), http://leginfo.legislature.ca.gov/faces/
    billNavClient.xhtml?bill_id=201320140SCA5.

16 SB-185, 2011-2012 Leg., Reg. Sess. (Cal. 2011) (Public postsecondary
    education), http://leginfo.legislature.ca.gov/faces/billAnalysisClient.
    xhtml?bill_id=201120120SB185.

17 Alexandria Malatesta, *California Governor Vetoes Affirmative Action Bill,*
    Jurist, Oct. 9, 2011, https://www.jurist.org/news/2011/10/california-governor-
    vetoes-bill-affirmative-action-bill.

18 *Registration by Political Party,* California Secretary of State (Feb.
    10, 2011, and Feb. 10, 2013), https://elections.cdn.sos.ca.gov/ror/ror-odd-
    year-2019/historical-reg-stats.pdf.

19 *A Health Profile of California's Diverse Population: 2011-2012 Race/Ethnicity
    Health Profiles,* UCLA Center for Health Policy Research, http://
    healthpolicy.ucla.edu/health-profiles/race_ethnicity/Documents/
    AllRaceEthnic/AllGroupsInfographic.pdf.

20 Press Release, Office of State Senator Ed Hernandez, Senator Hernandez
    Advances Constitutional Amendment for Equal Opportunity in Education
    (Aug. 20, 2013), https://web.archive.org/web/20140302143337/http://sd24.
    senate.ca.gov/news/2013-08-20-senator-hernandez-advances-constitutional-
    amendment-equal-opportunity-education.

21 David A. Lehrer et al., *Viewpoints: A Step Backward on Higher Education
    Enrollment,* Sacramento Bee, Mar. 2, 2014, https://web.archive.org/
    web/20140302040003/http://www.sacbee.com/2014/02/08/6138480/viewpoints-
    a-step-backward-on.html.

22 *Id.*

23 *SCA-5 Bill Analysis,* Senate Committee on Elections and Constitutional
    Amendments, Cal. Leg., http://www.leginfo.ca.gov/pub/13-14/bill/sen/
    sb_0001-0050/sca_5_cfa_20130816_110047_sen_comm.html.

24 Gene D. Block, *The Impact of Proposition 209 and Our Duty to Our Students,*
    Office of the Chancellor, University of California-Los Angeles
    (Feb. 24, 2014), https://chancellor.ucla.edu/messages/the-impact-of-
    proposition-209-and-our-duty-to-our-students.

25 *Id.*

26 Thomas J. Espenshade & Alexandria Walton Radford, No Longer
    Separate, Not Yet Equal: Race and Class in Elite College
    Admission and Campus Life 359 (2009).

27 Steven Boroweic, *Woman at Center of South Korean Political Scandal: 'I've*

Committed Wrongs for Which I Deserve to Die', L.A. Times, Oct. 31, 2016, https://www.latimes.com/world/asia/la-fg-korea-protests-20161031-story.html.

28 *Id.*

29 Anthony Caso, *California's SCA 5 and Racial Preferences in Education*, 16 Engage Issue 3 (Dec. 10, 2015), https://fedsoc.org/commentary/publications/california-s-sca-5-and-racial-preferences-in-education.

30 Frank Shyong, *Affirmative Action Amendment Divides State's Asian Americans*, L.A. Times, May 18, 2014, https://www.latimes.com/local/la-me-asian-divisions-20140519-story.html.

31 Josie Huang, *In California, a Vocal Minority of Asian Parents Helped Defeat Affirmative Action Once Before. This Time It Could Be Harder*, Laist, June 12, 2020, https://laist.com/2020/06/12/affirmative_action_california_aca_5_sca_5_asian_americans_chinese_universities_education_black_lives.php.

32 Leo Zou, *Asian Americans Furious at Proposal Allowing California Colleges to Choose Students by Race*, South China Morning Post, Mar. 6, 2014, https://www.scmp.com/news/world/article/1441993/asian-americans-furious-proposal-allowing-colleges-choose-students-race.

33 Shyong, *supra* note 30.

34 Caso, *supra* note 29.

35 Zou, *supra* note 32.

36 *Id.*

37 Shyong, *supra* note 30.

38 *Editorial: The Quest for Diversity at California's State Universities*, L.A. Times, Mar. 28, 2014, https://www.latimes.com/opinion/editorials/la-ed-proposition-209-20140328-story.html.

39 Katy Murphy & Jessica Calefati, *Affirmative Action Proposal for California Universities Runs into Asian-American Opposition*, S.J. Mercury News, Mar. 13, 2014, https://www.mercurynews.com/2014/03/13/affirmative-action-proposal-for-california-universities-runs-into-asian-american-opposition.

40 *Id.*

41 Josie Huang, *SCA 5: A Political Coming-of-Age Story for Chinese-Americans*, 89.3KPCC: Multi-American (Mar. 21, 2014), https://www.scpr.org/blogs/multiamerican/2014/03/21/16152/sca-5-chinese-americans-immigrants-asian-americans.

42 Phillip Matier & Andrew Ross, *Leland Yee Joins Effort to Stop Affirmative Action Measure*, S.F. Chron., Mar. 16, 2014, https://www.sfchronicle.com/bayarea/matier-ross/article/Leland-Yee-joins-effort-to-stop-affirmative-5322954.php.

43 Huang, *supra* note 41.

44 Laurel Rosenhall, *California Lawmakers Shelve Effort to Bring Back Affirmative Action*, Sac. Bee, Mar. 17, 2014, https://www.sacbee.com/news/local/education/article2593314.html.

45 Josie Huang, *Affirmative Action Bill SCA 5 'Dead for the Year'*, KPCC89.3: Multi-American (Mar. 17, 2014), https://www.scpr.org/blogs/

multiamerican/2014/03/17/16109/affirmative-action-bill-sca-5-dead-for-the-year.

46 Paul Guppy, *A Citizen's Guide to Initiative 200: The Washington State Civil Rights Initiative*, WASHINGTON POLICY CENTER (Sept. 1, 1998), https://www.washingtonpolicy.org/publications/detail/a-citizens-guide-to-initiative-200-the-washington-state-civil-rights-initiative.

47 *Washington Referendum 88, Vote on I-1000 Affirmative Action Measure (2019)*, BALLOTPEDIA, https://ballotpedia.org/Washington_Referendum_88,_Vote_on_I-1000_Affirmative_Action_Measure_(2019) [hereinafter *Washington Referendum 88*].

48 asianadmin, *Our New Year's Resolution—We'll Fight Against Racism Towards Chinese Americans*, WA ASIANS FOR EQUALITY (Jan. 25, 2020), https://waasians4equality.org/2020/01/25/new-years-resolution-fighting-against-racisim-towards-chinese-americans.

49 John Carlson, *I Helped Get Affirmative Action Banned in WA. Here's What I Think of the Plan to Bring It Back*, CROSSCUT (Apr. 25, 2019), https://crosscut.com/2019/04/i-helped-get-affirmative-action-banned-wa-heres-what-i-think-plan-bring-it-back.

50 asianadmin, *An Open Letter from Asian Americans to WA State Legislature in Opposition to I-1000*, WA ASIANS FOR EQUALITY (Apr. 23, 2019), https://waasians4equality.org/2019/04/23/an-open-letter-from-asian-americans-to-wa-state-legislature-in-opposition-to-i-1000.

51 *Washington Referendum 88, supra* note 47.

52 asianadmin, *Call to Re-elect Senator Mark Mullet of the 5th LD*, WA ASIANS FOR EQUALITY (July 23, 2020), https://waasians4equality.org/2020/07/23/reelect-senator-mark-mullet-of-the-5th-ld.

53 Post from Kan Qiu, Let People Vote Reject R-88, FACEBOOK (July 30, 2019), https://www.facebook.com/groups/704096406714719/permalink/743240916133601.

54 *Washington Referendum 88, supra* note 47.

55 asianadmin, *The Secretary of State Certified Referendum Measure 88, New Campaign Site Launched to Defeat I-1000 in the Fall*, WA ASIANS FOR EQUALITY (Aug. 8, 2019), https://waasians4equality.org/2019/08/08/the-secretary-of-state-certified-referendum-measure-88-new-campaign-site-launched-to-defeat-i-1000-in-the-fall.

56 *Washington Referendum 88, supra* note 47.

57 *Id.*

58 John Carlson, *Tech Workers and Asians Against Racial Preferences*, WALL ST. J., Oct. 25, 2019, https://www.wsj.com/articles/tech-workers-and-asians-against-racial-preferences-11572040678.

59 *Id.*

60 *Referendum 88: Letting Washington Voters Decide on Affirmative Action*, MYNORTHWEST.COM (May 6, 2019), https://mynorthwest.com/1372031/referendum-88-affirmative-action-washington.

61 *Id.*

62 *Id.*

63 Christopher F. Rufo, *Asian-Americans for Equal Opportunity*, City Journal (Oct. 8, 2019), https://www.city-journal.org/asian-americans-affirmative-action.

64 *Id.*

65 *Washington Referendum 88, supra* note 47.

66 *Id.*

67 Carlson, *supra* note 58.

68 *Id.*

69 *Id.*

70 Rufo, *supra* note 63.

71 asianadmin, *supra* note 55.

72 Edward Blum, Annual Report Letter, Students for Fair Admissions, Aug. 16, 2020, at 1, http://samv91khoyt2i553a2t1s05i-wpengine.netdna-ssl.com/wp-content/uploads/2016/08/2016-08-16-2016-Year-End-Review.pdf.

73 *Id.*

74 Complaint, Students for Fair Admissions, Inc. v. President and Fellows of Harvard College, 397 F. Supp. 3d 126 (D. Mass. 2019) (No. 14-cv-14176-ADB), at ¶ 1, https://www.clearinghouse.net/chDocs/public/ED-MA-0002-0001.pdf.

75 *Id.* at ¶¶ 5, 210.

76 *Id.* at ¶ 6.

77 *Id.* at ¶ 6.

78 *Id.* at ¶ 7.

79 *Id.* at ¶ 8.

80 Josh Gerstein, *Judge: Harvard Need Not Disclose Discrimination Against Jews*, Politico: Under the Radar (Sept. 7, 2016), https://www.politico.com/blogs/under-the-radar/2016/09/harvard-discrimination-jews-227842.

81 Expert Report of Peter Arcidiacono, Students for Fair Admissions, Inc. v. President and Fellows of Harvard College, 397 F. Supp. 3d 126 (D. Mass. 2019) (No. 14-cv-14176-ADB), https://samv91khoyt2i553a2t1s05i-wpengine.netdna-ssl.com/wp-content/uploads/2018/06/Doc-415-1-Arcidiacono-Expert-Report.pdf [hereinafter Expert Report of Peter Arcidiacono].

82 *Id.* at 3-4.

83 *Id.* at 7.

84 *Id.* at 4.

85 Heather Mac Donald, *Harvard Admits Its Preferences*, The New Criterion, Nov. 2019, https://newcriterion.com/issues/2019/11/harvard-admits-its-preferences.

86 Expert Report of Peter Arcidiacono, *supra* note 81.

87 *Id.* at 8.

88 *Id.* at 9-10.

89 *Id.* at 10.

90 United States Statement of Interest in Opposition to Defendant's Motion
    for Summary Judgment, Students for Fair Admissions, Inc. v. President
    and Fellows of Harvard College, 397 F. Supp. 3d 126 (D. Mass. 2019)
    (No. 14-cv-14176-ADB), at 1, https://www.justice.gov/opa/press-release/
    file/1090856/download.

91 Press Release, U.S. Dep't of Justice, *Justice Department Files Statement
    of Interest in Harvard Discrimination Case Defending Claim That Harvard
    Intentionally Discriminates on the Basis of Race in Admissions*, Aug. 30, 2018,
    https://www.justice.gov/opa/pr/justice-department-files-statement-interest-
    harvard-discrimination-case-defending-claim-0.

92 Scott Jaschik, *Judge Upholds Harvard's Admissions Policies*, Inside Higher Ed,
    Oct. 7, 2019, https://www.insidehighered.com/admissions/article/2019/10/07/
    federal-judge-finds-harvards-policies-do-not-discriminate-against.

93 *Id.*

94 Brief of Appellant, Students for Fair Admissions v. President and
    Fellows of Harvard College (1st Cir. 2019) (No. 19-2005), at 27, http://
    studentsforfairadmissions.org/wp-content/uploads/2020/02/SFFA-Harvard-
    Opening-Brief-First-Cir-00117552859_Opening-Br-1.pdf.

95 Jaschik, *supra* note 92.

96 Wenyuan Wu, *Half Truths and Lies Filled Pro-Harvard Ruling on Discrimination
    Against Asian Americans*, Daily Caller, Oct. 25, 2019, https://dailycaller.
    com/2019/10/25/wu-harvard-asian-americans.

97 Jaschik, *supra* note 92.

98 Wu, *supra* note 96.

99 *Id.*

100 Jaschik, *supra* note 92.

101 Brief of Appellant, Students for Fair Admissions v. President and Fellows of
     Harvard College, *supra* note 94, at 22.

102 Peter Arcidiacono, Josh Kinsler & Tyler Ransom, *Asian American
     Discrimination in Harvard Admissions*, Apr. 21, 2020, http://
     samv9ikhoyt2i553a2t1so5i-wpengine.netdna-ssl.com/wp-content/
     uploads/2020/04/realpenalty.pdf.

103 Scott Jaschik, *Appeals Court Backs Harvard on Affirmative Action*,
     Inside Higher Ed., Nov. 12, 2020, https://www.insidehighered.com/
     quicktakes/2020/11/12/appeals-court-backs-harvard-affirmative-action.

104 Letter from Eric S. Dreiband, Assistant A. G., Civil Rights Division, to Peter
     S. Spivack, *Notice of Violation of Title VI of the Civil Rights Act of 1964* (Aug.
     13, 2020) [hereinafter *Notice of Violation*], https://www.justice.gov/opa/press-
     release/file/1304591/download.

105 Press Release, Asian American Coalition for Education, AACE Applauds
     Justice Department's Finding Affirming Yale's Anti-Asian Discrimination
     in Admissions (Aug. 14, 2020), http://asianamericanforeducation.org/en/
     pr_20200814 [hereinafter AACE Applauds Justice Department's Finding].

106 *Notice of Violation*, *supra* note 104, at 1.

107 *Id.*

108 *Id.* at 3.

109 *Id.*

110 *Id.* at 1.

111 *Id.* at 2.

112 *Id.* at 3.

113 *Id.*

114 *Id.*

115 *Id.* at 2.

116 *Id.*

117 *Id.* at 4.

118 *Id.*

119 *Id.*

120 *Id.*

121 Anemona Hartocollis, *Justice Dept. Accuses Yale of Discrimination in Application Process*, N.Y. TIMES, Aug. 13, 2020, https://www.nytimes.com/2020/08/13/us/yale-discrimination.html.

122 *Id.*

123 AACE Applauds Justice Department's Finding, *supra* note 105.

124 Jon Schweppe, *Justice Dept. Threatens Yale's Taxpayer Funding After Discrimination AGAINST White, Asian Students*, NATIONAL PULSE (Aug. 19, 2020), https://thenationalpulse.com/news/doj-threatens-yales-taxpayer-funding-conservatives-must-use-this-victory.

125 Hartocollis, *supra* note 121.

126 Aaron Sibarium, *Racial Piety Short-Circuits the Ivy League*, AMERICAN MIND (Aug. 24, 2020), https://americanmind.org/post/racial-piety-short-circuits-the-ivy-leagues.

127 *Id.*

128 *Id.*

129 *Id.*

130 *Notice of Violation*, *supra* note 104, at 3.

131 Hartocollis, *supra* note 121.

132 Melissa Korn & Sadie Gurman, *Justice Department Drops Yale University Admissions Lawsuit*, WALL ST. J., Feb. 3, 2021, https://www.wsj.com/articles/justice-department-drops-yale-university-admissions-lawsuit-11612370047.

133 ACA-5, 2019-2020 Leg. Reg. Sess. (Cal. 2020) (repealing Section 31 of Article I thereof, relating to government preferences), https://leginfo.legislature.ca.gov/faces/billTextClient.xhtml?bill_id=201920200ACA5.

134 *Id.*

135 *University of California Endorses Affirmative Action Measure*, ABC NEWS, June 15, 2020, https://abcnews.go.com/US/wireStory/university-california-endorses-affirmative-action-measure-71261515.

136 *The Early Effects of Prop. 209: Background Statistics and Trends*, TOC

FOUNDATION, https://www.tocfoundation.org/the-early-effects-of-prop-209-background-statistics-and-trends.

137 *Report of the UC Academic Council Standardized Testing Task Force*, U. OF CALIFORNIA ACADEMIC SENATE, Jan. 2020 [hereinafter *Report of the Standardized Testing Task Force*], at 8, https://senate.universityofcalifornia.edu/_files/underreview/sttf-report.pdf.

138 *Id.*

139 *College Entrance Exam Use in University of California Undergraduate Admissions*, U. OF CALIFORNIA OFFICE OF THE PRESIDENT, May 21, 2020, at 7, https://regents.universityofcalifornia.edu/regmeet/may20/b4.pdf.

140 *Cohort Graduates Meeting UC/CSU Requirements by Race/Ethnicity, California Public Schools*, ED-DATA: EDUCATION DATA PARTNERSHIP, http://www.ed-data.org/ShareData/Html/40603.

141 *Report of the Standardized Testing Task Force, supra* note 137, at 5.

142 *Cohort Graduates by Race/Ethnicity, California Public Schools*, ED-DATA: EDUCATION DATA PARTNERSHIP, http://www.ed-data.org/ShareData/Html/40604.

143 Nikki Graf, *Most Americans Say Colleges Should Not Consider Race or Ethnicity in Admissions*, PEW RESEARCH CENTER, Feb. 25, 2019, https://www.pewresearch.org/fact-tank/2019/02/25/most-americans-say-colleges-should-not-consider-race-or-ethnicity-in-admissions.

144 Press Release, Public Policy Institute of California, Most Favor Vouchers, Yet Most Give Local Schools Good Grades (Apr. 19, 2017), https://www.ppic.org/press-release/most-favor-vouchers-yet-most-give-local-schools-good-grades.

145 AACE Applauds Justice Department's Finding, *supra* note 105.

146 Ashley Fan, *Affirmative Action Vote Splits Asian Americans*, WOODLAND DAILY DEMOCRAT, Aug. 26, 2020, https://www.dailydemocrat.com/2020/08/26/affirmative-action-vote-splits-asian-americans.

147 *Id.*

148 *Id.*

149 *Id.*

150 *Notice of Violation, supra* note 104, at 3-4.

151 Alexei Koseff, *California Effort to Restore Affirmative Action Divides Asian Americans*, S.F. CHRON., June 24, 2020, https://www.sfchronicle.com/politics/article/California-effort-to-restore-affirmative-action-15361618.php.

152 *Id.*

153 *Id.*

154 Gail Heriot, *Undoing Ban on Race/Sex-Based Preferences Will Harm Students*, REAL CLEAR POLITICS, May 16, 2020, https://www.realclearpolitics.com/articles/2020/05/16/undoing_ban_on_racesex-based_preferences_will_harm_students_143219.html.

155 Sohini Ashoke, *Flawed Affirmative Action System Hurts Asian Americans*, ORACLE, Sept. 15, 2017, https://gunnoracle.com/13792/uncategorized/flawed-affirmative-action-system-hurts-asian-americans.

156 *Id.*

157 *Id.*

158 *Id.*

159 *Id.*

160 *Id.*

161 J.K. Yamamoto, *JACL Hears Both Sides of Affirmative Action Debate*, HOKUBEI MAINICHI, Aug. 31, 1995, at 2, cited in Lance T. Izumi, *Confounding the Paradigm: Asian Americans and Race Preferences*, 11 NOTRE DAME J. L.E.P.P. 128, http://scholarship.law.nd.edu/cgi/viewcontent.cgi?article=1708&context= ndjlepp.

162 Ashoke, *supra* note 155.

A CLASS ACT? SOCIAL-CLASS AFFIRMATIVE ACTION AND HIGHER EDUCATION

1 *See* Erika Torpey, *Measuring the Value of Education*, U.S. BUREAU OF LABOR STATISTICS (Apr. 2018), https://www.bls.gov/careeroutlook/2018/data-on-display/education-pays.htm; *see also* Sarah R. Crissey, *Educational Attainment in the United States: 2007*, U.S. CENSUS BUREAU SPECIAL STUDIES, Jan. 2009, http://www.census.gov/prod/2009pubs/p20-560.pdf; Ron Haskins, Harry Holzer & Robert Lerman, *Promoting Economic Mobility by Increasing Postsecondary Education*, ECONOMIC MOBILITY PROJECT, May 2009; Robert M. Hauser et al., *Occupational Status, Education, and Social Mobility in the Meritocracy* (Center for Demography & Ecology, University of Wisconsin-Madison, Working Paper No 96-18, July 1996), http://www.ssc.wisc.edu/cde/cdewp/96-18.pdf.

2 *See* College Board, *2016 College-Bound Seniors: Total Group Profile Report* 4 (College Board scores correlated with parental income); Catherine Rampell, *SAT Scores and Family Income*, N.Y. TIMES: ECONOMIX (Aug. 17, 2009), http://economix.blogs.nytimes.com/2009/08/27/sat-scores-and-family-income; DOUGLAS S. MASSEY ET AL., THE SOURCE OF THE RIVER: THE SOCIAL ORIGINS OF FRESHMEN AT AMERICA'S SELECTIVE COLLEGES AND UNIVERSITIES (2003) (children of higher-income families disproportionately attend the more selective colleges and universities).

3 Eugene Robinson, *Obama Cools on Affirmative Action*, TRUTHDIG (May 15, 2007), http://www.truthdig.com/report/item/20070515_obama_cools_on_affirmative_action.

4 *See, e.g.*, RICHARD D. KAHLENBERG, THE REMEDY: CLASS, RACE, AND AFFIRMATIVE ACTION (1996); ANTHONY P. CARNEVALE & STEPHEN J. ROSE, SOCIOECONOMIC STATUS, RACE/ETHNICITY, AND SELECTIVE COLLEGE ADMISSIONS (2003).

5 CAL. CONST. art. I, § 31(a) (prohibiting the state from discriminating against or granting preferential treatment to any individual or group on the basis of race, sex, or national origin in the operation of public education, employment, and contracting). *See also* MICH. CONST. art. I, § 26 (banning racial preferences in all state public schools); NEB. CONST. art. I, § 30 (banning discrimination based on race in public employment, contracting,

and education); Wash. Rev. Code § 49.60.400 (2011) (effective Dec. 3, 1998) (banning discrimination based on race in public employment, education, and contracting); Fla. Exec. Order No. 99-281 (Nov. 9, 1999), http://www. dms.myflorida.com/media/general_counsel_files/one_florida_executive_ order_pdf (banning racial or sex-based preferences in public employment, education, or contracting).

6 *See* Larry Alexander & Maimon Schwarzschild, *Grutter or Otherwise: Racial Preferences and Higher Education*, 21 Constitutional Commentary 3 (2004).

7 Kahlenberg, *supra* note 4, at 42-52 (with extensive documentation that those granted preferences under racial affirmative action are often from more prosperous families than those who receive no preference).

8 For scholarly studies, *see, e.g.*, Michael Hout, *Americans' Occupational Status Reflects the Status of Both of Their Parents*, PNAS (Proceedings of the National Academy of Sciences of the United States of America) (2018) (offering a statistical case for substantial decline in social mobility in recent decades), https://www.pnas.org/content/115/38/9527; *see also* Julia Isaacs, Isabel V. Sawhill & Ron Haskins, *Getting Ahead or Losing Ground: Economic Mobility in America*, Brookings Institution (2016), https://www.brookings.edu/ wp-content/uploads/2016/06/02_economic_mobility_sawhill.pdf; Greg Duncan, William Rodgers & Timothy Smeeding, *W(h)ither the Middle Class: A Dynamic View*, in Poverty and Prosperity in the USA in the Late Twentieth Century 240-271 (Dimitri B. Papadimitriou & Edward N. Wolff eds., 1993) (arguing that social mobility is static or declining); Daniel P. McMurrer & Isabel Sawhill, *Economic Mobility in the U.S.*, Urban Institute (Oct. 1, 1996), http://webarchive.urban.org/publications/406722.html. For news media reports, *see* Janny Scott & David Leonhardt, *Shadowy Lines That Still Divide*, N.Y. Times, May 15, 2005, at 1 (the first in an eleven-part series on class in America, emphasizing impediments to class mobility); *Meritocracy in America: Ever Higher Society, Ever Harder to Ascend*, Economist, Dec. 29, 2004.

9 *See* Bruce Bartlett, *Class Struggle in America?*, 120 Commentary 33 (July-Aug. 2005) (criticizing the *New York Times* series, *supra* note 8); *see also* Scott Winship, *The American Dream Abides*, National Review (May 15, 2017), https://www.nationalreview.com/2017/05/american-dream-social-mobility-opportunity; Chul-In Lee & Gary Solon, *Trends in Intergenerational Income Mobility*, 91 Review of Economics and Statistics 766, 766-72 (2009) (statistical analysis suggesting little change in intergenerational social mobility in recent decades).

10 *See* William R. Cline, *U.S. Median Income Has Risen More Than You Think*, Cato Journal, Winter 2019, https://www.cato.org/cato-journal/winter-2019/ us-median-household-income-has-risen-more-you-think; *see also* Deloitte Insights, *Income Inequality in the United States: What Do We Know and What Does It Mean?* (July 12, 2017) (suggesting that income inequality is a serious social problem but conceding that absolute incomes have generally risen

in every quintile even as income inequality has increased), https://www2.
deloitte.com/us/en/insights/economy/issues-by-the-numbers/july-2017/rising-
income-inequality-gap-united-states.html.

11 ANNE F. THURSTON, ENEMIES OF THE PEOPLE: THE ORDEAL OF THE
INTELLECTUALS IN CHINA'S GREAT CULTURAL REVOLUTION 287 (1988).

12 *See, e.g.*, Rene Goldman, *The Rectification Campaign at Peking University: May-
June 1957*, 12 CHINA QUARTERLY 138, 138-53 (1962).

13 ANNE APPLEBAUM, GULAG: A HISTORY 264 (2003).

14 *See* THOMAS SOWELL, AFFIRMATIVE ACTION AROUND THE WORLD: AN
EMPIRICAL STUDY 23 (2004).

15 ROBERT E. KLITGAARD, CHOOSING ELITES 161 (1985). *See also* WILLIAM
BOWEN & DEREK BOK, THE SHAPE OF THE RIVER: LONG-TERM
CONSEQUENCES OF CONSIDERING RACE IN COLLEGE AND UNIVERSITY
ADMISSIONS 88 (1998).

16 *See* Paul A. Westrick et al., *Validity of the SAT for Predicting First-Year
Grades and Retention to the Second Year*, COLLEGE BOARD (2019), https://
collegereadiness.collegeboard.org/pdf/national-sat-validity-study.pdf; S.A.
Hezlett, N.R. Kuncel, M.A. Vey, A.M. Ahart, D.S. Ones, J.P. Campbell, &
W. Camara, *The Predictive Validity of the SAT: A Meta-analysis, in* D. Ones &
S. Hezlett (Chairs), PREDICTING PERFORMANCE: THE INTERFACE OF I-O
PSYCHOLOGY AND EDUCATIONAL RESEARCH, symposium conducted at the
16th Annual Convention of the Society of Industrial and Organizational
Psychology (April 2001).

17 KAHLENBERG, *supra* note 4, at 159.

18 Richard H. Sander, *Experimenting with Class-Based Affirmative Action*, 47 J.
LEGAL EDUC. 472, 486 (1997).

19 KAHLENBERG, *supra* note 4, at 142 (arguing for preferences for those below
the socioeconomic median "in the applicant pool").

20 CAROL M. SWAIN: THE NEW WHITE NATIONALISM IN AMERICA: ITS
CHALLENGE TO INTEGRATION (2002). *See also* CAROL M. SWAIN (ED.), RACE
VS. CLASS: THE NEW AFFIRMATIVE ACTION DEBATE (1996).

21 WILLIAM G. BOWEN, MARTIN A. KURZWEIL, EUGENE M. TOBIN & SUSANNE
C. PICHLER, EQUITY AND EXCELLENCE IN AMERICAN HIGHER EDUCATION
(2005).

22 U.S. Census Bureau, *Place of Birth for the Foreign Born Population in
the United States*, Table B05006 (2019), https://data.census.gov/cedsci/
table?q=ACSDT1Y2016.B05006&tid=ACSDT1Y2019.B05006.

23 Abby Budiman, *Key Findings About U.S. Immigrants*, PEW RESEARCH CENTER
(Aug. 20, 2020), https://www.pewresearch.org/fact-tank/2020/08/20/key-
findings-about-u-s-immigrants.

24 *Id.*

25 U.S. Census Bureau, *Nativity Status and Citizenship in the United States: 2009*,
https://www2.census.gov/library/publications/2010/acs/acsbr09-16.pdf.

26 *Id.* at 5, Table 2.

27 Steven A. Camarota & Karen Ziegler, *Immigrants in the United States: A Profile of the Foreign-Born Using 2014 and 2015 Census Bureau Data*, CENTER FOR IMMIGRATION STUDIES, Oct. 2011, at 11, https://cis.org/sites/cis.org/files/immigrant-profile_0.pdf.

28 U.S. Census Bureau, *Educational Attainment in the United States: 2019*, March 30, 2020, table 2 ("BothSexes"), https://www.census.gov/content/census/en/data/tables/2019/demo/educational-attainment/cps-detailed-tables.html.

29 *Id.* at Ex. 20; *see also* Annual Update of the HHS Poverty Guidelines, 70 FED. REG. 3637-3638 (Jan. 20, 2011).

30 Camarota & Ziegler, *supra* note 27, at 21.

31 *See generally* HUGH DAVIS GRAHAM: COLLISION COURSE: THE STRANGE CONVERGENCE OF AFFIRMATIVE ACTION AND IMMIGRATION POLICY IN AMERICA (2002) (supporting affirmative action for African Americans, Indians, and long-resident Mexican Americans, but opposing it for recent non-white immigrants).

32 *See, e.g.,* Rebecca Tan, *No Cooperation with ICE: Montgomery's New Ban Is Strongest in DC Region*, WASH. POST, July 22, 2019 ("Police in Montgomery...have refused since 2014 to cooperate with ICE agents on immigration enforcement"), https://www.washingtonpost.com/local/md-politics/no-cooperation-with-ice-montgomerys-new-ban-is-strongest-in-dc-region/2019/07/22/46b85870-ac7d-11e9-a0c9-6d2d7818f3da_story.html; Michael J. Wishnie, *State and Local Police Enforcement of Immigration Laws*, 6 U. PA. J. CONST. L. 1084 (2004) (many local police departments reluctant to enforce immigration laws).

33 CAL. EDUC. CODE § 68130.5 (persons "without lawful immigration status" are exempt from paying non-resident tuition at the California State University and the California Community Colleges, so long as they meet the residency requirements of the statute). This statute, by charging higher tuition to out-of-state U.S. citizens and legal residents than to illegal aliens in California, appears to flout a federal law which prohibits states "from providing a post-secondary education benefit to an alien not lawfully present unless any citizen or national is eligible for such benefit." Illegal Immigration Reform and Immigrant Responsibility Act, § 505, 110 Stat 3009-672; 8 U.S.C. 1623. The California State Supreme Court upheld the statute as constitutional in 2010. *See* Martinez v. Regents of the Univ. of Ca., 241 P.3d 855 (Cal. Sup. Ct 2010), *cert. den.* 180 L. Ed. 2d 245 (2011). *See also* Denise Oas, *Immigration and Higher Education: The Debate Over In-State Tuition*, 79 U.M.K.C. L. Rev. 877 (2011); National Conference of State Legislatures, *Tuition Benefits for Immigrants*, Jan. 16, 2019, http://www.ncsl.org/research/immigration/tuition-benefits-for-immigrants.aspx.

34 National Conference of State Legislatures, *supra* note 33.

35 The Civil Rights Act of 1964 forbids discrimination on the basis of "national origin" by public colleges, 42 U.S.C. § 2000c-6(a)(2), or by any program or activity receiving federal financial assistance, 42 U.S.C. § 2000d. While these provisions do not refer explicitly to legal aliens, other federal statutes do—for

example, the Immigration and Nationality Act, 8 U.S.C. § 1324(b), which forbids employment discrimination against legal aliens. In general, state government—which would include public colleges and universities—may not discriminate against legal aliens except where authorized or required by federal law; *see* Graham v. Richardson, 403 U.S. 365, 372 (1971); and even the federal government may not discriminate invidiously against legal aliens, although the courts are usually deferential to federal immigration and nationality laws; *see* Mathews v. Diaz, 426 U.S. 67, 78-84 (1976). *See also* CAL. CIV. CODE § 3339 (aliens entitled to all employment remedies under the state civil rights laws).

36 U.S. Census Bureau, *Nativity Status and Citizenship in the United States: 2009*, *supra* note 25.

37 Steven A. Camarota & Karen Ziegler, *Immigrant and Native Fertility 2008 to 2017*, CENTER FOR IMMIGRATION STUDIES, Mar. 2019, at 1 (in 2017, the total fertility rate for immigrant women was 2.18; for native women, it was 1.76), https://cis.org/sites/default/files/2019-03/camarota-fertility19.pdf.

38 Emma Lazarus, *The New Colossus* (1883).

39 Nicholas A. Jones, Karen R. Humes & Roberto R. Ramirez, *Overview of Race and Hispanic Origin: 2010*, U.S. CENSUS BUREAU, Mar. 2011, http://www.census.gov/prod/cen2010/briefs/c2010br-02.pdf.

40 *But see* Jamilah King, *Census: Interracial Marriage May Be on the Decline*, COLORLINES, May 26, 2010, https://www.colorlines.com/articles/census-interracial-marriage-may-be-decline.

41 National Healthy Marriage Resource Center, *Interracial Marriage and Relationships: A Fact Sheet*, https://www.healthymarriageinfo.org/wp-content/uploads/2017/12/Interracial-Marriage-and-Relationships.pdf.

42 Brittany Rico, Rose M. Kreider & Lydia Anderson, *Growth in Interracial and Interethnic Married-Couple Households, Race, Ethnicity and Marriage in the United States*, U.S. CENSUS BUREAU (July 2018), https://www.census.gov/library/stories/2018/07/interracial-marriages.html.

43 GEORGE ORWELL, THE ROAD TO WIGAN PIER 154 (1937).

44 Sander, *supra* note 18, at 472.

45 KAHLENBERG, *supra* note 4, at 132-36.

46 Richard H. Sander, *Fair Housing in Los Angeles County: An Assessment of Progress and Challenges, 1970-1995*, Report for the City and County of Los Angeles, at 74 (1996).

47 *See, e.g.*, Mitchell Langbert, *Homogeneous: The Political Affiliations of Elite Liberal Arts College Faculty*, 31 ACADEMIC QUESTIONS 186 (2018); *see also* Adam Bonica et al., *The Legal Academy's Ideological Uniformity*, 47 J. LEGAL STUD. 1 (2018).

48 Sander, *supra* note 18, at 478.

49 KAHLENBERG, *supra* note 4, at 180.

50 Camilo Maldonado, *Price of College Increasing Almost 8 Times Faster Than Wages*, FORBES (July 24, 2018) ("between the academic years ending in 1989 and 2016, the cost for a four-year degree doubled, even after inflation"),

https://www.forbes.com/sites/camilomaldonado/2018/07/24/price-of-college-increasing-almost-8-times-faster-than-wages/. Tuition at public and private colleges and universities rose at between double and triple the rate of inflation over the three decades from 1980 through 2010. *See* The College Board, *Trends in College Pricing 2010*, 13, https://research.collegeboard.org/pdf/trends-college-pricing-2010-full-report.pdf. *See also* Ronald G. Ehrenberg, *The Economics of Tuition and Fees in American Higher Education*, Cornell University ILR School Working Papers (2007), https://digitalcommons.ilr.cornell.edu/cgi/viewcontent.cgi?referer=&httpsredir=1&article=1068&context=workingpapers&sei-redir=1.

51 *See* Meredith Kolodner, *States Moving College Scholarship Money Away from the Poor, to the Wealthy and Middle Class*, HECHINGER REPORT (July 22, 2015), https://hechingerreport.org/states-moving-college-scholarship-money-away-from-the-poor-to-the-wealthy-and-middle-class; *see also* Fay Vincent, *No Merit in These Scholarships*, EDUCATIONAL POLICY INSTITUTE (June 2005); Robert H. Frank, *Intense Competition for Top Students Threatening Financial Aid Based on Need*, N.Y. TIMES, Apr. 14, 2005, at C2.

52 *See* generally David O. Lucca, Taylor Nadauld & Karen Shen, *Credit Supply and the Rise in College Tuition: Evidence from the Expansion in Federal Student Aid Programs*, Federal Reserve Bank of New York Staff Reports (Staff Report No. 733 July 2015, revised Feb. 2017), https://www.newyorkfed.org/medialibrary/media/research/staff_reports/sr733.pdf; *see also* Lawrence E. Gladieux, *Federal Student Aid Policy: A History and an Assessment*, in FINANCING POSTSECONDARY EDUCATION: THE FEDERAL ROLE (1995), http://www.ed.gov/offices/OPE/PPI/FinPostSecEd/gladieux.html.

53 *See* Matthew Quirk, *The Best Class Money Can Buy*, 296 ATLANTIC 128 (2005) ("enrollment management" and the "cutthroat quest for competitive advantage" among colleges and universities).

54 *See* John Staddon, *Administrative Bloat: Where Does It Come From and What Is It Doing?* JAMES G. MARTIN CENTER FOR ACADEMIC RENEWAL (June 19, 2019), https://www.jamesgmartin.center/2019/06/administrative-bloat-where-does-it-come-from-and-what-is-it-doing.

55 *See The Annual Report on the Economic Status of the Profession, 2017-2018*, ACADEME 4 (Mar.-Apr. 2018), American Association of University Professors, https://www.aaup.org/sites/default/files/ARES_2017-18.pdf.

INDEX